Globalization, Privatization and Free Market Economy

Globalization, Privatization and Free Market Economy

EDITED BY
C. P. RAO

QUORUM BOOKS
Westport, Connecticut · London

Library of Congress Cataloging-in-Publication Data

Globalization, privatization and free market economy / C.P. Rao,
  editor.
       p.   cm.
    Includes bibliographical references and index.
    ISBN 1–56720–075–3 (alk. paper)
    1. International economic relations.   2. Competition,
International.   3. Privatization.   4. Free enterprise.   I. Rao, C.
P.
    HF1359.G588   1988
    337—dc21   97–32994

British Library Cataloguing in Publication Data is available.

Library of Congress Catalog Card Number: 97–32994
ISBN: 1–56720–075–3

First published in 1998

Quorum Books, 88 Post Road West, Westport, CT 06881
An imprint of Greenwood Publishing Group, Inc.

Printed in the United States of America

The paper used in this book complies with the
Permanent Paper Standard issued by the National
Information Standards Organization (Z39.48–1984).

10 9 8 7 6 5 4 3 2 1

To

VENKU

for continuous support and encouragement

Contents

Globalization, Privatization and Free Market Economy

CHAPTER 1

Introduction

C. P. RAO

Globalization, privatization and liberalization have become dominant forces shaping societies and economies the world over. With the fall of communism and the decline of socialism in most parts of the world, these processes have accelerated in the 1990s. These three processes are interrelated phenomena. Globalized economies are likely to be more privatized and liberalized economies. On the other hand, privatization and liberalization facilitate the process of globalization of a country or a region. Hence, it is essential that these processes be addressed collectively. This is the major objective of this volume.

Globalization, privatization and liberalization are multidimensional phenomena that have implications not only for the economic but also the sociocultural and environmental aspects of countries and societies. As a secondary objective, these multidimensional aspects are included in this volume.

The three phenomena that form the focus of this volume also have differing impacts on different units of analysis. For purposes of understanding and analyzing these three forces, the units of analysis can be conceived at regional, country, industry and organizational levels. The chapters in this book deal with all of these, reflecting the multilevel aspects of globalization, privatization and liberalization forces shaping world economies.

This volume is divided into six parts. Part I deals with the conceptual issues of meaning, definitions and differing interpretations and perspectives. Part II addresses the regional issues reflecting the emerging regional integration rather than global integration and the implications of the regional for the global. Part III is concerned with global investment issues and places special emphasis on the big emerging economies. Part IV is devoted to exploring the implications of globalization for certain managerial concerns dealing with human resource management, international marketing strategy and technology transfer. Part V addresses the varied experiences of specific developing countries in adopting globalization, privatization and liberalization policies and practices. Finally, Part VI presents the issues relating to the specific industry sectors and industries.

CONCEPTUAL ISSUES

In Chapter 2, O'Sullivan deals with the concept of globalization taking a broader view of it to include both its economic and political perspectives. O'Sullivan traces the multidimensionality of the concept and its impacts and explores implications from the perspectives of both the proponents and opponents of globalization. The conceptual exploration addresses the potential socioeconomic problems and conflicts that may result from pursuing globalization policies and practices. The author also identifies the realistic outcomes of globalization in the form of: (1) the end of Western international hegemony; (2) the cultural change; (3) the erosion of national sovereignty; and (4) environmental pollution. In the concluding section O'Sullivan draws attention to the emerging problems of local versus global, globalization and human rights, national identity in a globalized world and, finally, the creation of appropriate new international institutions to facilitate the globalization process.

In Chapter 3, Nwankwo explores the privatization issues based on experiences in Great Britain. Concurrent with globalization of economies and societies, privatization of public sector enterprises usually follows and intensifies. Privatization is being vigorously pursued in all countries—industrialized, newly industrialized, developing and formerly communist countries. However, as Nwanko rightly argues, the traditional categorization of private versus public enterprise has become inadequate. In its place, he introduces the concept of the national enterprise, an emergent organization form that seems to be more relevant in today's global competitive environment.

In Chapter 4, Banerjee addresses the linkage between globalization, economic development and ecology. Countries adopt globalization, privatization and liberalization policies and practices so as to accelerate their economic and social development. The environmental and ecological consequences of such unsustainable economic growth could have adverse sociocultural impacts. This chapter discusses various dimensions of globalization, together with its relationship to economic development and its ecological consequences; critically examines the emergence of a new environmental paradigm; and presents the implications of globalization for Third World countries in particular.

REGIONAL ISSUES

Historically, attempts at regional economic integration have preceded the recent globalization developments. In recent years, at the same time that globalization forces have been shaping the world economies, regional economic integration, both formal and informal, has intensified. This regional trend raises some troubling questions about the compatibility of regionalism and globalism. Some of these questions are addressed in Part II.

In Chapter 5, Oumlil and Rao discuss the implications of the emerging regional trading blocs for member and nonmember countries and their enterprises. In particular, they point out that rampant regionalism may be detrimental to those countries that are left out of such regional groupings. They also maintain that closely knit trading blocs may inhibit the emergence of true multilateral free trade on a global scale, which is the ultimate objective of globalization.

In Chapter 6, Kirpalani focuses on the NAFTA market and management training for successful entry into that market. After presenting the various salient features of NAFTA, he specifically describes the management education and training requirements for outside international managers seeking to enter the regional market. Specifically, the management training issues relating to content, methods of delivery, location of training and type of instructors are discussed.

GLOBAL INVESTMENT ISSUES

One of the major consequences of globalization, privatization and liberalization is the acceleration in foreign direct investment flows. While foreign direct investment has been increasing for some time among the developed triad countries, in recent years it has spread to other parts of the world, especially to the giant emerging economies such as China and India. The privatization and liberalization policies pursued by these emerging economies have created new opportunities for foreign direct investment. As a result, international investors now face difficult problems such as choosing countries, evaluating risk-return relationships and assessing profitability in private and public sectors. These global investment issues are addressed in this section, particularly in the context of two burgeoning economies—India and China.

The first chapter in Part III, by Anand and Delios, empirically examines the patterns of Japan's direct investment in India and China. Japanese investments in China are considered to be larger and broader in scope than those in India and are often reflected in the overall global strategies of Japanese firms. In contrast Japanese investments in India are market exploring investments spurred by incentives by the host government and typically reflect a multidomestic strategy. The authors conclude that not only is Japan's direct investment in China larger than that in India, but also that accruing benefits of technology and management expertise transfer are more substantial in the case of China than in India. The chapter explores the consequent policy implications for the host countries.

Chapter 8, by Duggal and Cudd, is an empirical study reflecting the U.S. investors' perception of the risk-return relationship to their investments in India since 1991, the year when liberalization of the Indian economy began. The major finding of this chapter is that U.S. stockholders do not perceive investment opportunities in India to be positive net present value projects. Duggal and Cudd believe that the higher perceived risk of the Indian investments may slow down the pace of future of U.S. investments in that country.

Next, in Chapter 9, Ramaswamy and Renforth investigate the relative profitability of private versus public sector enterprises in India and assess the effects of competitive intensity in making such comparisons. Not surprisingly, private sector firms have clearly outperformed the public sector counterparts. However, these differences in profitability seem to be accentuated when competitive intensity is high and minimized when it is low. This relationship suggests that competitive intensity has moderated the relationship between ownership status and commercial profitability. Consequently, industry's competitive market structure must be considered when evaluating the effects of ownership form on performance. Ramaswamy and Renforth raise some interesting questions that have implications for privatization policies and public sector programs.

MANAGERIAL ISSUES

The macrolevel developments associated with globalization, privatization and liberalization have created many managerial challenges at the microlevel. First, all managerial functions have become global in scope and complexity, and competitiveness has intensified. Technology and its management has become the bedrock of managerial efficiency. Manufacturing, sourcing, marketing, financing, human resource management and management information systems have all become global in scope. Organizational survival and growth have come to depend on how successfully organizations manage these managerial functions both individually and collectively in an integrated manner. Part IV addresses three of these broader managerial issues emanating from the three forces shaping world business today.

In Chapter 10, Subbarao addresses the issue of managing diverse human resources for globalization. He discusses the diversity of human resources in two developed countries, the United States, and Canada, as well as in three developing countries, India, Malaysia and Sri Lanka. The public policies of these nations that are influencing the management of a diverse workforce are analyzed separately as equality, equity, job preference and job reservation models. Subbarao introduces a representation model for managing human resources in workplaces that compete in global markets. He also examines the problems related to the multicultural workforce in both developed and developing countries.

Chapter 11, by Yadav and Szymanski, deals with the effects of free market reforms on market openness, market attractiveness and international marketing strategies. The authors identify the critical factors that managers consider when they are evaluating the adequacy of reforms in a target market and the impact of such factors on perceptions of market openness and market attractiveness and, in addition, on the international marketing strategy development among firms. Finally, Yadav and Szymanski present a conceptual model and some preliminary research findings.

Venaik, in Chapter 12, discusses the issues of technology acquisition by firms in developing countries through licensing and joint ventures. By utilizing the transaction cost analysis framework, Venaik demonstrates that under a given set of product–market conditions, the joint venture mode is more advantageous than licensing for firms in developing countries seeking to obtain technology from multinational corporations (MNCs). In contrast to most of the literature on technology transfer from MNCs in developed countries to firms in developing countries, Venaik examines the problem from the perspective of the recipient of technology rather than that of the provider.

COUNTRY-SPECIFIC EXPERIENCES

The experiences of individual countries vary widely with regard to adopting globalization, privatization and liberalization policies and practices. Some countries, such as the Southeast and East Asian countries, have been more successful in integrating their economies into the global economy than other countries. Given the greater diversity of developing countries, it would be instructive to focus on the specific experiences of these countries. From this perspective, Part V present the developing countries' experiences.

In Chapter 13, Gulati proposes that effective globalization of the Indian economy depends on blending Western technology with the Indian ethos. To support his argument, he points to the success of the Southeastern and East Asian countries in globalizing their economies through their ability to blend their cultural Confucian ethic with Western technology. As a parallel, he contends that in order to successfully globalize its economy India must blend the Hindu ethic with technology. In this regard, Gulati assigns the core cultural values of a society a central role in the process of globalization. In other words, cultural adaptability to the demands of technology and market values assimilation is a prerequisite for successful globalization.

In Chapter 14, Razzaque critically examines globalization, privatization and liberalization in the context of Bangladesh. According to this author, blind emulation of other successful country approaches (in this case the Asia-Pacific neighbors of Bangladesh) is not always appropriate or even feasible. Country-specific factors such as image problems, overly ambitious policies, the rise of religious fundamentalism, inadequate infrastructure, wide-scale corruption and poor selling due to bureaucratic wrangling and lack of support and information are formidable impediments to transforming Bangladesh into a globalized economy.

The last chapter in this section, by Nik-Yacob, addresses the issue of whether the inheritors of business are any less entrepreneurial than the initiators among the Malays of Peninsular Malaysia. Nik-Yacob investigates the similarities and diferences between these two types of entrepreneurs in terms of their background profiles and innovative tendencies. She has found that inheritors and initiators tend to share many aspects, especially their individual profiles, innovative tendency and business perception. The conclusion is that in a rapidly globalizing economy both inheritors who are traditionally wealthy and initiators who are traditionally self-starters stand to gain to the overall benefit of the society.

SECTORAL AND INDUSTRY-SPECIFIC ISSUES

The different industrial sectors and industries in any economy are affected by globalization, privatization and liberalization forces in quite different ways. Some industries, such as the automobile, electronics and steel are more readily globalized than other industries, which are purely local. The same is true with regard to privatization affecting different industries to different degrees. Even the government that is most committed to privatization will hesitate to privatize either defense or social service-related industries. For some industries such as pharmaceuticals and other knowledge-based industries, intellectual property protection becomes critical in the global spread of such enterprises. Three of these issues are addressed in Part VI.

The first chapter in this section, by Majkgård and Sharma, discusses the impact of international business relationships on service quality in business services global marketing. International business transactions are greatly influenced by buyer–seller relationships, mutual trust, commitment and adaptation, aspects that are accentuated by the inherent characteristics of the business services trade. Because the service sector is becoming a significant part of overall international trade and will likely continue to do so with increasing globalization, privatization and liberalization trends, it is vital that we understand the complexities of services transactions in the international context. Majkgård and Sharma based their findings on face-to-face interviews with the decision makers in two international service firms in Sweden.

In Chapter 17, Rao investigates the linkage between intellectual property protection and foreign direct investment in the global pharmaceutical industry. He contends that intellectual property protection (IPR) is only one of many factors that influence foreign direct investment (FDI) decisions, even in the pharmaceutical industry, which attaches great importance to IPR. With data and examples, the author establishes that the recently concluded Trade Related Intellectual Property Rights (TRIPS) agreement by the Uruguay Round will have little effect on the flow of pharmaceutical FDI into the developing countries. The main driving forces for FDI in the global pharmaceutical industry are the global marketing strategies driven by market forces and technological developments in the industry.

In the final chapter of this volume, Muranda and Jaensson deal with domestic and global environmental changes and their impact on the international marketing strategies of the textile industry in Zimbabwe. They trace the forces that caused the poor performance of Zimbabwe's textile and clothing sector, including the government's long-standing protectionist policies, economic structural changes in the domestic market, limited vision of opportunities in different international markets and inability to adapt strategy to quick changes in both the domestic and global markets. The textile firms' lack of experience and knowledge of the wider external markets has become a great obstacle to their ability to internationalize their operations.

PART I

Conceptual Issues

CHAPTER 2

Concept and Reality in
Globalization Theory

NOËL O'SULLIVAN

Globalization seems to be the most fashionable economic concept of the 1990s.[1] The precise meaning of this term, however, is far from clear. Sometimes it is used in a relatively restricted descriptive sense to refer to a variety of trends in contemporary economic and political life. It is also used in a much broader sense to refer to the emergence of "new forms of world interdependence, in which . . . there are no 'others.' ''[2] The concern here is with a closer consideration of both the narrower and broader conceptions of globalization, in order to to decide whether in fact any new or distinctive developments in the world order may be said to constitute a uniquely late-modern, or postmodern, kind of global identity.

The chapter is presented in five parts. The first considers briefly the great dream (or myth) that has inspired defenders of globalization. The second looks at the most important doubts that have been expressed about it. The third tries to step back from the dream and the doubts, in order to give a more analytical account of the globalization concept. The fourth part considers the political options that are open to us in responding to it. The final part attempts to give some idea of the problems that the future holds for societies, both developed and developing, which commit themselves to competition in the global market.

THE DREAM THAT HAS INSPIRED THE CONCEPT OF
GLOBALIZATION

In order to understand why talk of globalization has become fashionable, it is necessary to remember that it is not merely an analytical concept, but also a highly emotive one. Its emotive appeal is at two levels, one of which is political, while the other extends much deeper. At the political level, the appeal is partly

to liberal and democratic hopes for the spread of democracy and peace throughout the world, but partly also to more right-wing dreams about the final destruction of socialism as a luxury no one can afford any more, in the face of the
global competition threat.

Beyond this diverse political appeal, the concept of globalization exercises a
deeper, quasireligious emotional appeal for those concerned about the environment and, more generally, about the attitude toward the world implicit in modern
science and technology. In order to understand this quasireligious appeal, we
must remember that the idea of globalization draws on a myth that has ancient
roots in Western culture—the myth, that the whole world is really one single
nation. As the French scholar Gilbert Larochelle recently remarked, this myth
"borrows its principal characteristics from stoicism, medieval Christianity, six-
teenth and seventeenth century *iusnaturalism*, eighteenth century cosmopolitan-
ism and twentieth century universalism."[3]

The present concern, however, is not to trace in detail the historical links
between the age-old dream of a universal society and the contemporary concept
of globalization, but simply to identify the main assumptions on which the
contemporary version of the dream depends. There are four such assumptions.
Since the critics of the dream have a good bit to say about each of them, they
will only be very lightly sketched in at this point.

The first assumption is that the world is becoming a global economy in which
the accelerated development of transport and communication technology makes
traditional spatial and territorial frontiers increasingly irrelevant. This is the process for which Marshall McCluhan coined the term *global village* in the early
1960s.[4] The second assumption is that a spontaneous, unregulated world economy is the best way of securing economic harmony, and in any case, is preferred
by business. The third is that the nation-state is rapidly becoming an inappropriate basis for modern economic and political life. Finally, the fourth assumption is that the world is tending toward the creation not only of a single global
economy, but also a single homogeneous culture.

So much for the assumptions behind the dream. What we must now consider
are the doubts that a variety of contemporary skeptics have expressed about the
dream.

THE DOUBTS ABOUT GLOBALIZATION

The skeptics may be divided into three different groups, each of which has
expressed different but related fears about the consequences of globalization.

The First Group of Skeptics

This first line of attack comes from two extremely successful European capitalists. One is the British businessman, James Goldsmith, and the other is the
Hungarian financier, George Soros.

Goldsmith retired from business in 1990. Soon thereafter, in 1994, he co-founded a new political movement, *L'Autre Europe*. His recent book, *The Trap* (1994), ended with the assertion that we must reject the whole concept of global free trade and replace it with regional free trade. Goldsmith gives tree main reasons for this conclusion. The first is that globalization just won't work. "The four billion people [from China, India, Vietnam, Pakistan, Bangladesh and the former Soviet empire, among others] who are joining the world economy," he insists, "have been part of a wholly different society, indeed, a different world. It is absurd to believe that [we can ignore cultural differences and] suddenly create a global free trade area, a common market with, for example, China without massive changes leading to consequences we cannot anticipate."[5]

The second reason is that globalization is a formula for disaster for advanced industrial societies. It is a disaster, because "GATT [and the World Trade Organization that has replaced it] makes it almost imperative for enterprises in the developed world to close down their production, eliminate employees and move their factories to low-cost labour areas."[6] Goldsmith was asked, in this connection, whether developed nations have a moral obligation to open their markets to the Third World. His reply leads to his third reason for rejecting globalization.

The third reason is that a global free market would impoverish the developed world without significantly improving the economic situation of the mass of the population in the Third World.[7] Globalization, in other words, is disastrous not only for the developed world but also for the Third World, where it means the destruction of the rural communities in which most of the Third World population still lives. Goldsmith quotes in his support Vandana Shiva, who is the director of the Indian Research Foundation for Science, Technology and National Resource Policy, and also the Science and Environment adviser of the Third World Network. In India, she says, global free trade "will mean a further destruction of our communities, uprooting of millions of small peasants from the land, and their migration into the slums of overcrowded cities. GATT destroys the cultural diversity and social stability of our nation . . . GATT, for us, implies recolonization."[8]

The rejection of global free trade does not mean, Goldsmith explains, "closing off any region from trading with the rest of the world. It means that each region is free to decide whether or not to enter into bilateral agreements with other regions."[9] Nor does it mean that free movement of capital is abolished, but only that a company wanting to sell in a particular region would have to invest in that region.[10]

It will be instructive to turn now to another capitalist, George Soros, the Hungarian financier who made more than $1 billion when Britain was forced out of the European exchange-rate mechanism. Soros's critique of globalization overlaps with that of Goldsmith, but approaches issues from a slightly different angle.

For Soros, the term *globalization* is just a way of concealing what is really the most striking feature of the world today, which he describes as "dynamic disequilibrium.'' In practice, Soros believes, this disequilibrium makes the breakdown of free markets and the rise of protectionism almost inevitable, and the only viable policy is to recognize this and work for it intelligently. Soros is pessimistic not only about the economic aspects of globalization, but also about the foreign policy implications. The root of the problem here, he believes, is the crucial change that has occurred in Western culture: the replacement of the traditional concern with freedom by something very different, which is ''a narrower concept—the pursuit of self-interest.'' In foreign policy, this change has meant the rise of geopolitical realism. In simple terms, the West has given up its concern for defending any international moral principles; instead, it is now concerned solely with national economic interest.

As the net result of all this, Soros believes, the democracies are unlikely to face up to the danger of an era of nationalist conflict that may now be opening up. In particular, the amoral, ''geopolitical'' mode of thinking means that they are unlikely to take a stand against the neofascist nationalist dictatorships that Soros thinks may arise in ex-communist countries like the former Yugoslavia, and possibly in Russia itself. The outcome is that we are deluded if we think the term *globalization* points forward to a new era of free markets and peaceful democratic government: it is, rather, as if we have gone backwards, to the interwar situation.

This, then, is the skeptical view of globalization taken by two hawk-eyed capitalists both of whom have made fortunes from free markets. Of the many interesting issues they raise, only the most important will be singled out for comment here. This is their defense of protectionism as a response to globalization. In the case of Europe at least, it does not seem to offer a viable answer. As Martin Jacques recently remarked, protection is more likely to intensify than alleviate the difficulty of the European world ''by nurturing inefficiency and delaying structural adjustment.'' Even more disturbingly, Jacques observed, protectionist sentiment is ''symptomatic of a deeper failure on the part of Europe to understand what is happening.'' What has happened is, above all, that the time has gone when Europe could complacently take it for granted that it was in a position to have a go at doing everything. The only salvation, he suggested, is for Europe to recognize that

it must specialise, concentrate on what it is good at, find its global niche. If it fails to do that, then the future will be like the last decade, but writ even larger: declining regions, lost employment, a reduction in social cohesion and marginalised groups. . . . The niche that Europe must fill is to move up-market, specialise in value-added, knowledge-based activities, take advantage of its cultural lead in education, research and development. There is no way back to labour-intensive manufacturing: that is the road to nowhere.[11]

Jacques added that no niche is of course forever: the successful societies ''will be those that are fleet of foot and whose ethos is change.''[12]

The Second Group of Skeptics

This group consists mainly of Marxists and can be covered very briefly because, ironically, the Marxist critique of globalization converges at many points with the one developed from within the capitalist fold by Soros. For present purposes, the American thinker, Immanuel Wallerstein, provides a good summary of the Marxist position.

From the Marxist standpoint, globalization is merely the extension of capitalist exploitation over the whole world. Its great vehicle is the multinational corporation, on the growth of which Marxist literature is often particularly illuminating. That literature will be passed over in the present connection, however, in order to get straight to Wallerstein's main theme. Globalization, Wallerstein argues, has in fact brought liberation and prosperity—but only to the middle-class part of the world, which makes up no more than 20 percent of the world's total population. As far as the other 80 percent are concerned, it has meant only misery. The idea of Hayek and the New Right, that global economic development creates a "trickle-down" effect, is not borne out by the facts. The reality is that global capitalism has entailed two misfortunes, both of which converge with concerns already expressed by Soros. One is "the steady diminution, even the total elimination, of the role of [the] small community structures" within which most of that 80 percent lived their lives.[13] The other is the constant worldwide growth of what he calls "anti-systemic forces"—forces such as nationalism and fundamentalism—which are created, in part at least, by the globalization process itself. The way out of this destructive situation is not through a struggle between capitalism and socialism. That is not what the future is about. What it is about is choosing between "a transition to a relatively classless society versus a transition to some new class-based mode of production (different from historical capitalism but not necessarily better)."[14]

The difficulty with Wallerstein's position becomes most clearly apparent if, for the sake of argument, one agrees with what he has to say. In that case, two problems emerge. The first is that, insofar as he claims to offer a distinctively Marxist position, he is committed to attributing the evils of globalization to capitalist exploitation by the advanced economies. But the theoretical difficulty is to explain the exact sense in which "exploitation" is involved. To be precise, the Marxist theory of exploitation entails an ultimately *unilateral* or *one-way* process of domination. The most striking feature of the globalization process, however, is that the supposed victim nations actually want economic development, capitalist or otherwise. One can try to explain this fact away, as Marxism does, with the aid of a more or less elaborate theory of global "false consciousness." But the point is that this is just to explain away the *reciprocal, two-way* character of globalization by imposing the simplistic logic of a conspiracy theory upon it.

The second difficulty emerges the moment one looks more carefully at Wallerstein's claim that globalization poses a choice between "a transition to a relatively classless society versus a transition to some new class-based mode of production (different from historical capitalism but not necessarily better).'' As Hannah Arendt noted long ago, the transition to a classless society is likely to mean in practice the transition to an amorphous mass society. Unfortunately, a change of that kind is likely to produce far more problems than it solves—many of them, incidentally, being akin to those for which Wallerstein castigates capitalism. Marxism, that is to say, seems to offer us a distinction without a difference, when it comes to suggesting how we might respond to globalization in a constructive, noncapitalist way.

The Third Group of Skeptics

This is a miscellaneous group of academics and publicists; among them, the views of Max Singer and the late Aaron Wildavsky are worth special mention. They deny that a global world order of any kind is emerging, maintaining that what is happening instead is that the world is being divided into ''zones of peace,'' containing 15 percent of the world's population and made up of the stable, rich and powerful democracies, and ''zones of turmoil,'' which contain everyone else and consist of 85 percent of the world's population.[15] What is happening, to be precise, is that for those living in the zones of turmoil, life will continue to be nasty, poor, brutish and short, which is how Hobbes described the state of nature. For those in the zone of peace, however, things look increasingly good. There, war is becoming increasingly unthinkable and democracy increasingly secure.

Another skeptical thinker worthy of note is Samuel Huntington.[16] Huntington also rejects the idea that a peaceful global order based on democracy and free market integration is emerging, or is likely to emerge, and he also rejects the optimism of Singer and Wildavsky about the future of the zone of peace. According to Huntington, the sources of future conflict will not be reduced even if the post–cold war world moves towards a global order based on capitalism, free markets and democracy.

It is my hypothesis that the fundamental source of conflict in this new world will not be primarily ideological or primarily economic. The great divisions among human kind and the dominating source of conflict will be cultural. Nation states will remain the most powerful actors in world affairs, but the principal conflicts of global politics will occur between nations and groups of different civilizations. The clash of civilizations will dominate global politics.[17]

But why, one may ask, should differences between civilizations lead to conflict? Huntington's view is that the impact of modernization stimulates the need for a sense of group identity which states cannot fully satisfy, since the primary sense of identity can only be provided by religion, culture or a sense of race.

Since these considerations cut across state divisions, the quest for identity will likely pave the way for a global clash of civilizations.

In the light of these skeptical reactions, it would be natural to conclude that the concept of globalization is at best a mere euphemism for some extremely disturbing world developments. A more measured response begins to emerge, however, if we step back from the debate between the defenders of globalization and their skeptical critics in order to consider four novel aspects of the present world situation for which we need, in some form or another, a concept of internationalization or globalization. It is when these four aspects are taken into account that we come, in particular, to the "reality" of globalization referred to in the title of this chapter. What, then, are the four novel aspects of the world situation?

THE REALITY OF THE GLOBALIZATION PROCESS

The First Novel Aspect of Globalization: The End of Western International Hegemony

Writing in 1934, Oswald Spengler repeated the brutal message he had proclaimed in *The Decline of the West* in 1918, at the end of the First World War. It was not only Germany that lost the war, he said: more generally, the war "was a defeat for the white races, and the Peace of 1918 was the first great triumph of the coloured world."[18] The white ruling nations, he continued, have "lost the feeling of the self-evidence of their power and are not even aware that they have lost it . . . they have ceded the choice of the hour to America and, above all, to Asia, whose frontier now [includes Russia]."[19] In a word, Europe has ceased to be the political center of world history. It was not until the decades after the Second World War that the great shift in world power that Spengler had identified was completed.

More recently, the American scholar Samuel Huntington restated Spengler's message in a more up-to-date and dispassionate way. "With the end of the Cold War," Huntington wrote, "international politics moves out of its Western phase, and its center-piece becomes the interaction between the West and non-Western civilizations and among non-Western civilizations . . . the peoples and governments of non-Western civilizations no longer remain the objects of history as targets of Western colonialism but join the West as movers and shapers of history."[20] This, then, is the first distinctive aspect of our time for which the term *globalization* is required.

The Second Novel Aspect of Globalization: Cultural Change

Like the first aspect, the second aspect of globalization was already beginning to emerge before the Second World War. Writing in 1931, the French thinker, Paul Valéry (1871–1945), asked himself what was the most novel feature of the age in which he was living. "I noticed almost immediately," he records, "a major event, a fact of outstanding significance, which its very greatness, its obviousness, its novelty, or rather its essential singularity, had kept hidden from us who are its contemporaries."[21] What was this "fact of outstanding significance" that Valéry had noticed?

It was, Valéry explained, the fact that a new "period of inter-relation" was now replacing the "period of discovery."[22] What marks the new period is the fact that "The age of uncharted areas, of unoccupied territories, of places which nobody owns, and therefore the age of free expansion, is at an end. . . . *The age of a finite world is now beginning.*"[23] There is nothing more remarkable, he said, than this "linking together of all parts of the globe."[24]

If we now jump a quarter century to the postwar period, Peter Drucker emphasized in particular growing cultural homogeneity as the most striking difference between an "international" economy, which we have had for at least three centuries, and a "global" (or world, as Drucker himself called it) economy. In an *international* economy, Drucker wrote, each country "is a separate unit with its own economic values and preferences, its own markets, and its own largely self-contained information."[25] In a *world* (or *global*) economy, by contrast, there are common appetites, common demands, and a large body of common information. The result, Drucker noted, is that in a global economy, the most important difference may one day be the simplest of all differences—the differences, that is, between the haves and the have nots.

The Third Novel Aspect of Globalization: The Erosion of National Sovereignty

During the interwar era, most Western thinkers tended to remain blind to the advent of the new global age: thinkers like Spengler and Valéry were exceptional. What obscured it from sight for most of their contemporaries was the triumph of the principle of national sovereignty. Even when the trend towards a global economy was recognized, nationalist sentiment was so powerful that any speculations about globalism generally took for granted the indefinite future existence of the nation-state as the basis of European life. This was evident, for example, in the proposals of the French prime minister, Aristide Briand, for a united Europe. The Spanish philosopher Jose Ortega y Gasset was one of the relatively small number of interwar thinkers to transcend nationalist sentiment when he envisaged the emergence of a European identity in *national* terms, to be embodied in a United States of Europe. It was only the spiritual and political inspiration provided by such an ideal, Ortega maintained, that would permit what he believed to be the bankrupt system of nation-states to cope with the ideological challenge posed by Soviet communism.[26]

In recent years, by contrast, it has become commonplace to talk of the end of the sovereignty of the nation-state and the "de-centering" of politics. Such is the theme of Ulrich Beck, for example, in Germany,[27] a theme echoed in

Britain by Anthony Giddens[28] and in the United States by, for example, the former White House aide James Pinkerton, who struck a lucky phrase when he called for a "new paradigm" for modern government. *The Times* of London, at any rate, was so impressed by Pinkerton's phrase that late in 1993 it sponsored a conference on his proposal. In a leading article in which it subsequently explained what the new paradigm was about to its readers, *The Times* announced that the new model of government would be "pluralist, decentralised and entrepreneurial, rather than bureaucratic, centrally managed and highly regulated." In addition, the new paradigm would emphasize "intermediary institutions and subsidiarity as the basis of good government."[29]

By this time, the thought is bound to have occurred that what is termed the "decentering" of politics is really just a "globalized," so to speak, version of the old Marxist vision of the withering away of the state. This conclusion has in fact been drawn by some commentators. Thus, Michael Hirsh, for example, wrote in *Newsweek* that "The state is withering and global business is taking charge." Not only are nation-states becoming increasingly impotent, he added, but so also are international institutions such as the European Union, the North Atlantic Treaty Organization, the United Nations and the International Monetary Fund.[30]

The Fourth Novel Aspect of Globalization: Pollution of the Environment

In a well-known essay called "Economic Possibilities for Our Grandchildren," published in 1930, J. M. Keynes tried to cast his mind far forward into the distant future and predict how the world would have changed in a hundred years' time. Since a good part of that hundred years has now elapsed, his prediction remains of considerable interest.

What is striking about this essay is his optimism. "I look forward," Keynes wrote, "to the greatest change which has ever occurred in the material environment of life for human beings in the aggregate." The essence of this change, he explained, is that "there will be ever larger and larger classes and groups of people from whom problems of economic necessity have been practically removed."[31] In a word, humankind would be well advanced on the path to a final solution to the economic problem.

What is relevant at present is a danger which Keynes' optimism conceals from him, although it is one that now seems obvious to us. This is the progressive pollution of the environment that was to be brought about by economic and technological progress. Half a century later, this concern had acquired an increasingly prominent position on the political agenda. But what was to be done? During the past quarter of a century, two wholly different kinds of answer have emerged.

The most radical, and least consequential, answer calls for a profound spiritual change in the individual's spiritual attitude toward the world. If it is asked what such a spiritual change would imply in practical political terms, an answer is provided by the American vice-president, Al Gore, who has demanded what he terms a Global Marshall Plan.[32] Such a plan, Gore stresses, is no pragmatic affair but requires that we should "change the very foundation of our civilization" by moving it toward the philosophy of Gandhi.[33] The prospect of the spiritual revolution this requires actually happening, needless to say, is somewhat remote.

At the opposite extreme to the demand for a spiritual revolution as the only stable basis for a global order is the response by the director of the Hudson Institute during the 1970s. In *The Next Two Thousand Years* (1976), Herman Kahn remarked that it had become popular to blame technology for the environmental pollution we face today, and to draw the conclusion that we should "try to slow technological advance by halting economic growth." This attitude, Kahn declared, is "thoroughly misguided," since technology itself provides the means to overcome pollution:

The limits to growth model—with its conclusion that continued economic growth causes pollution that will inevitably overwhelm us—is undoubtedly incorrect. Our principal argument is that although the fraction of our GNP needed to control pollution may increase over the near term, it is likely to remain a very small part of the whole GNP. Secondly, we conclude that from now on, *if the choice is made*, the air, water and landscapes can become cleaner over time—along with continued economic growth.[34]

In between the two extremes of neo-Buddhist spirituality and undimmed technological confidence lies a variety of rather limited but more or less viable responses to the global spread of technological problems. One is the naive hope that the need to do anything at all would simply disappear if the concept of "sustainable development" advanced in the Bruntman Report (1987) replaced the present ideal of unlimited growth. Another, more realistic, view is more pessimistic. Viable responses, in this view, are possible only on issues that are not politically inflammable—and these tend, by definition, to be relatively minor issues.

THE ROLE OF NATIONAL GOVERNMENTS IN THE CONTEXT OF GLOBALIZATION

Having considered the novel aspects of globalization, the problem that now arises is to determine more precisely the nature of the role left for national governments to play in the new era. Four very different answers have been suggested by Western thinkers.

The first answer is the minimalist, stripped-down conception of government envisaged by the American Republican leader Newt Gingrich in his book *Contract with America*. The trouble with this view is that it ignores (among other things) the growing internal problems of unemployment and an underclass—the problems, that is, of exclusion—faced by all developed societies.

The second view is that proposed by Anthony Giddens. Giddens rejects Gingrich's minimalism in favor of a position that sets out to bring into view "the new ties between the regional and the global" by emphasizing the dual, two-way nature of globalization. More precisely, Giddens maintains, governments must promote a process of "double democratisation," a concept that he takes over from David Held. What this means is that democracy must not only be "filtered downwards," but must also "reach upwards and outwards." It must, that is, be made to penetrate into every sphere of life, and not just the narrowly political part of it. To embrace democracy in this active fashion is, for Giddens, the only way of coming to terms with "the waves of democratisation sweeping across the world."[35]

The trouble with this position is the enormous weight that it places on an extremely vague conception of democracy. Above all, what Giddens fails to allow for is the most important feature of the Western experience of democracy, which is its ambiguity. It is ambiguous in the sense that it is normally associated with constitutional government of the American and British kind, but it is in fact just as compatible with despotic forms of government based on extraconstitutional charismatic leadership. This is the lesson that Rousseau taught over two centuries ago. For some reason, however, Giddens chooses to ignore it.

The third view is most clearly formulated by Paul Hirst.[36] Far from making the sovereign nation-state an anachronism, Hirst maintains, globalization is likely to make it even more indispensable than it has been in the past. "Even if national states become less effective in deciding the affairs of their societies," Hirst remarks, "national political institutions remain central in setting up the rules whereby various political bodies and social agencies play their games. This may not be 'sovereignty' in the old sense, and the state may be highly pluralistic, but such a society [still] requires a public power that ensures the rule of law?"

Finally, other thinkers have offered a fourth, more military reason for maintaining that the dispensability of the nation-state has been exaggerated. This reason concerns, more specifically, new sources of instability that have arisen in the post–cold war era. The nature of these sources is well brought out by, for example, Martin Van Creveld, the Israeli military analyst. Van Creveld has recently argued that the lost portions of state sovereignty would simply mean that the initiative in the international order increasingly passed away from large states into the hands of drug barons, nationalist and fundamentalist zealots, terrorists and small maverick states flooded with arms in the aftermath of the collapse of the Soviet Union.[37] Even those who reject pessimism of Creveld's kind sometimes only seem to succeed in making the ground for pessimism even deeper. John Keegan, for example, suggested that established states will not in fact suffer the loss of sovereignty and consequent destabilization forecast by Creveld, but that this is only because they will, with popular encouragement, defend their position by acquiring the kind of powers over their citizens formerly associated with totalitarian dictatorships.[38]

CONCLUSIONS

This review of the different views of globalization suggests three conclusions. The first involves the distinction between a *global society*, on the one hand, and the *globalization process*, on the other. In a word, it is possible to speak of the globalization process, but not of a global society, disappointing as that may be for the more optimistic kind of liberal democrat. In this connection, the concept of a global society is essentially a Western one, inspired by the universalistic tradition of thought mentioned at the beginning of this chapter. The point is worth stressing because this universalistic way of thinking is profoundly at odds with, for example, "the particularism of most Asian societies and their emphasis on what distinguishes one people from another."[39] The globalization process, by contrast, refers simply to a set of trends that are primarily economic and technological. The second conclusion, to which we now turn, concerns the likely social and political consequences of globalization in this latter sense.

Specifically, it may be suggested that the globalization process will inescapably create at least four major problems for both developed and developing states.

The First Problem Is the Emergence of Militant "Identity Politics," Involving the Assertion of the Local Against the Global

Perhaps the greatest difficulty of all, for developed and developing states alike, will be one that was quite unforeseen by Western universalistic theory of the kind that characterized traditional liberal and socialist thought. This is that globalization does not necessarily mean cultural homogenization. On the contrary, the assertion of the universal, as Bhikhu Parekh has observed, tends to call forth the assertion of the particular.[40] J. P. Arnason voiced a similar thought when he remarked that globalization, instead of being a process of homogenization, "should rather be understood as a new framework of differentiation."[41]

The potentially militant implications of this reassertion of the local and particular against the globalization process has already been noticed in connection with Huntington's work. A decade ago, however, a notable French publicist, Régis Debray, had already issued a prophetic warning. Modernity, he wrote, "will be archaic or it will not be at all. And when humanity 'in progress' is civilised by its own hand, it simultaneously becomes savage in its head and heart." This is why globalization has the seemingly paradoxical result of renewing "the escalation of tribal conflict and the resurrection of religion, not only on the periphery but at the very centre of the industrial world."[42] The hope that a peaceful postmodern affirmation of difference or otherness might eventually be made possible by a harmonious multicultural interpenetration of the local and the global, or the particular and the universal, to a point where both terms became meaningless, was dismissed out of hand by Debray. Such a hope merely evades what globalization actually entails, which is a rout:

Let the music begin: Shi'ites against Sunni or Arabs against Persians, Alawites against Sunnis, Cypriot Turks against Cypriot Greeks, Druzes against Marionites, Jews against Muslims, Kurds against Arabs and Persians, Moors against Berbers, Sikhs against Hindus, Singhalese against Tamils, Germanics against Slavics, and Slavics against Turks, the Catholic against the Orthodox, the believers against the atheists, Hazaras and Pashtuns against Russian occupants, Baluchi against Punjabi, Vietnamese against Khmer Rouges and Chinese against Vietnamese or vice-versa.[43]

It may be objected that this is at most a passing stage of the globalization process, since exposure to the modern media and modern products gradually erodes traditional ethnic differences, along with the significance of traditional territorial loyalties. Yet the reply offered by Gilbert Larochelle is worth pondering. It is that identity politics do not depend on the survival of actual differences, since the boundless power of the human imagination can provide an endless supply of symbolic ones that are equally effective.[44]

Is there then no ground at all for optimism about the consequences of the globalization process? Does it not, at least, promote solidarity in some degree, simply through the greater spirit of tolerance which (it is hoped) men and women must surely acquire when the media and communications technology break down the starker forms of the "them" and "us" mentality of tribal thinking? M. Featherstone has offered the most judicious conclusion on this matter, which is to the effect that the outcome of globalization may point in several mutually incompatible directions. "With globalization," Featherstone writes, "the person who was unequivocally outside now becomes a neighbor, with the result that the inside/outside distinction fails. This can lead to responses of ecumenism, tolerance and universalism in which everyone is included, or resistance to globalization in the form of counter movements such as the various non-Western fundamentalisms which react against Westoxication."[45]

Beside Featherstone's conclusion may be set the aptly worded conclusion of Gilbert Larochelle. "The image of the 'global village,' " Larochelle notes, is "only valid insofar as the global does not erase the village."

Globalization and the Problem of Human Rights

The second major issue presented by globalization is whether it is likely to promote increasing recognition of individual rights in non-Western societies, or rather to bring about the increasing rejection of such a concern, on the ground that the concepts of the individual and of rights associated with the Western model of civil association are alike destructive imports from an alien culture.

Doubts about the universal relevance of the Western civil model, with its related concept of freedom, impersonal law, freedom of choice and universal tolerance, are not confined to non-Western thinkers searching for an autonomous national identity. In the West, thinkers like Ernest Gellner, for example, have argued that the ideal of civil association presupposes a conception of man that is not to be found outside the Western world. This Gellner describes as "modular man"—a kind of man, that is, whose life is divided and compartmentalized in a way in which life is not in societies with more organic forms of communal identity.[46] Gellner's position is misleading, however. While he is correct in saying that the emergence of the civil ideal in the West occurred in tandem with the emergence of modular man, it does not follow that civil association cannot be detached from the modular experience of life. This, indeed, is precisely what has happened in non-Western societies like Malaysia in which elements of the civil ideal have been implemented.

In principle at least, then, the civil model may be applied to the globalization process. How far it is actually applied in practice, however, is a different matter, and one on which profitable speculation is impossible at the present stage.

The Problem of Legitimation

Closely related to the problem of the implications of globalization for human rights is the problem of legitimation faced by states that feel themselves threatened by globalization. The danger already touched on is apparent: such states may instead seek legitimation through rejection of global tendencies, turning instead to the assertive "politics of identity." To the extent to which they do so, they are likely to find themselves impelled towards one or other of two extremes.

At one extreme there lies, as in the case of Russia, the prospect of *authoritarian nationalist populism*, of a potentially fascist kind. In the case of India, the BJP represents a similar response. At the other extreme lies the possibility of another response, of the kind found in Turkey, for example. This is the resort to *fundamentalism* of various kinds.

Even in the apparently stable industrial democracies of the West, the problem of legitimacy has been rendered potentially acute as a result of pressure from the global market to cut back on costly social democratic policies, with a consequent reduction in the strategies available for dealing with the existence of an underclass. The tax revolt now evident in advanced societies is likely to make the problem of exclusion still worse.

For the sake of argument, however, let us assume for a moment that Fukayama is right to regard democracy in one form or another as the fate of both the developed and the developing nations caught up in the globalization process. In that case, what must be remembered is that democracy, which is based on an ideal of self-government, has no intrinsic connection either with good government or with the creation of a free society. This was implied in what has already been said about the lack of any intrinsic connection between the civil model, with its commitment to the rule of law, and the democratic one, with its rival commitment to the popular will. It will be useful, however, to recall the crucial point made long ago by Alexis de Tocqueville, in a form that applies to both developed and developing states.

What de Tocqueville argued was that, to the extent to which states became prosperous, democracy was very likely to create a new form of dictatorship or (he might well have added), to give an existing one new sources of life, in some cases. De Tocqueville emphasized that this new form of despotism was likely to be benign, with a form of paternalistic managerialism replacing the atrocities formerly associated with it. He stressed, however, that this did not make democratic despotism any the less incompatible with human dignity.

The fact that many contemporary thinkers speak, as has been seen, of the decline of the centralized, sovereign state in the face of globalizing tendencies does not mean that de Tocqueville's misgivings have become irrelevant: the real object of his attack was the tendency to tolerate arbitrary power, provided it seemed well-intentioned. Unfortunately, there is nothing to suggest that this tendency would automatically disappear with decentralization. On the contrary, this problem is more likely to reemerge, albeit in new guise, in the new, localized centers in which power is presently thought to be in process of being relocated. In developing societies, this may not be a novel development, but in developed ones, it is a misfortune that the imperatives of globalization may help to induce rather than to obviate.

The Problem of Creating Appropriate New International Institutions

The most demanding cooperative task created by globalization is that of devising institutions to cope with the problems it creates. These institutions will by no means always be governmental ones, but in the nature of things there are, and will continue to be, problems that can only be dealt with by agreed governmental action. Such cooperation will entail, as Hobbes put it, covenants without the sword and will have all the limitations of such covenants. Success in creating relevant institutions will, needless to say, be directly related to the nature and scale of the problem involved.

In practice, the real problem (and the discouraging reality) seems to be that even when there is agreement on the need for global action, translating the agreement into operative policy is frequently impossible. An excellent example is provided by the 1987 Montreal Protocol on Substances That Deplete the Ozone Layer, finally signed by 24 countries. Even a measure of this kind, whose value no one contested, only won the support of developing nations like India and China when the West finally agreed (in 1990) to compensate them for the loss of revenue they would otherwise have suffered from ceasing to manufacture chlorofluorocarbons (CFCs).[47]

Finally, the third conclusion is a very general thought—to the effect that before a satisfactory response to globalization can be worked out, it is necessary above all to learn the main lesson that the history of twentieth-century politics has to teach.

This lesson is that economics is *not* the driving force of history, although much of the contemporary discussion of globalization appears to assume that it is. On the contrary, the lesson to be learned by looking at what happened in Russia in 1917, for example, or more recently in 1989; or by looking, once again, at the rise of fascism, is that *the political enjoys primacy over the economic*. To recall this lesson is the best way of avoiding the danger of discussing globalization primarily, or even exclusively, in economic and technological terms.

NOTES

I am indebted to Ümit Cizre-Sakallioglu, Simon Lee and Bhikhu Parekh for conversations on this subject.

1. The literature is now vast, but interesting examples are: S. Hall, D. Held and T. McGrew (eds.), *Modernity and Its Futures* (Oxford: Polity Press/Open University, 1992), especially chapter 2, "A Global Society," by T. McGrew; Z. Mlinar (ed.), *Globalization and Territorial Identities* (Aldershot: Avebury, 1992); G. Parry (ed.), *Politics in an Interdependent World* (Aldershot: Edward Elgar, 1994); M. Featherstone (ed.), *Global Culture: Nationalism, Globalization and Modernity* (London: Sage, 1990); A. Giddens, *The Consequences of Modernity* (Oxford: Polity Press, 1994); D. Held, *Democracy and the Global Order: From the Modern State to the Cosmopolitan Governance* (Oxford: Polity Press, 1995); B. Axford, *Global System* (Oxford: Polity Press, 1995); R. Falk, *On Humane Governance: Towards a New Global Politics—The Womp Report of the Global Civilization Project* (Oxford: Polity Press, 1995); R. Harvey, *The Return of the Strong: The Drift to Global Disorder* (London: Macmillan, 1995).

2. A. Giddens, *The Consequences of Modernity* (Oxford: Polity Press, 1994), 175.

3. G. Larochelle, "Interdependence, Globalization and Fragmentation," in Z. Mlinar (ed.), *Globalization and Territorial Identities* (Aldershot: Avebury, 1992), 155.

4. M. McLuhan, *The Gutenberg Galaxy* (Toronto: University of Toronto Press, 1962).

5. J. Goldsmith, *The Trap* (London: Macmillan, 1994), 34.

6. Ibid., 36.

7. Ibid., 29–30.

8. Ibid., 32.

9. Ibid., 36–37.

10. Ibid., 36.

11. *The Sunday Times*, November 13, 1994, 16.

12. Ibid.

13. Immanuel Wallerstein, *Historical Capitalism* (London: Verso, 1983), 101.

14. Ibid., 107.

15. *The Real World Order* (Chatham, NJ: Chatham House Publishers, 1994).

16. S. Huntington, "The Clash of Civilizations?" *Foreign Affairs* 72(3) (1993): 22–49.

17. Ibid., 22.

18. *The Hour of Decision* (London: Allen and Unwin, 1934), 209.

19. Ibid., 210.

20. Huntington, "The Clash of Civilizations?" 23.

21. Paul Valéry, *Reflections on the World Today*, trans. F. Scarfe (London: Thames and Hudson, 1951), 21.

22. Ibid., 22.

23. Ibid., 21–22 (emphasis in original).

24. Ibid., 22.

25. P. F. Drucker, *The Age of Discontinuity* (New York: Harper and Row, 1978), 81.

26. See K. Wilson and J. van der Dussen (eds.), *The History of the Idea of Europe* (London: Routledge, 1995), 104–105 (on Briand), 129 (on Ortega).

27. Ulrich Beck, *Risk Society: Towards a New Modernity* (London: Sage, 1992), 195, 230–231.

28. See, for example, Giddens's article, "Government's Last Gasp?" *The Observer*, July 9, 1995.

29. *The Times*, December 3, 1993.

30. Hirsh is quoted and paraphrased by Giddens in his article, "Government's Last Gasp?" in *The Observer*, July 9, 1995.

31. J. M. Keynes, *Essays in Persuasion* (London: Macmillan, 1931), 372.

32. Al Gore, *Earth in the Balance* (London: Earthscan Publications, 1992), 295 et seq.

33. Ibid., 14.

34. H. Kahn, *The Next Two Thousand Years* (London: Sphere, 1977), 150–151 (emphasis in original).

35. Giddens, in *The Observer*, July 9, 1995.

36. References here are to P. Hirst, *Renewal* 2(4) (October 1994). See also P. Hirst and G. Thompson, "The Problem of Globalisation," *Economy and Society* 21(4) (1992): 99, 357–396; and P. Hirst and G. Thompson, "Globalisation, Foreign Direct Investment and International Economic Governance," *Organisation* 1(2) (1994).

37. M. Van Creveld, *On Future War* (London: Brassey's, 1991).

38. In *The Daily Telegraph*, March 23, 1995.

39. Huntington, "The Clash of Civilizations?" 41.

40. B. C. Parekh, *New Community* 21(2) (April 1995): 147–152.

41. J. P. Arnason, "Nationalism, Globalization and Modernity," in Featherstone (ed.), *Global Culture*, 224.

42. R. Debray, *Les empires contre l'Europe* (Paris: Gallimard, 1986), 27.

43. Ibid., 27–28.

44. G. Larochelle, "Interdependence, Globalization and Fragmentation," in Mlinar (ed.), *Globalization and Territorial Identities*, 139.

45. M. Featherstone, "Global Culture: An Introduction," in Featherstone (ed.), *Global Culture*, 11.

46. "The Importance of Being Modular," in J. A. Hall (ed.), *Civil Society* (Oxford: Polity Press, 1995), 278–300.

47. T. Brenton, *The Greening of Machiavelli* (London: Earthscan, 1994), 140–143.

CHAPTER 3

Privatization and Organizational Taxonomy: The Case of the National Enterprise

SONNY NWANKWO

Conceptually, privatization entails changing organizational status from public to private and from a monopoly to a competitive situation. In practice, the outcome may be different. Many privatized utilities conform to the traditional notion of neither the public nor the private enterprise. The broad dichotomy of the public-private model of enterprise classification no longer provides adequate insight into the workings of organizations in today's environment. The new challenges emanating from the increasingly complex nature of modern environment require a new philosophy of organizational classification—a reconceptualization of conventional paradigms.

This chapter, based on the United Kingdom's privatization experience, notes the importance of an emergent organizational form—the national enterprise—which has not been well explored in the existing literature. The chapter offers a framework for identifying and delineating the boundaries of this organizational type. It is suggested that a clear articulation of the national enterprise concept might be useful to governmental strategies in planning the process of transforming state-owned enterprises.

INTRODUCTION

The most common approach to the classification of enterprise organizations is to distinguish between the public and the private. Although the public-private dichotomy may provide a useful guide, it is nevertheless inadequate for constructing a general taxonomy (Perry and Rainey, 1988). It no longer provides a comprehensive description of the subtleties and varieties of a broad range of modern enterprise organizations.

This chapter accordingly advances the concept of the national enterprise, which is intended to overcome some of the obvious weaknesses of the public-private model. It does this by (1) specifying the domain of the national enterprise—identifying its major attributes and the configurations different national enterprises create at particular points in their development, and (2) highlighting the implications of the national enterprise concept as an aid to the successful management of public-to-private transitions. The need to signify the existence of national enterprises and to clarify the range of forms they can take is urgent, given the trend for many developing economies to embark on transitions from public to private systems and the dangers that are often inherent in moving wholesale from one side of the public-private continuum to the extreme of the other (Ivanov et al., 1994).

The motivation for this chapter stems from the author's involvement in researching the privatization experience in different national settings. However, the United Kingdom is used here as a contextual base mainly because its program of ''rolling back the frontiers of the state'' has been more far-reaching than that in any comparable country (Miller, 1994) and, indeed, has been the hallmark of the Conservative government since the premiership of Margaret Thatcher (Marsh, 1991).

PRIVATIZATION AND ORGANIZATIONAL CLASSIFICATION

The weakness of current paradigms about what privatization is and the organizational forms it creates has become more apparent as the consequences of privatization are analyzed (Ivanov et al., 1994; Nwankwo, 1993 and 1994). At a broader level, there is growing speculation about how organizations might be characterized in the future (Drucker, 1992; Mitroff, Mason and Pearson, 1994). The conventional textbook approach to enterprise classification has accordingly come under severe strain, leading some researchers to assert that it no longer works (Hinterhuber and Levin, 1994; Mitroff, Mason and Pearson, 1994). A new approach is, therefore, necessary to produce a more sensible explanation and understanding of modern organizations, especially those that differ markedly from the popular typologies in the degree to which they might be characterized.

THE PUBLIC-PRIVATE ORGANIZATIONAL PARADIGMS

The literature is replete with studies addressing the similarities and differences between public and private enterprise organizations. Among the relationships that have been examined are control systems; equity ownership; managerial autonomy; work-related employee attitudes; performance norms and outcomes; social roles; political influences; and economic incentives and strategic decision processes (Aryee, 1992; Perry and Rainey, 1988; Rainey, Backoff and Levine, 1976; Yarrow, 1987).

Although more recent studies have viewed public and private typologies as a continuum (rather than a dichotomy), very little help is on offer in terms of providing a framework useful for resolving the underlying taxonomical complications (Dunsire et al. 1988; Perry and Rainey, 1988; Sikorski, 1993). The framework proposed here offers useful strategic insights into the delicate act of managing organizational change from traditional public forms of organization to privatized ones. Due acknowledgment is, however, given to the literature base which reveals the existence of organizations that neither conform nor subscribe to the traditional assumptions about public and private entities—organizational types that are collectively referred to as the third sector (Etzioni, 1973; McGill and Wooten, 1975). Nevertheless, since the third sector cannot be comfortably positioned along a continuum at the extremes of which lie, respectively, the pure public and pure private enterprises, they may be unaffected by the dialectics of the public-to-private transition (Nwankwo, 1994).

To discuss this nascent organizational type, it is necessary, first, to set out the criteria for defining the concept of an enterprise and within it, the public-private configuration.

THE ENTERPRISE CONCEPT

Popular attempts at defining the concept of an enterprise include Ramanadham's (1984) two-factor framework, Bohm's (1981) tripartite characteristics and Liebenstein's (1965) three tests.

Formulating a generally agreeable definition of an enterprise is obviously problematic. However, it is pertinent to demarcate the boundaries of an enterprise in order to isolate public and third sector organizations that are not "enterprises." On the basis of synthesis drawn from the general literature, the following generalizations can be made about the common paradigm for enterprise:

- An enterprise is profit oriented. Theorists have argued against the reality of the notion of profit maximization behavior in enterprises (Koutsoyiannis, 1980: chs. 14–18), but none argues against the fundamental import of the profit motive.

- Resource generation and utilization and the associated notion of viability seem inextricably intertwined with the whole enterprise concept. The manner in which resources are generated and deployed differentiates the enterprise from other organizations. This differentiation is created by the degree of involvement in commercial activities, the extent to which revenue is derived directly from those activities and the level of dependence on market performance for survival.

- By implication, for an enterprise to become and remain viable and profitable, its products and services must not only be offered at a price to consumers but prices should reflect the real economic costs of activities.

- An enterprise is managed by personnel who have much discretion over how the organization's resources will be attracted and utilized.

The United Kingdom's "privatized sector" satisfies these basic criteria of an enterprise. In the section that follows, we examine the broad distinction that currently is being made between public and private versions of the enterprise.

The Public Enterprise

Views on the public enterprise are widely varied (Bohm, 1981; Curivon, 1986 Ramanadham, 1984). Broadly, it may be defined as the enterprise that is publicly owned and controlled. A more rigid and universal definition may be elusive and may even seem undesirable in view of conceptual difficulties and the diversity of legal and organizational forms prevalent in the literature.

Nevertheless, it can be inferred from the general literature that public enterprises have three defining characteristics: they are government owned and controlled; they are engaged in commercial (business) activities; and they have sociopolitical goals alongside the primary economic goals. These characteristics are not precise, either in a conceptual or an operational sense partly because of the taxonomical problems.

The Private Enterprise

The private enterprise refers to the enterprise that is privately owned and controlled by the market. Two principal factors have been applied in explaining the private enterprise: (1) ownership and (2) management of benefits (Ramanadham, 1984). The crucial point of the private enterprise is that the organization and its management are solely answerable to the owners via the board of directors. As a consequence, management activities reflect the supremacy of shareholders' interests.

Weaknesses of the Public-Private Distinction

Several areas of weakness consequently arise and have been addressed in several works (Coursey and Bozeman, 1990; Dunsire et al., 1988; Nwankwo, 1994; Perry and Rainey, 1988; Rainey, Backoff and Levine, 1976) which include—for emphasis;

Ownership and control: The intractable controversy over issues such as where the public concept ends and the private concept begins (for example, over what proportion of public/private equity holdings classifies an enterprise in either domain) shows that ownership per se does not fully capture the dimensions of the public-private distinction. For example, privatized utilities represent the grey area where the public-private distinctions seem particularly weak. Experience in these industries has revealed the fallacy of assuming that ownership and control are the same thing (Majone, 1994).

The case of British Telecom (BT) is particularly insightful. At the time of privatization in 1984, the government retained a 48.6 percent equity holding in the company (the largest single block shareholding). After the second and third flotations, the government divested itself of its holding. But the resultant change in equity structure did not result in any change in the regulatory control. Hence, BT is no freer now to respond to the dictates of market forces than it was in 1984.

With regard to British Gas, some early observers did argue that the change of ownership from public to private could be viewed as significant because the market behavior of the privatized British Gas did not seem different from that of any previous state utility (Kay, 1987; Odell, 1987). Although privatization was supposed to introduce the discipline of the competitive mechanism, the initial market power of British Gas conferred by control over the grid largely insulated it from the chill winds of competition. However, following the government's adoption of a report by the Monopolies and Mergers Commission (MMC, 1993), the industry has been going through a major transformation—with full competition expected in 1998. Previously, only large industrial users could choose their suppliers. Beginning in April 1996, competition was extended to domestic consumers in some parts of the country. British Gas, however, is still tightly controlled and cannot respond to the challenges of free competition in the manner of a private enterprise.

In general, transfers of ownership by themselves have not succeeded in altering the market characteristic of some of the privatized utilities. This is confirmed in, for example, Parker (1992) where he provides a schema to illustrate that there has been little movement from the North (monopoly) to the South (perfect competition) attendant upon privatization (see Figure 3.1). Much of the movement has been from the West (public/political ownership but not control) to the East (private ownership).

Public versus private interests: Some enterprises, due to the nature of their products/markets, belong to the realm where it may be very difficult to separate public from private interests. The result is that such enterprises are closely monitored, for example, through specially tailored regulatory agencies. (U.K. examples include Oftel, Ofwat, Offer, Ofgas for telecommunications, water, electricity and gas industries, respectively.) Furthermore, the notion of public interest is value-laden and notoriously difficult to define or measure. It may not, therefore, be possible to capture the public-private distinction on the basis of public versus private interests.

IDENTIFYING THE NATIONAL ENTERPRISE

Having provided a definition of an enterprise and discussed the mainstream theoretical distinction between the public and private enterprise and some of the weaknesses in the current model for distinguishing between one and the other, it is now possible to isolate the national enterprise from other organizational types that have been mentioned in the general literature (Shipp and Cravens,

Figure 3.1
A Schema of Privatization

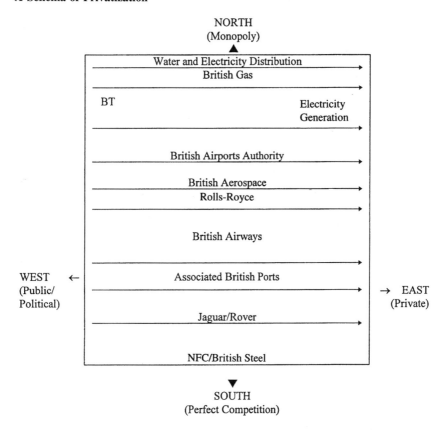

1994; Etzioni, 1973; Hinterhuber and Levin, 1994; Mitroff, Mason and Pearson, 1994; Sternberg, 1933).

The Concept of the National Enterprise

The national enterprise may be defined as the enterprise that is privately owned but still publicly controlled (type I in Figure 3.2), or publicly owned but controlled primarily by the market (type II).

The concept is derived by application of a series of criteria that seek to explain whether such an enterprise

• is publicly owned

• was once publicly owned

• is a natural monopoly

Figure 3.2
A Conceptual View of the National Enterprise

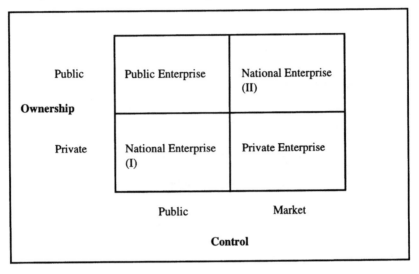

- is a national flag bearer
- dominates the sector of its primary activity
- provides social/political goods.

These criteria may be combined in several different ways in order to define a national enterprise. Accordingly, the approach is, to view a national enterprise as one that exhibits the generic characteristics of an enterprise and that is rated on a sufficient number of the above criteria (see Table 3.1). The following sections flesh out how these criteria are to be applied.

Public ownership/control: Enterprises of interest here are those Posner (1979) referred to as "one who sells and buys in the market place, but relies on the government to act as banker." Ownership per se is not absolutely crucial in marking the boundaries of the national enterprise. Classifying enterprises on the basis of government's equity involvement is fraught with complications. The determinant factor is the control system. This indicates the degree to which the enterprise is effectively controlled through public policy initiatives in order to achieve public interest objectives such as those highlighted by Majone (1994). In this respect, one would be interested in finding out the extent of government's involvement in making investment decisions, in the management of trade surpluses (profits) and in the appointment of key executives.

Enterprises that fall into this category are those that display the public enterprise features specified earlier. Examples include British Rail (BR), Post Office, British Nuclear Fuels (BNFL) and regional transport companies such as the

London Underground and tramway. There are no longer many large enterprises left in this category in the United Kingdom.

Once publicly owned (and still culturally bound to the public ethos): The list of companies falling into this category is now very large, although the great majority (well over one hundred) have entered the private sector via a trade sale or management buyout rather than via a public offer for sale. Considerable evidence shows, as in the examples of British Airways, British Petroleum and BT, that it takes many years to "privatize" attitudes and culture within large organizations, although this has been less problematic in respect of, for example, the National Freight Consortium.

Some privatizations are of more recent vintage, and there may still be a strong residual adherence to practices better suited to public ownership and control. However, the strength of this factor is clearly less than that of public ownership as such. The issue here is not whether ownership is private or public. Rather, the key question is under what conditions will managers be more likely to act in the public interest.

In theory, all privatizations via public issue of shares since Margaret Thatcher are of interest. Realistically, the chances of some of the privatized enterprises (e.g., Amersham International, Jaguar, Enterprise oil, National Bus Company, British Leyland) returning to the public sector are quite remote. However, it may not be sensible to begin to make distinctions as to which enterprises are more likely candidates for re-nationalization because some of the earlier nationalizations seem to defy economic logic and can only be explained by public choice theory (Dunsire et al., 1988). Broadly, all privatized companies will be scored on this attribute.

Natural monopolies: These typically are characterized by the presence of economies of scale, high sunk cost and strong entry barriers. From this it follows that natural monopoly features are generally associated with utility companies such as gas, water, electricity, coal, rail and telecommunications. These utilities are not natural monopolies in their entirety. Advances in technology, for example, have greatly eroded the natural monopoly features in the telecom sector. Only certain aspects of their operation qualify—in effect, the network, and for gas and electricity, their "grids." The supply into the grid and distribution from grid to customers are not natural monopolies. This point was glossed over at the time of early privatizations such that, while BT was privatized in its entirety, the electricity generators were separated from the grid and the grid from the distribution companies. This issue is currently being addressed in respect of the planned privatization of British Rail.

A strong case may be made for retaining public ownership of a grid; the Labour party is committed to a reversal of the present government's privatization program in some sector. Nevertheless, the case for public ownership is not absolute. This is because, even where ownership is passed into private hands, it is possible to stimulate public ownership via special share restrictions combined with a tough regulatory regime. It has always been fallacious to argue

Table 3.1
The National Enterprise Attribute Score

Organizations	Public Enterprise	Privatized Enterprise	Natural Monopoly	Tailored Regulation	Sectoral Dominance	National Flag Bearer	Common Goods Provider	Golden Share or Other Restriction	Total Score (Max = 8)
Regional Electricity Companies	0	1	1	1	1	0	1	1	6
Water Companies	0	1	1	1	1	0	1	1	6
British Gas	0	1	1	1	1	0	1	1	6
Electricity Generators	0	1	1	1	1	0	1	1	6
British Airports Authority	0	1	1	1[1]	1	0	1	1	6
British Telecom	0	1	1[2]	1	1	0	1	1	6
British Rail	1	0	1	1	1	0	1	0	5
Regional Transport Companies[3]	1	0	1	1	1	0	1	0	5
Post Office	1	0	1[2]	1	1	0	1	0	5
British Aerospace	0	1	0	0	0	1	1	1	4
British Airways	0	1	0	0	1	1	0	1	4
Rolls-Royce	0	1	0	0	0	1	0	1	3

ATTRIBUTES

British Coal	1[2]	0	0	0	1	0	1	0	3
British Nuclear Fuels	1	0	0	0	1	0	1	0	3
National Health Service	0[4]	0	0	1	1	1	1	0	3
Associated British Ports	0	1	0	0	1	0	1	0	3
British Petroleum	0	1	0	0	0	1	0	0	2
Cable & Wireless	0	1	0	0	0	0	0	1	2
Sealink	0	1	0	0	0	0	0	1	2
Enterprise Oil	0	1	0	0	0	0	0	1	2
British Steel	0	1	0	0	0	0	0	1	2
Amersham International	0	1	0	0	0	0	0	1	1
National Express	0	0	0	0	0	0	0	0	1
Glaxo	0	0	0	0	0	0	0	0	0
National Westminster Bank	0	0	0	0	0	0	0	0	0
Guinness	0	0	0	0	0	0	0	0	0
Imperial Chemical Industries	0	0	0	0	0	0	0	0	0
Marks and Spencer	0	0	0	0	0	0	0	0	0

1. By Civil Aviation Authority.
2. Effect is largely wearing off over time.
3. Applies, for example, to London Underground but not to, for example, to South Yorkshire Transport.
4. Not strictly an "enterprise" in terms of the discussion, but some charges are made (prescriptions) and hospitals are permitted to "opt out."

37

that major utilities can be left to their own devices in a free market if they are allowed to retain monopoly elements at the time of privatization. Either strong competition must be introduced at the time (which may be difficult to achieve), or a regulatory body must be created in order to exercise surrogate ownership controls.

Tailored regulation: Accordingly, the creation of a regulatory body *specifically* in respect of a single company or companies is also to be viewed as a defining characteristic of a national enterprise. However, it must be recognized that in certain cases, for example, BT, an attempt was made to introduce competition at the time of privatization. Further competition has been introduced subsequently, so it is appropriate to score it fully in respect of its natural monopoly element and its regulatory body. Other utilities in this category include electricity, gas and water.

Market or sectoral dominance: The extent of dominance associated with an enterprise in a given economic sector constitutes another issue that sheds light on the concept of national enterprise. Such dominance may be defined according to Shepherd (1985) as existing where one firm controls over 40 percent of the market and is more than twice the size of the next largest firm.

The greater the dominant firm's market share, the closer it moves toward becoming a textbook monopoly. However, the key factor is that, even though its market power is not absolute, a dominant firm can behave more or less as though it were a monopoly.

Sectoral dominance is commonly associated with a regulatory body in the sense that the official definition of a monopoly for regulatory purposes is a firm that controls one-quarter of a specific market. However, in practice, many unitary monopolies, though falling within the terms of reference of antitrust legislation, have been left wholly to their own devices, while the others have typically only been required to modify their behavior in some minor way. Thus, regulation is significant only where it is industry specific.

It is evident, therefore, that there is no presumption that market dominance and tailored regulation go hand in hand, and they can both be treated as shedding light independently on the concept of the national enterprise.

National flag bearer (national champion): This may be taken to be, quite literally, an organization that flies the national flag (in the case of the United Kingdom, the Union Jack—for example, British Aerospace (BAe). For our purposes, however, it will be taken to be a company that is prominent in international markets where it is regarded as symbolic of the state of the economy, and where that factor is played up in the way in which the organization represents itself to the outside world.

This is clearly a two-way process. Where a company affects a symbolic image, the government is necessarily under pressure to support that image in some way. Such support may be extremely substantial. For example, the government negotiates reciprocal landing rights with other countries, which it then awards to specific U.K. carriers. British Airways has traditionally received the lion's share of international landing rights in this way.

Equally, Rolls-Royce engines are a potent symbol of the excellence of British engineering (which is in need of such symbols now that the Victorian era is but a memory). As this indicates, a company does not cease to be a flag bearer simply by virtue of its transferral into the private sector. From a practical perspective, therefore, a national flag bearer is a company that the government either has been, is or will be protecting against certain market circumstances.

Among these circumstances, the most obvious and traumatic is the threat of bankruptcy. In this respect, it may be noted that Rolls-Royce and British Leyland (as was) only came into public ownership as a result of bankruptcy. Clearly, therefore, no government, be it ever so right wing/free market in its outlook, will let a national flag bearer disappear without trace.

At a less dramatic level, the government might refuse to allow a company to fall into foreign ownership. This might be the direct result of a special share provision at the time of privatization (for example, Rolls-Royce), but it might also be inferred from the government's behavior (for example, in forestalling the Kuwait Investment Organisation [KIO] takeover of British Petroleum [BP] after the abortive 1987 privatization). In certain cases, such as British Steel, it is necessary to presume that the government would behave in that way were a similar circumstance to arise, so there are certain ambiguities at the margin.

One additional difficulty is that it is possible to make out a case for the belief that whenever a company has sectoral dominance, it cannot be permitted to go to the wall. Since such an argument is hypothetical, it may be impossible to lay to rest satisfactorily. A discretion has been exercised to the effect that a company that is manifestly a flag bearer should be scored on the merit of this criterion.

Special (golden) share: The retention of the golden share represents a key feature of the national enterprise. The golden share is a generic name for the special rights preference share held by the government. (Face value usually equals one pound.) It is a share "which may secure a certain kind of national interest and guarantee the company independence" (Yamamoto, 1992: 116). It is widely believed that the government uses the golden share to express political sensitivity over possible foreign takeovers of large U.K. companies. This happened recently when the government signaled its intention to block the bid approach by Southern Company of the United States over National Power (*Financial Times*, May 3, 1996). Chiefly, this share imposes the following restrictions and conditions on privatized enterprises:

• restriction on shareholding by a specific individual

• restriction on the property disposal of business belonging to the group

• restriction on the closure and dissolution of the company

• condition of representative appointment

- restriction on shareholding by foreigners
- condition of domestic director specification

These provisions, intended to preserve the national interest, may be seen as the final band that ties the state and the privatized enterprises. It is thus doubtful whether those companies with a special share can be truly defined as private companies (see Table 3.2).

In many cases (e.g., British Steel, Jaguar, Enterprise Oil, Amersham International), the special share was given a terminal date whereby it would have to be redeemed on or before that date. In other cases (e.g., BAe, BT, British Gas, Sealink), the share is open-ended. Here again, there might be a case for the first cases to be scored only a half point, while the second are scored a full point. From a practical point of view and judging from how the government has sought to apply its special share privileges, such distinction might be unnecessary. For example, it might be difficult to explain why the government, in the last week of April 1996, blocked PowerGen's (U.K.-based electricity generator) bid for Midland Electricity (regional electricity distribution company) as well as an offer by National Power (generator) for Southern Electric (distributor) but in the first week of May 1996 allowed the offer by two U.S. utility groups led by General Public Utilities of New Jersey to go through. As an industry insider noted, "this is a game that doesn't have any rules; you get the feeling that they are making it up as they go along."

Provision of social/political goods: The focus here is on the wider noneconomic functions of organizations that include political, social and environmental considerations. In particular, it encompasses situations in which there are significant differences between social costs and benefits, and the enterprise is obligated, or chooses, to provide socially desirable but economically unprofitable goods and services.

At a more fundamental level, there is a common goods provision in respect of utilities in that they are obligated to supply customers in outlying areas or to transport any goods whatsoever upon request. In other words, characteristically a national enterprise does not have complete freedom to choose its customers.

On the political front, the major consideration is in respect of defense-related goods and services where, for reasons of safety of the realm, the government wishes to ensure that British companies produce certain commodities. This may require specific contracts to be awarded to such companies by the government, even where the product could more economically be provided by some other party. It has been suggested that such companies (e.g., BAe) may become so dependent on public contract that they begin to take on attributes of government agencies. This seems rather speculative because, with defense contracts, the Ministry of Defence is now more willing to buy abroad.

Table 3.2
Principal Restrictions Entrenched by Special Shares

Company	15% Voting Restrictions	15% Restriction on Foreign Ownership	Restriction on Issue of New Voting Shares	British Chief Executive	Government-Appointed Directors	Disposal of Assets	Restriction on Winding up or Dissolution
Amersham International	✓		✓			✓	✓
British Gas	✓		✓				
British Telecom	✓		✓		✓		
Rolls-Royce	✓	✓	✓*	✓		✓	✓
Britoil	(1)		✓	✓			✓
BAA(2)	✓						✓
British Aerospace		✓		✓+	✓		✓
Jaguar	✓			✓		✓	✓
Cable & Wireless	✓		✓			✓	✓
Enterprise Oil	(1)		✓				✓
National Power	✓		✓				✓
PowerGen	✓		✓				✓
RECs	✓		✓				✓
Water Authorities	✓		✓				✓

Special Clauses
(1) Temporary majority of votes when person seeks to obtain control.
(2) Provision concerning the ownership of control of the designated airports (Heathrow, Gatwick and Stansted).
* For two years.
+ All Directors.

Source: Adapted from Veljanovski (1989), p. 216.

SYSTEMIC CONSIDERATIONS: A SYNTHESIS

The process of attributing scores to individual companies has proven to be a difficult exercise (see Table 3.1), and it is probable that individual readers will take issue with some of them. However, it is unlikely that the overall pattern of scores will be materially affected in the process. Still, it is to be hoped that this study will be the first of a number that will help clarify the meaning of the national enterprise, and its purpose is to provoke discussion as much as it is to lay down a definitive approach to the problem.

In terms of Table 3.1, it is possible to argue that a score of 3 is the dividing point in the data. The organizations with very low scores (0–1) are predictable enough, and no one could possibly claim that they could be deemed to be national enterprises. There are 6 such among the 28 organizations listed.

Interestingly, six organizations with a low score of 2 were once public enterprises. This fact, besides reminding us that any evaluation of national enterprise status takes place at a point in the evolution of the organization being evaluated, also demonstrates that an organization can be privatized and in the process lose almost all its national enterprise characteristics. It may be argued that these characteristics were not very strong in the first place, but British Steel represents one interesting illustration of a company that required massive state subsidies over a period of many years, and yet has grasped the mettle post-privatization and turned itself into a paragon of private sector virtue compared to the major (often state-owned) operators elsewhere in the European Union. The obvious implication is that a public-to-private status change alone is no guarantee that an organization will act in the stereotypical private way. Genuine market competition holds the key to understanding the changes in organizational systems and structures needed to achieve private sector organizational transformation.

The nearest parallel that scores in excess of 3 is British Airways (BA), which has recently been voted the world's best airline (which is not the way customers felt in pre-privatization days). Nevertheless, BA differs from British Steel insofar as it controls more of its market (via landing rights); has a strict regulatory regime geared to safety standards; and flies the flag for Britain. Although Virgin Airlines may be permitted to nibble at the edges of its routes, BA is too important a national flag bearer to be treated as the equivalent of TWA or Continental in the United States, which have been permitted to become bankrupt because there are other major operators in the market. In these respects, it shows a set of characteristics that incline one to put it in the national enterprise category, although it is one of those organizations where a case both for and against could be made.

The high scores are also predictable enough insofar as it is clear that such organizations either remain in public ownership or have been released to a free market by the act of privatization. They tend to exhibit elements of natural monopoly, to dominate their sectors, to provide common goods and to be tightly regulated as a consequence of these factors. These are exhibited more clearly in the case of privatized water companies and electricity distribution companies, which tend to give the lie to assertions by their top managers that they are just like other standard market operator (and hence executives should receive competitive salaries). According to our schema, they remain unambiguously national enterprises, and this has been barely affected by the nominal transfer of ownership.

The difficulties arise in the middle ground score of 3, of which there are four examples. Interestingly, one of these is yet to be privatized, namely, British Coal, but most of the pits are currently being shut down and the rest will be privatized. Thus, this latter group will sit fairly comfortably outside the national enterprise definition, especially when account is taken of the fact that its sectoral dominance will be much reduced and the degree of competition from other fuels much more severe. Nevertheless, at the present time, it is sensibly allocated to the national enterprise category.

The National Health Service, as currently constituted, cannot be deemed an enterprise, but it is slowly beginning to operate more like a private sector organization. However, it is difficult to use it to shed much light on our problem of definition. BNFL is also something of an oddity. An Act of Parliament requires the state to hold a majority shareholding because of its nuclear activities, but it has long been a profitable company, with full order books until the year 2003. On balance, BNFL has to be allocated to the national enterprise category.

Thus, out of a list of 28 organizations, 16 qualify for classification as national enterprises. Of these, 6 are state-owned but 10 have been privatized. What the latter share is a tendency to market dominance, with consequent great potential to operate against the public interest. It follows logically that there is only one straightforward way to denationalize a national enterprise, namely, through the introduction of market competition.

One final point is worthy of note. Given the government's slow but steady process of disengagement from the marketplace (evident in the outright privatization or continual withdrawal of financial support to a widening range of organizations), many more organizational transitions may follow the pattern shown in Figure 3.3. For utility industries such as telecommunications and Gas, exposure to full competition, as it is now beginning to unfurl, will necessitate a migration from the national enterprise domain to the private sector. Contrarily, it is possible for the national enterprise, depending on political exigencies, to fall back into more political control as to occasion renationalization. Although this has not happened, there is a veiled threat by the Labour party, if elected, to reverse any possible privatization of British Rail. Organizations providing ancillary services that the government is becoming reluctant to fund and that may not be sustainable under market control might be allowed to undertake passage to the third sector where they either settle permanently or are subsequently taken into market or political control.

Figure 3.3
Possible Organizational Transitions

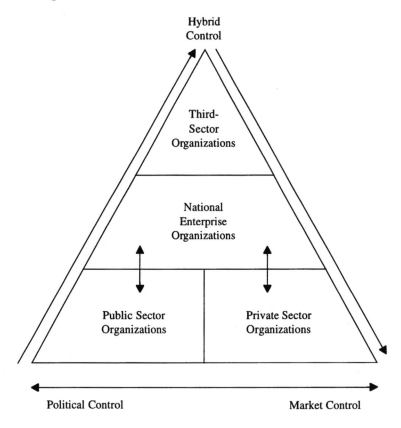

CONCLUSIONS

Following from the U.K. experiment in the 1980s, many countries in the developing world and the emerging democracies of Eastern/Central Europe have embarked on a privatization policy as a way of freeing their economies from perceivably unattractive bureaucratic control. The problems being encountered are many and varied (Cameron, 1992; Frydman and Rapaczynski, 1993; Ivanov et al., 1994). These problems may stem in part from the fact that many adopters of the privatization experiment have not addressed some of the conceptual issues, such as those relating to the goals and limitations of privatization as a policy instrument in widely diverse social contexts. This has resulted in a whole variety of implementation problems; a major one, for example, is the task of confidence building among the citizens and major institutional stakeholders such as the banks and citizen action groups. Sections of the populace, for instance, may worry about the sale of enterprises previously seen as symbols of collective ownership and may be less than supportive due to misconceptions about the free market system such as no interference and survival of the fittest.

One way of addressing these problems is by articulating the concept of the national enterprise which should demonstrate, for example, that whereas the assets of some enterprises might be in private hands, those enterprises may not necessarily shirk traditional public service objectives or fall outside the political purview. To this extent, the concept of the national enterprise provides an alternative strategic route towards a market economy. This type of route, and clear articulation of it, are particularly pertinent now that many developing (as well as erstwhile command) economies are beginning to chart a course geared toward removing the government of business from the business of government.

REFERENCES

Aryee, S. 1992. Public and Private Sector Professionals: A Comparative Study of Their Perceived Work Experience. *Group and Organisation Management* 17(1): 72–85.

Bohm, A. 1981. The Concept, Definition and Classification of Public Enterprises. *Public Enterprise* 1(4): 72–78.

Cameron, C. 1992. A Comparison of Privatisation in Capitalist and Socialist Countries. *International Journal of Social Economics* 19(6): 55–60.

Coursey, D. and Bozeman, B. 1990. Decision Making in Public and Private Organisations: A Test of Alternative Concepts of "Publicness." *Public Administration Review* 50(5): 523–535.

Cravens, D., Shipp, S. and Cravens, S. 1994, July–August. Reforming the Traditional Organization: The Mandate for Developing Networks. *Business Horizons*: 9–28.

Curwen, P. 1986. *Public Sector: A Modern Approach*. Brighton: Wheatsheaf Books.

Drucker, P. F. 1992, September–October. The New Society of Organisations. *Harvard Business Review*: 95–104.

Dunsire, A., Hartley, K., Parker, D. and Dimitriou, B. 1988. Organisational Status and Performance: A Conceptual Framework for Testing Public Choice Theories. *Public Administration* 66: 363–388.

Etzioni, A. 1973, July–August. The Third Sector and Domestic Missions. *Public Administration Review*: 314–323.

Foster, C. 1992. *Privatisation, Public Ownership and Regulation of Natural Monopoly*. Oxford: Blackwell Publishers.

Frydman, R. and Rapaczynski, A. 1993, June. Privatisation in Eastern Europe. *Finance and Development* 27(3): 10–13.

Hinterhuber, H. and Levin, B. 1994. Strategic Networks—The Organisation of the Future. *Long Range Planning* 27(3): 43–53.

Ivanov, D., Montanheiro, L., Nwankwo, S. and Richardson, B. 1994. Privatisation Policy: A Comparative Analysis of the Public-to-Private Programmes in the UK and Bulgaria. In P. Curwen, B. Richardson, S. Nwankwo and L. Montanheiro (eds.), *The Public Sector in Transition*. Sheffield: Pavic Publications, 389–400.

Kay, J. 1987. *The State and the Market: The UK Experience of Privatisation*. London: Group of Thirty, Occasional Paper No. 23.

Koutsoyiannis, A. 1980. *Modern Microeconomics.* London: Heinemann.

Liebenstein, H. 1965. *Economic Theory and Organisational Analysis.* N.P.: Harper International Reprints.

Majone, G. 1994. Paradoxes of Privatisation and Deregulation. *Journal of European Public Policy* 1(1): 53–69.

Marsh, D. 1991. Privatisation under Mrs. Thatcher: A Review of the Literature. *Public Administration* 69: 459–480.

McGill, M. and Wooten, L. 1975, September–October. Management in the Third Sector. *Public Administration Review:* 444–455.

Miller, A. 1994. Privatisation: Lessons from the British Experience. *Long Range Planning* 27: 125–136.

Mitroff, A., Mason, R. and Pearson, C. 1994. Radical Surgery: What Will Tomorrow's Organisation Look Like? *Academy of Management Executive* 8(2): 11–21.

Monopolies and Mergers Commission, Gas and British Gas plc. 1993. Cm 2314–2317 (3 vols.). London: HMSO.

Nwankwo, S. 1993. Rethinking the Public-Private Distinction in Organisation Theory. In J. Chandler and J. Darwin (eds.), *Waves of Change: Strategic Management in the Public Sector.* Sheffield, UK: Sheffield Business School, 378–410.

Nwankwo, S. 1994, December 11–13. Public-to-Private Organisational Transition: The Bankruptcy of Current Paradigms. Paper presented at the 20th Annual Conference of the European International Business Academy, Warsaw, Poland.

Odell, P. 1987, December. *Gas Market Regulation in Europe and Liberalisation in Britain.* London: Public Issues Conference.

Parker, D. 1992. Privatisation Ten Years On: A Critical Analysis of Its Rationale and Results. *Economics* 27: 155–163.

Perry, J. and Rainey, H. 1988. The Public-Private Distinction in Organization Theory: A Critique and Research Strategy. *Academy of Management Review* 13: 182–201.

Posner, M. 1979. *Public Enterprises in the Market Place.* London: Nationalised Industries Chairmen's Group, Occasional Paper No. 1.

Rainey, H., Backoff, R. and Levine, C. 1976, March–April. Comparing Public and Private Organisations. *Public Administration Review:* 233–244.

Ramanadham, V. 1984. *The Nature of Public Enterprises.* London: Croom Helm.

Shepherd, W. 1988. *The Economics of Industrial Organisations.* New York: Prentice-Hall.

Sikorski, D. 1993. A General Critique of the Theory on Public Enterprise. *International Journal of Public Sector Management* 6: 17–40.

Sternberg, E. 1993, November–December. Preparing for the Hybrid Economy: The New World of Public-Private Partnerships. *Business Horizons:* 11–15.

Veljanovski, C. 1989. *Privatization and Competition.* London: Institute of Economic Affairs.

Yamamoto, T. 1992. Privatisation and National Interest. *The Waseda Business and Economic Studies* (28): 99–120.

Yarrow, G. 1987. *Does Ownership Matter?* London: Institute of Economic Development.

CHAPTER 4

Globalization, Economic Development and Ecology: A Critical Examination

SUBHABRATA BANERJEE

Globalization is fast becoming one of the buzzwords of the 1990s. Advances in telecommunications and information technology as well as the increased permeability of national boundaries have contributed to the ever-increasing pace of globalization. The literature in marketing and other business disciplines has focused mainly on the economic dimension of globalization. This chapter discusses various dimensions of globalization, its relationship with economic development, and its ecological consequences. The chapter critically examines the emergence of a "new environmental paradigm" and discusses the implications of globalization for Third World countries.

INTRODUCTION

The last few years have seen tumultuous changes in the social and political arena of the globe. Formerly restricted markets have now eagerly embraced the principles of market economies, and the focus of many corporations has shifted to these emerging markets. As transnational corporations and the "developed" countries scramble for a foothold in the huge Chinese and other Asian markets, it appears that the center stage for world trade has shifted to the Asia-Pacific theater. Rapid advances in information technology, increased competition in global markets and the increased permeability of national boundaries have all contributed to the ever-increasing pace of globalization in virtually all business sectors. Terms like "global product," "global consumer," "global village," "global marketplace" and "global economy" are commonplace in the business press and academic journals.

While we can marvel at the phenomenon of a global consumer and a global product (a family in Boise, Idaho, watching the latest episode of "The Simpsons'' on television in their living room, drinking Diet Coke, and snacking on Kentucky Fried Chicken could easily have counterparts consuming the same products in San Cristobel, or Ahmedabad, or Ankara, or Phnom Penh), other phenomena like global warming are less reassuring. Economic growth and the expansion of world markets have come at the price of environmental destruction, a price that many people feel the world cannot afford to pay. The last 25 years have seen increasing public concern about the destruction of the natural environment. Concern about forest depletion, global warming and other ecological problems is now universal, and if ''globalization'' is one of the buzzwords of the 1990s, then ''sustainable development'' is not far behind. Most of the serious environmental problems facing the world have resulted from industrial development, and ''sustainable development'' as defined by the Brundtland report (World Commission, 1987) is an attempt to modify current growth patterns that can sustain the biophysical environment.

The global market economy of the 1990s emerged from the political changes around the world following the breakup of the Soviet Union. The ''development'' process in the Third World was well underway. Industrialization and economic growth were the key objectives set for the developing world. The main assumption underlying these processes was that economic growth was the key to eradicate poverty and raise the standard of living for the poor in developing or underdeveloped countries. Globalization makes the same promise: increased access to resources and markets, tarriff-less geographical boundaries and increased efficiency in resource utilization will generate wealth for the poorer countries. At the root of most of the arguments for globalization is the assumption that the benefits of globalization far outweigh the costs. Global environmental destruction is one such cost. This chapter examines the concepts of globalization, economic development and biophysical environment and their interrelationships.

GLOBALIZATION, MODERNITY AND DEVELOPMENT

What exactly does globalization mean? Concepts related to globalization include internationalization, multidomestic marketing, and multinational or transnational marketing, suggesting that the basic criterion is transactions across national boundaries. In the marketing and strategic management literature, globalization is conceptualized as a means to gain competitive advantage by locating different stages of production in different geographic regions according to the particular region's comparative advantages. This conceptualization focuses only on the economic aspects of globalization: social, cultural and political factors are only considered in the context of achieving economic advantage. Thus, being ''culturally sensitive'' in global markets is being able to sell one's product with enough ingenuity to avoid possible pitfalls arising from the seller's ignorance of local customs. International marketing textbooks discuss such cultural pitfalls in great detail: however, the cultural context of globalization is always framed by the economic.

Broader conceptualizations of globalization can be found in other disciplines such as sociology and anthropology. Waters (1995:3) defined globalization as "a social process in which the constraints of geography on social and cultural arrangements recede and in which people become increasingly aware that they are receding." This conceptualization, with its much broader scope, allows for the examination of a number of consequences of globalization, not just economic but social, cultural and political ones.

While there are a few different conceptualizations of globalization, researchers seem to be in agreement that there are at least three dimensions of globalization: economic, political and cultural (Waters, 1995). The economic aspects of globalization stem from the spread of the capitalist world economy and the resulting expansion of geographical boundaries for the production and consumption of goods and services. The need for cheap raw materials, cheap labor and new markets saw the expansion of the capitalist world economy from one that was primarily Eurocentric to one that encompassed the entire world (Wallerstein, 1990). This process was achieved by various means and often involved overcoming political resistances (frequently through military means) in the new "markets." The political aspects of globalization involved establishing control over markets and raw materials through either the use of direct military power or the establishment of international institutions (through diplomacy) that control such markets. The rise of the nation-state is an example of the political aspect of globalization, although it is argued that advances in telecommunications and information systems and the resulting constructions of institutions that transcend territorial boundaries are making the nation-state obsolete (Smith, 1990).

If the economic and political aspects of globalization involve material and power exchanges, the cultural aspect of globalization involves the "expression of symbols that represent facts, meanings, beliefs, preferences, tastes and values" (Waters, 1995:8). In fact, these symbolic exchanges are increasingly displacing economic and political exchanges in the spread of global mass culture. Traditional barriers of language pose no problems to what Appadurai (1990) calls "mediascapes" or modern means of cultural production such as satellite television and film. However, the new "global culture," despite its manifestations through consumption of global products and symbols in different parts of the globe, is essentially the culture of dominant groups in that it remains centered in the West (Hall, 1991).

Thus, it is important to realize that despite its "worldwide" connotation, globalization is essentially a Western notion inextricably linked with economic development. It is a Western world view which in economic terms defines the world as a market that can be exploited to generate wealth. While foreign trade and appropriation of resources can be traced back to colonial times, globalization has its historical roots in the modern era where control of raw materials across the globe and control of world markets (along with the consolidation of military strength) can sustain a nation's competitive and economic advantage. World trade was the basis of globalization, and global trade relations in the modern era set up the dichotomy of "developed" versus "underdeveloped or developing" countries. Since progress was defined solely in economic terms, the fundamental problem for the underdeveloped countries in the post–World War II era was how to become a developed country (Escobar, 1995). Developmental plans at the regional, national and international levels were formulated and implemented, but despite more than 50 years of development, the benefits to the poorer countries are at best equivocal. The march to progress and modernity in many cases has created more problems: exacerbation of poverty, environmental destruction, displacement of peasant populations, cultural and social alienation and unequal distributions of income. Despite the failure of several development projects in Latin America and Asia, the desirability of economic growth was unquestioned; in cases where the benefits were not immediately apparent, the problems of infrastructural deficiencies and lack of capital in Third World countries were the commonly cited causes.

The underlying assumption in all development projects was that technological advancement and industrialization would lead to economic development. This, in turn, would have positive effects on the social, political and cultural arenas of developing countries. However, development was constructed primarily as a process of increasing growth rates measured by Western standards. Social advancement for the poorer nations of the world was conceived in economic terms, although in many such cultures there was no clear separation of the economic from the social and cultural. Economics became the engine that drove the development discourse, and the "progress" of the rest of the world was evaluated using Western theories and models of economics. Thus, growth became paramount: the assumption that growth equals development was never challenged. Poorer countries needed to embark on planned economic growth through industrialization and capital accumulation. Development, that is, the transition from the traditional to the modern, would automatically follow. This argument constructed the world in terms of a modern-traditional dichotomy where the traditional was seen as backward and progress was defined as a transition to the modern (Escobar, 1995). This dualistic construction represents the ontological position of several Western theories (including, as we shall see later, in the conceptualization of the biophysical environment) and is a defining characteristic of Western culture. One important consequence of the dualistic construction was the unchallenged domination of science as the only valid system of knowledge. As these modes of existence became consolidated, older schemes of knowledge, especially in agriculture and land management, were replaced by modern "scientific" techniques of production, leading to a host of ecological problems, as we will see in the next section.

ECOLOGICAL CONSEQUENCES OF ECONOMIC DEVELOPMENT: THE EMERGENCE OF ENVIRONMENTAL ECONOMICS

Meanwhile, a host of environmental problems arose due to unbridled economic growth. One of the earlier efforts to highlight the ecological consequences of economic growth was made by Rachel Carson (1962) in her book *Silent Spring*. Most of her predictions on the harmful effects to toxic chemicals on marine life, nuclear accidents and radiation hazards, and the damaging effects of pesticides like DDT on plant, animal and human life were accurate. Probably the first serious attempt to question the "grow or die" aphorism of economic theory came from a series of studies by Meadows et al. (1972). In their book *The Limits to Growth*, they concluded that unchecked economic growth could lead to depletion of natural resources and the planet would lose its carrying capacity and its ability to produce food for its ever-growing population. However, Meadows et al. (1992) also concluded that it was possible for economic growth to be environmentally sustainable, although the options for this type of growth remained unclear.

In an attempt to expand the theoretical boundaries of their discipline to accommodate ecological issues, some researchers in the field of economics attempted to include the biophysical environment in current economic accounting systems. These environmental economists critically evaluated certain assumptions made in current economic theory. For instance, land, labor and capital are the three major factors of production addressed in conventional economics. The underlying assumption is that these factors are interchangeable and replaceable by other forms of capital (Gilman, 1992). However, if the notion of land includes the biophysical environment, the level of substitution declines dramatically. The natural capital (the air we breathe, the ozone layer) cannot be replaced by other forms of capital, and many natural resources are nonrenewable and irreplaceable. Given the ultimate natural constraint of the planet, human well-being depends not on unbridled economic growth and consumption but rather on how available natural resources are used (Korten, 1992).

Researchers in environmental economics are calling for accounting practices that include environmental impact and account for natural capital (Morison and Gray, 1991; Surma and Vondra, 1992). Gray (1992) distinguishes between two kinds of natural capital: critical natural capital pertains to parts of the biosphere that cannot be expended at any cost (the ozone layer, the rainforests, wetlands and critical habitats) and sustainable capital (renewable resources like water, land, timber). The function of an accounting system that sustains life on earth involves keeping organization decision makers informed about the ways natural resources and the planet's capital are being depleted. This is a process of internalizing what neoclassical economics treats as "externalities." Information about natural capital employment should also be provided to society. One approach to calculate the depletion of natural capital is to attempt to compute a "sustainable cost" or additional costs that must be borne by the firm at the end of the accounting period which would maintain the planet at its initial level of natural capital. Recognizing these costs will indicate that income has been greatly overestimated. If these costs are to be deducted from company profits, then it is doubtful that any company has ever made a "sustainable" profit in recent years (Gray, 1992).

The same shortcoming is reflected in current systems of accounting for a country's "wealth." Traditional accounting methods and market-based information cannot accurately reflect the effects of environmental degradation. Current national accounting systems do not include natural resources in balance sheets and hence present a misleading picture of well-being. Depreciation of natural capital is not recorded, and while environmental cleanup costs are included in national income statements, environmental damages are not considered (Lutz and Munasinghe, 1991). Indonesia is a case in point. Touted as a model for all Third World countries to follow, Indonesia had an annual GNP growth rate of 7.1 percent in 1990. However, after accounting for resource depletion (Indonesia's major industry is timber), the growth rate declines to a more modest 4 percent (Passel, 1990). Many traditional economic indicators like GNP and GDP fail to account for environmental costs. For instance, the environmental disasters of the Exxon Valdez oil spill actually showed up as a gain in the United States' gross national product (GNP) because of the products and services involved in the cleanup of the oil spill (Reilly, 1990).

Neoclassical economics does not directly address externalities, the assumption being that society and other external entities would take steps in controlling the problem. Environmental destruction results from economic growth due to the expansion of polluting, but profitable technologies and the costs of environmental degradation are typically not borne by the producer but by society in the form of "externalities" (Commoner, 1974).

Environmental economists view the physical environment as a collective or public good and evaluate the natural environment in terms of their future value instead of their present utility for resource extraction. Possible future benefits of preserving the natural environment are, in some circumstances, greater than present benefits of resources extraction (Krutilla, 1967). This future demand for natural environments is termed an option value. Option values take into account the notion of irreversibility. For example, if some natural environment is destroyed irreversibly by the construction of a hydroelectric power plant, it will not be possible to exercise an option on the natural environment in the future (Petulla, 1980). Environmental and social costs should be taken into account when evaluating development projects that are associated with irreversible conversions of the natural environment (Krutilla and Fisher, 1974). Development decisions are taken by both firms and policymakers, and virtually all decisions involve irreversible changes to the natural environment. Outcomes of these decisions influence the welfare of society, and some element of social risk is always involved due to environmental degradation (Norgaard, 1975).

Neoclassical economics follows the doctrine of the "sovereign consumer" who dictates the proper functioning of the marketplace. Consumer preferences are ruled by prices the consumer is willing to pay for products or services. The problem with this approach is that external effects like pollution are not included in the market transaction. Some economists recommend taking social costs into account while determining production costs. Since business tends to ignore costs that are borne by society, economists recommend that pollution taxes or incentives for pollution-free production processes be applied. The effect of pollution taxes would tend to raise prices for goods which have adverse effects on the environment, lowering demand for these products and consequently lowering pollution that results from their manufacture. The objective of this approach is to put a price on an external factor—pollution, for instance—and thus internalize this factor after estimating the external cost of pollution. Traditional cost-benefit analysis is then used when arriving at a decision. These approaches however, remain limited in their efforts to reduce environmental degradation since they do not take into account the concept of social risk, irreversibility and option values (Petulla, 1980). Also, given the uncertain nature of predicting consequences of pollution or other environmental hazards, measuring social costs is a problem. Ultimately, a monetary value is being applied to the destruction of natural capital to evaluate development, and the computation of such a value is almost impossible in many cases, given the complexities of ecosystems in the natural environment.

Environmental economists are attempting to modify the neoclassical model to include relationships with the biophysical environment, with a view to determine growth areas that do not irreversibly damage the environment. As noted earlier, their motto is "sustainable development," which has become the buzzword of the 1990s. Economists and politicians have called for national economic plans, Third World industrial development and industry growth to be based on sustainable development. The Brundtland report (World Commission, 1987) defines sustainable development as a process by which present needs can be met without compromising the ability of future generations to meet their own needs. Sustainable development involves concepts like futurity or intergenerational equity, welfare (including income and nonfinancial aspects like environmental quality) and equity or the equitable distribution of economic costs and benefits (Jacobs 1990, cited in McIntosh, 1991).

These concepts appear to challenge traditional views of neoclassical economics and have important implications for development and growth. Many basic assumptions are challenged by an environmental paradigm. For an economist, growth means an increase in GNP, whereas for an environmentalist, it may mean consumption of natural resources and a resulting increase in entropy.[1] Sustainable development is an attempt to combine environmentally sustainable growth with an added focus on intergenerational equity and equitable distribution of wealth between groups and nations (McIntosh, 1991). However, as we will see in a later section, the notion of sustainable development in a market economy can have negative consequences for the nations of the Third World. The market economy assumes that all potential buyers have access to resources available and that the price mechanism will regulate demand and supply. Given the scenario of exhaustible resources, this assumption breaks down as most potential buyers (future generations) cannot access the market, or as Martinez-Alier (1987) elegantly states, "individuals not yet born have ontological difficulties in making their presence felt in today's market for exhaustible resources."

All economic activity takes place within the natural constraints of the planet and is bounded by the planet's carrying capacity. Treating the ecological effects of economic activity as "externalities" that can be accommodated does not reflect the complexities of ecosystems. Relationships in ecology are never linear; they comprise a series of highly complex interrelationships, and any attempt to isolate or control a single activity is reductionist and therefore inaccurate. The following section discusses the salient principles of ecological theory and the problems it poses to the neoclassical economic paradigm.

ECOLOGICAL THEORY AND THE NEW ENVIRONMENTAL PARADIGM

Since all human activity is performed within the biophysical environment, the effects of such activity on the biophysical environment cannot be ignored. Ecological theory or ecosystem theory examines how humans, plants, soils, microorganisms, water and air function together as an integrated community (Petulla, 1980). In the past, many ecologists ignored human activity from the working of the ecosystem and focused on the natural system. Fundamental concepts of ecology involve all elements that support life, including inorganic substances (e.g., carbon, nitrogen), organic compounds (proteins), climatic factors (rainfall, temperature), green plant producers, macroconsumers (animals) and microconsumers (bacteria and fungi). All these constituents are functionally interdependent, and their relationships can be analyzed in terms of energy transfer, food chains, diversity patterns and feedback systems (Petulla, 1980). However, human intervention in this ecosystem, especially at the rate at which these systems are being destroyed, poses serious environmental problems. Human, social, technological and economic systems all interact with the ecosystem and consequently are subject to the same laws that govern the ecosystem (Gray, 1992; Odum, 1971). The diversity of natural systems (and hence their strength) can be easily weakened by human interventions.

Examples of the negative consequences of human intervention abound: the extinction of entire animal and plant species in the rainforests, plant species extinction due to monoculture in agriculture or forestry and soil erosion due to uncontrolled deforestation and grazing by domestic animals. The artificial simplification of an ecosystem by monoculture and agricultural production increases the vulnerability of the entire crop to attacks from pests. A diverse blend of species would be more resistant to these attacks. Increased use of fertilizers and pesticides tends to yield only short-term benefits as soil contamination and new strains of pests evolve.

The ecological effects of the so-called Green Revolution leading to massive increases in food production in Third World countries is well established. Energy inputs increased, soil erosion accelerated, soil fertility declined dramatically, and fertilizers and pesticides contaminated the food chain and the environment (Martinez-Alier, 1987; Shiva, 1989). Land in many parts of the world that produced crops for countless centuries are now virtually barren due to overgrazing and soil erosion.

The fundamental premise underlying the laws of ecology is the interrelatedness of all processes within the ecosystem, including human activity. Commoner (1972) summarized the basic principles of ecology:

1. Every separate entity is connected to all the rest.

2. Everything has to go somewhere.

3. You cannot get something for nothing from it.

4. Nature knows best.

Although some of these principles may seem facetious, the following anecdote will highlight the interrelatedness of all components of an ecosystem:

The Parachuting Cats

In Borneo in the early 1950's, the World Health Organization was faced with the problem of malaria among the Dayak people in Borneo. They had an answer that was short, simple, and wrong, which was to spray DDT all over the place to kill the mosquitoes that carried malaria. The mosquito population declined, the incidence of malaria declined, and everybody declared the program a success.

They discovered, however, that the roofs of people's houses were falling in on their heads. It seemed that the DDT had poisoned wasps which parasitized thatch-eating caterpillars. Without the wasps the caterpillars proliferated, they ate the thatch in the roofs, and the roofs fell in.

WHO found it had a worse problem, which was that the DDT had built up in the food chain—it got into the insects, which were eaten by little lizard-like creatures called geckos, which were eaten by the cats. The cats died, the rats flourished, and the WHO was faced with an outbreak of sylvatic plague and typhus, which it itself had created. It was then obliged to parachute live cats into Borneo. (Lovins, 1977)

This story illustrates the dangers of following a classical problem-solving approach with a narrow and static view of the environment. It exposes only the tip of the iceberg about complex interrelationships in an ecosystem. New and more difficult paradoxes arise when one includes the social, technological, economic and human environment in the picture.

Modern Western culture has evolved from a long-standing anthropocentric tradition wherein humans are viewed as being superior to the rest of nature (White, 1967). The development of scientific knowledge emphasized this dualistic tradition, and the assumption that the domination and mastery of nature through scientific and technological advancements were the basis of humanity's existence was never in question. The dualistic tradition was reinforced by beliefs that individuals are masters of their destiny, and that the earth is an unlimited source of resources and opportunities for humans. Catton and Dunlap (1980) call this paradigm the "Dominant Western Worldview." This paradigm is obviously unacceptable from an ecological perspective, and problems arising from depletion of resources and deterioration of the natural environment are forcing many scholars and scientists to realize that humans are not exempt from ecological constraints. Moreover, the societal implications of the environmental crisis prompted researchers in diverse fields to pay attention to the natural environment. For instance, environmental sociology examines relationships between social and environmental variables. The acceptance of the natural environment as being relevant to the human condition challenged traditional assumptions about the dichotomy between humanity and nature (Dunlap and Catton, 1979). This new environmental paradigm stresses the interdependence of the natural environment and human societies and recognizes that scientific and technological advances cannot overturn basic ecological principles (like entropy). Consequently, the environmental paradigm recognizes that there are limits to growth (Catton and Dunlap, 1980).

Current economic theory does not question the validity of the goal of unlimited economic growth: this is seen as desirable and remains unquestioned. Economics is also accused of grossly simplifying the world (Daly, 1980; Gray, 1992). While this may be necessary to model complex systems, any form of reductionism necessarily violates existing structures, and actions based on the model are invalid. To incorporate the biophysical environment into current economic theory and to internalize what has been traditionally treated as "externalities" require a reappraisal of assumptions underlying present paradigms. The major assumptions underlying the environmental paradigm are listed in Table 4.1.

We have discussed the relationships between globalization and economic development and the ecological problems associated with these phenomena. We have also discussed how some researchers have attempted to address these problems at a theoretical level and have called for a new paradigm to reflect ecological concerns. Do these new concepts and theories really challenge conventional theories of economic growth? Do they call for an absolute rejection of the old paradigm? Or are they merely attempts to explain the anomalies in current theory?

Table 4.1
Comparison of Paradigm Assumptions

	Neoclassical	Environmental
Goals	Maximize wealth through consumption and economic expansion	Survival and quality-of-life issues
	Economic growth	Sustainable development
Context of external environment	Social, political, cultural, economic	Social, political, cultural, economic, biophysical
Resource constraints	Financial, human, technological	Financial, human, technological, natural
Progress	Unlimited growth and resources	Limits to growth, limited resources
Strategy focus	Resource conservation and utilization	Resource conservation
Nature of relationship	Anthropocentric, reversible processes	Holistic, irreversible processes
Time span	Short to medium, focus on present and immediate future	Ecological time span, long-term, future generations
Stakeholder groups	Shareholders, customers, public, institutions	Shareholders, customers, public, institutions, planet preservation, future generations

Sources: Adapted from Catton and Dunlap (1979) and Throop (1993).

ENVIRONMENTAL ECONOMICS, SUSTAINABLE DEVELOPMENT AND THE NEW ENVIRONMENTAL PARADIGM: A CRITICAL REEXAMINATION

It is important to realize that all the arguments discussed earlier emanate from a Western capitalist framework. The problems and solutions facing the world have been articulated from this perspective alone, and the assumption that these arguments represent reality for the rest of the world must be questioned. The rise of social and environmental movements in many parts of the world prompted a reevaluation of theories of growth and development. This led to what some researchers have called a new paradigm. Let us examine this so-called paradigm shift critically. While it is true that some major assumptions of the neoclassical paradigm have been challenged, an examination of the solutions proposed by environmental economists does not indicate any rejection of the market economy. Valuation of natural resources may have changed, but fundamentally nature is still treated as capital that must be utilized. Perhaps the mode of utilization differs—it is more "efficient" yielding less waste or incorporating more recyclability—but essentially the objectives have not changed. The tools of economic analysis continue to operate with minor alterations: by depreciating nature and accounting for this depreciation in corporate and national income accounts, we have a more "realistic" picture of the ecological consequences of economic activity. Thus, the environment is constructed as something that could be managed to sustain growth and development.

On closer examination this "new" paradigm does not appear to be fundamentally different from earlier articulations in terms of the basic goals and values that are being expounded. Interpreting the paradigm through an examination of sustainable development indicates that the major difference is that the biophysical environment is addressed more explicitly. The fundamental precepts of development have not undergone any significant change: growth remains paramount, and it is recast as sustainable growth. It is unclear what sustainability really means: what are we trying to sustain? the biophysical environment? development? or both? From a purely ecological perspective, development and ecological preservation are inherently incompatible.

The environment in the new paradigm is still seen as "external" to human existence. In fact, as Escobar (1995) argues, the rise of ecological concerns during the period of industrialization saw the transformation of nature into "the environment," a construct that reproduced the economic realities of industrialization. This view of nature implied that the environment was just another external factor that could affect economic growth. With proper environmental management, economic growth could proceed as before. The assumption that it was the environmental that needed to be "managed" and not humans is still not challenged. Alternative views of nature, such as those of indigenous peoples in different parts of the world, are either marginalized or romanticized through profitable ventures such as ecotourism. The basic tenets of growth are far from abandoned: certain variables are reshuffled, some accounting practices are changed, and emission controls are tightened, but the market continues to be the mechanism through which progress is defined.

CONCLUSIONS AND IMPLICATIONS FOR THE THIRD WORLD

Globalization, with its corollaries of global products, global consumers and the global marketplace, appears to signify "the crystallization of the entire world as a single place" (Robertson, 1987). The questions are: what economic, political or cultural parameters does this process of globalization render invisible? What groups of people or regions are excluded from this discourse? Does it imply cultural homogenization or cultural heterogenization? Historically, the flow of "knowledge" has been unidirectional: from the West to the rest of the world, from the developed countries to the underdeveloped countries. In many cases, especially among the countries of the Third World, globality is an imposed condition that even defines the locale. It is here that globalization has far-reaching consequences, and we will now discuss four aspects of globalization that are of particular importance to Third World countries.

First, there is a need to question the uncritical acceptance of the benefits of globalization by Third World countries. This is by no means an easy task: while the Western-educated middle-class elite eagerly embrace the proliferation of commodities, the silent majority of the population, who cannot afford most of the products in the market, recede further into the background. The benefits of industrial development in countries like India and Brazil were enjoyed by a small minority of the population while widening the gap between rich and poor and creating a host of social and environmental problems (Guha, 1989). Globalization will ensure the continuation of this trend: the benefits of a "free" economy will be reaped by a minority of the population in Third World countries. Increased consumption levels will put more pressure on the environment, and the people who will be most adversely affected are those who depend on the land for their subsistence. Globalization and development continue to define reality for large segments of the world's population and in the process continue to render them invisible. As the world marvels at the rate of technological advances in communications and negotiates the potholes on the information superhighway, it is easy to forget that half the population of this planet has not made a telephone call.

Second, it is important to critically evaluate the so-called mutual benefits of global trading partners. The hegemonic forms of control exercised by the industrialized nations of the world remain firmly entrenched (one could argue that globalization is the manifestation of the continuing hegemony of industrialized countries) as the world gears up for the twenty-first century. The Third World has been told how to develop for most of this century. The ecological consequences of the development process have been integrated in the development paradigm, and now the Third World is expected to follow sustainable development. Not only do the developing countries have to purchase expensive polluting technologies from the industrialized nations, but also due to the need for sustainable development, the developing nations are compelled to purchase cleanup and recycling technologies as well.

Third, it is important to realize that just as many development policies were not applicable to Third World countries, the environmental solutions are just as incompatible. Western environmentalism, however radical, should be seen as being essentially Western in cultural content and is by no means applicable to the rest of the world. In industrialized countries, nature itself has become a commodity. Environmentalism is a quality-of-life issue: their citizens want clean air, clean beaches, the opportunity to acquire a suntan without worrying about skin cancer and so on. In many Third World countries, especially among the rural poor, environmentalism is a matter of subsistence and survival. These are people who depend on the land for their livelihood and for countless centuries have managed the land using their own systems of knowledge.

Fourth, globalization can ensure the disappearance of traditional forms of knowledge about ecology. The development process has always marginalized alternative forms of knowledge, and there is a real danger that globalization will ensure that these forms of knowledge disappear forever. Related to this point is the portrayal of Third World peoples as ''backward'' and ''ignorant.'' Evidence of this depiction can be found in the representation of the Third World in the media. As the Western media lament the destruction of the environment, the common questions raised by them are population explosion in Third World countries or the ''backward,'' ecologically unsound practices of aboriginal peoples, such as the ''slash and burn'' practice (Escobar, 1995). The fact that these communities have been ''slashing and burning'' for thousands of years without the kind of destruction that industrialization has wrought is ignored. (Only recently has the use of fire in land management been recognized by the Australian government as a legitimate and ecological sound practice. The aboriginals have been using this technique for over twenty thousand years.) What is never stated is the ecological damage caused by the consumption patterns of the West. The industrialized countries account for 25 percent of the world's population and use 86 percent of the world's resources. Somehow these facts never appear to be as significant as the ''ecologically unsound'' lifestyle of the peasants. Again, the dominant knowledge system has been used to frame a problem and articulate solutions without considering alternative explanations.

So what are the alternatives? Points of resistance can be found in both academic circles and the numerous grassroots movements that have sprung up in various parts of the world. The work done by authors such as Nandy (1989), Shiva (1989), Visvanathan (1991), Esteva (1987) and others focuses on alternatives to development (as opposed to development alternatives). The common theme of this stream of work centers on local culture and knowledge and the promotion of local grassroots movements (Escobar, 1995). Others advocate the use of appropriate local technologies and, in cases where technologies need to be imported, call for a critical evaluation of the relevance of those technologies (Dholakia, 1988). A common response to globalization is the return to the local. Escobar (1995) calls for the deconstruction of development and advocates conducting local ethnographies that map development practices in different communities. Whatever the particular mode of resistance, it is important that alternatives to development and alternative forms of knowledge be made visible using its own lenses rather than a visibility created by the mirror of the dominant Western paradigm.

NOTE

1. Entropy refers to the deterioration of existing natural resources and the amount of unavailable energy in the planet. Any increase in entropy results in a decrease in available energy (Rifkin, 1989).

REFERENCES

Appadurai, Arjun. 1990. Disjuncture and Difference in the Global Cultural Economy. In Mike Featherstone (ed.), *Global Culture: Nationalism, Globalization and Modernity*. London: Sage, 31–56.

Carson, Rachel. 1962. *Silent Spring*. Boston: Houghton Mifflin.

Catton, William R. and Dunlap, Riley E. 1980. A New Ecological Paradigm for Post-Exuberant Society. *American Behavioral Scientist* 24(1): 15–48.

Commoner, Barry. 1972. The Social Use and Misuse of Technology. In J. Benthal (ed.), *Ecology: The Shaping Enquiry*. London: Longman, 335–362.

Commoner, Barry. 1974. *The Closing Circle*. New York: Bantam Books.

Daly, Herman E. 1980. *Economy, Ecology, Ethics: Essays toward a Steady State Economy*. San Francisco: Freeman.

Dholakia, Nikhilesh. 1988. The Marketing of Development: An Exploration of Strategic Forms of Development. In Erdogan Kumcu and A. Faut Firat (eds.), *Marketing and Development: Towards Broader Dimensions*. Greenwich, CT: JAI Press, 63–78.

Dunlap, Riley E. and Catton, William R. 1979. Environmental Sociology. *Annual Review of Sociology* 5: 243–273.

Escobar, Arturo. 1995. *Encountering Development: The Making and Un-Making of the Third World, 1945–1992*. Princeton, NJ: Princeton University Press.

Esteva, Gustavo. 1987. Regenerating People's Space. *Alternatives* 12(1): 125–152.

Gilman, Robert. 1992. Design for a Sustainable Economics. *In Context* 32: 52–59.

Gray, Rob. 1992. Accounting and Environmentalism: An Exploration of the Challenge of Gently Accounting for Accountability, Transparency, and Sustainability. *Accounting, Organization and Society* 17(5): 399–425.

Guha, Ramachandra. 1989, Spring. Radical American Environmentalism and Wilderness Preservation: A Third World Critique. *Environmental Ethics* 11: 71–83.

Hall, Stuart. 1991. The Local and the Global: Globalization and Ethnicity. In Anthony D. King (ed.), *Culture, Globalization and the World System: Contemporary Conditions for the Representation of Identity*. London: Macmillan, 19–39.

Jacobs, Michael. 1990. *Sustainable Development*, Fabian Tract 538. London: Fabian Society, cited in McIntosh (1991).

Korten, David C. 1992. Development, Heresy, and the Ecological Revolution. *In Context* 32: 30–35.

Krutilla, J. V. 1967. Conservation Reconsidered. *American Economic Review* 57: 777–786.

Krutilla, J. V. and Fisher, A. C. 1974. *The Economics of Natural Environments*. Baltimore: Johns Hopkins University Press.

Lovins, Amory. 1977. *Soft Energy Paths*. Cambridge, MA: Ballinger.

Lutz, E. and Munasinghe, M. 1991, March. Accounting for the Environment. *Finance and Development* 28: 19–22.

Martinez-Alier, Juan. 1987. *Ecological Economics: Energy, Environment and Society.* New York: Basil Blackwell.

McIntosh, Andrew. 1991, July. The Impact of Environmental Issues on Marketing and Politics in the 1990's. *Journal of the Market Research Society* 33(3): 205–217.

Meadows, Donella H., Meadows, Dennis L. and Randers, Jorgen. 1972. *The Limits to Growth.* New York: Universe Books.

Meadows, Donella H., Meadows, Dennis L. and Randers, Jorgen. 1992. *Beyond the Limits: Confronting Global Collapse, Envisioning a Sustainable Future.* Post Mills, VT: Chelsea Green Press.

Morison, S. and Gray, Rob. 1991, July 12. Accounting for the Local Environment. *Public Finance and Accountancy* 117: 10–12.

Nandy, Ashish. 1989. Shamans, Savages, and the Wilderness: On the Audibility of Dissent and the Future of Civilizations. *Alternatives* 14(3): 263–278.

Norgaard, R. B. 1975. Scarcity and Growth: How Does It Look Today? *American Journal of Agricultural Economics* 57: 811.

Odum, Eugene P. 1971. *Fundamentals of Ecology.* 3rd ed. Philadelphia: W. P. Saunders.

Passel, Peter. 1990, November 27. Rebel Economists Add Ecological Cost of Price of Progress. *New York Times*, C4.

Petulla, Joseph M. 1980. *American Environmentalism: Values, Tactics, Priorities.* College Station: Texas A&M University Press.

Reilly, William K. 1990, Fall. The Green Thumb of Capitalism: The Environmental Benefits of Sustainable Growth. *Policy Review*: 16–21.

Rifkin, Jeremy. 1989. *Entropy: Into the Greenhouse World.* New York: Bantam.

Robertson, Roland. 1987. Globalization Theory and Civilizational Analysis. *Comparative Civilizations Review* 17: 20–30.

Shiva, Vandana. 1989. *Staying Alive: Women, Ecology and Development.* London: Zed Books.

Smith, Anthony. 1990. Towards a Global Culture? In Mike Featherstone (ed.), *Global Culture: Nationalism, Globalization and Modernity.* London: Sage, 171–191.

Surma, J. and Vondra, J. 1992, March. Accounting for Environmental Costs: A Hazardous Subject. *Journal of Accountancy*: 51–55.

Throop, Gary M. 1993. Strategy in a Greening Environment. Doctoral dissertation, University of Massachusetts, Amherst, MA.

Visvanathan, Shiv. 1991. Mrs. Brundtland's Disenchanted Cosmos. *Alternatives* 11(1): 147–165.

Wallerstein, Immunel. 1990 Culture as the Ideological Battleground of the Modern World-System. In Mike Featherstone (ed.), *Global Culture: Nationalism, Globalization and Modernity.* London: Sage, 31–56.

Waters, Malcolm. 1995. *Globalization.* London and New York: Routledge.

White, Lynn. 1967. The Historical Roots of our Ecological Crisis. *Science* 155: 1203–1207.

World Commission on Environment and Development. 1987. *Our Common Future.* New York: Oxford University Press.

PART II

Regional Issues

CHAPTER 5

Multinational Market Groups: Realities and Implications for Member and Nonmember Countries

A. BEN OUMLIL AND C. P. RAO

The dynamic global business environment is being greatly affected by the emergence of the regional trading blocs (e.g., NAFTA, the European Community, and the Southeast Asian countries). Although the full consequences of these united markets cannot yet be known, member and nonmember countries and their multinational firms can take steps now to prepare themselves to operate within these newly structured entities. The aim of this chapter is to examine these realities and their implications.

INTRODUCTION

Today's U.S. economy can be characterized as truly global. Our prosperity depends in large measure on the prosperity of our trade partners. It has been argued that free trade is good and that all parties benefit. This is especially true for the world's principal trading nations (i.e., the three major regional trading blocs of North America, the European Community, and industrialized Asia). While these blocs account for only 15 percent of the world's population, they produce 72 percent of its wealth.

NAFTA, the North American Free Trade Agreement between the United States, Canada and Mexico, is the world's largest single trading zone with over 360 million consumers (Wu and Gaspar, 1994). Given the proximity of the three countries to one another, this can be considered a natural trading bloc. Officially, NAFTA will gradually eliminate all tariffs and lower most other trade barriers between Mexico, Canada and the United States over a period of 10 years (Wu and Gaspar, 1994). Before NAFTA, the textile industry in the United States and Canada was highly protected. Wu and Gaspar have predicted that under NAFTA, U.S. and Canadian textile production will become more competitive through the use of Mexican labor. In addition, under the provision of the local content requirement, NAFTA should allow automobile production to increase in the three nations (1994).

In the 1990s, the eight East Asian countries as a group became the United States' most important trading partner. Asia's sudden growth as a competitor in world trade can be attributed to several coordinated events, especially the area's private domestic investment and rapidly growing human capital. Additional factors are East Asia's fundamentally sound development policies, timely government interventions, and rapid accumulation of physical capital (Wu and Gaspar 1994).

Latin America's trading blocs, though viable, currently operate on a much smaller scale. Their trade is primarily between each other and less with the larger trading blocs. For instance, in 1992 U.S. exports to Latin America, excluding Mexico, totaled $35 billion, less than U.S. exports to Singapore, Taiwan, and South Korea combined during the same time period (Wu and Gaspar, 1994).

ADVANTAGES OF REGIONAL TRADING BLOCS

Some argue that these new regional trade groupings are a faster route to global free trade. Over the years, GATT (the General Agreement on Tariffs and Trade) has encouraged free trade and the elimination of tariffs; however, some researchers (e.g., Joseph L. Brand) believe that it has failed to deal effectively with nontariff barriers such as import quotas and has therefore outlived its usefulness. They also cite statistics showing that trading blocs help reduce national tariffs and trade barriers and generate huge increases in trade among the partners. However, because GATT does not adequately address nontariff barriers and because Japan's exports therefore receive equal treatment, trading blocs have become an effective way of competing with Japan (Brand, 1991).

On the other hand, Panagariya (1994) emphasizes that future GATT rounds could facilitate the formation of regional trade blocs, owing to the decreasing level of trade between individual countries. The consolidation of countries into three regional trading blocs will make it much easier to adopt global reductions in trade barriers. These regional trading blocs can be laboratories for free trade initiatives (e.g., agreements on intellectual rights or service industries). In addition, trading nations have been both unable and unwilling to implement these initiatives on the global level. Consequently, regional trade groupings will inevitably become building blocks rather than obstacles in the move toward global economic integration (Lawrence, 1991).

Other researchers support the existence of trading blocs because they expect the "trade creation" among member states or among natural trading blocs like the United States, Mexico and Canada to be more than a "trade diversion" from nonmembers (Krugman, 1991). Neighboring high-income countries that are natural trading partners because of geographical proximity, complementarities in factor endowment and supply patterns could be net welfare-enhancing for the group itself without doing harm to nonmembers (Langhammer 1992). This simply means that the amount of trade between the member countries (i.e., the United States and Mexico) will increase, but this increase will not affect the amount of trade between nonmembers (i.e., the United States and Japan). Trade in these nonmember countries is anticipated to remain the same.

In addition to these reasons, Panagariya (1994) states that trade blocs, representing a large market enjoy more market power than individual countries. The net result is lower prices for the trading bloc members. When dealing with nonmember countries, member countries or a particular trading block need to observe the issue of reciprocation. Fear of retaliation for unfair trade practices assures a certain level of fair trade between different trading blocs/countries/members. Therefore, given the vital role that extraregional trade plays in their economies, it is not in the interest of any one trade region to strengthen trade barriers with the rest of the world (Lawrence, 1991). As Langhammer has observed, trade blocs can have a immense economic implications in addition to tariff removal: "For instance, they can provide technical assistance for policy reforms including monetary integration, debt relief, economic aid, free capital movement, and technology transfer" (Langhammer, 1992).

DISADVANTAGES OF REGIONAL TRADING BLOCS

Some researchers have urged caution concerning the emergence of regional trade blocs. For instance, "a world organized around regional trade blocks unconnected to a larger global trade framework would have devastating consequences for those nations left outside the regional blocks, particularly in the poorest and least developed of the world's nations." These outsiders, including some of the poorest and least secure in the world, "fear being left out in the cold" because they have less to offer to the rest of the world (Kinnock, 1994). These countries, preoccupied with the demands of their domestic market, are less prepared to become players in the world trade arena. Thus, as nonmembers, they will likely encounter trade barriers (e.g., tariffs or quotas) when they engage in trade with members of trading blocs. The outcome leaves these nonmember countries at a disadvantage and in desperate need to build their economies (Brand, 1991). Even if these poor nonmember countries were to join a trading bloc, they would gain less than their rich counterparts (Panagariya, 1994).

Others (e.g., Krugman, 1991) fear that negotiations between just three parties would also increase the potential for conflict. Larger trading blocs would be more powerful and would want to protect their markets by imposing restrictions on imports to nonmember countries. Accomplishing the goal of having only three main trading parties (the North American, Asian and European blocs) would require that a large number of countries would have to join together. These negotiations would be a daunting task (a case in point is the EC). In addition, in some cases, regional trade blocs would require the cooperation of

long-time political rivals (Panagariya, 1994). If these blocs were to turn hostile
toward each other, then significant trade gains could be lost (Petersen, 1992).
Therefore, small numbers of trading blocs does not necessarily mean faster progress in trade (Panagariya, 1994).

Another cautious observation concerns the possibility that major trading blocs
might lead to a regression away from multilateral free trade by restricting external trade. This regression is attributed to trade barriers and discriminatory
preferential trade. The net result could be a diversion away from the most efficient producer in the world to the least efficient producer within the bloc
(Brand, 1991; Lal, 1993).

Trade experts have proposed that the ideal goal is complete free trade or a
multilateral trading system. They believe that "regionalism is slower and less
efficient than multilateralism and will not produce any better results than a multilateral approach" (De Melo and Panagariya, 1992). In addition, regionalism
might act as an obstacle because it could make multilateral free trade more
difficult to obtain (Bollard and Mayes, 1992), ultimately diverting attention and
support away from the multilateral approach and to the second best approach
of regional trading blocs (Lal, 1993). Various researchers have argued that the
potential for increasing trade frictions between rival trading blocs could lead to
an intensification of trade barriers between them, which, over time, could erode
the multilateral trading system (De Melo and Panagariya, 1992; Lal, 1993).

CONCLUSIONS

Among the recommendations made in the reviewed literature are continuing
the extraregional commerce by the three big trade powers (the United States,
Japan, and the Eastern Caribbean) and using the regional trade integration as a
vehicle for multilateral liberalization (*The Economist*, 1992). Specifically, si-
multaneous liberalization in all the major countries would lead to minimal adjustment costs (Panagariya, 1994), and the ideal policy would be unilateral free
trade for each country (Krugman, 1991).

In conclusion, member and nonmember nations, together with their multinational companies, have been forced to face the new marketing realities created
by the unification of regional trading blocs. Although we do not yet know the
full consequences of these unifications, members and nonmembers and their
multinational companies can take steps now to prepare to operate within the
newly structured global/regional market. They will need not only effective strategies, but also contingency planning at an early stage. Through such flexible
strategies they can avoid being "trampled under foot" by the rising economic
power of the trading blocs.

REFERENCES

Bollard, Allan and Mayes, David. 1992, June. Regionalism and the Pacific Rim. *Journal
    of Common Market Studies*: 195–209.

Brand, Joseph L. 1991, October 17. The New World Order: Regional Trading Blocks. *Vital Speeches of the Day*: 155–160.

De Melo, Jaime and Panagariya, Arvind. 1992, December. The New Regionalism. *Finance and Development*: 37–40.

The Trouble with Regionalism. 1992, June 27. *The Economist* 323(7765): 79.

Kinnock, Neil. 1994, Summer. Beyond Free Trade to Fair Trade. *California Management Review*: 124–135.

Krugman, Paul. 1991, November–December. The Move Toward Free Trade Zones. *Economic Review*: 5–25.

Lal, Deepak. 1993, September. Trade Blocs and Multilateral Free Trade. *Journal of Common Market Studies*: 349–357.

Langhammer, Rolf J. 1992, June. The Developing Countries and Regionalism. *Journal of Common Market Studies*: 211–229.

Lawrence, Robert Z. 1991, Summer. The Reluctant Giant: Will Japan Take Its Role on the World Stage? *Brookings Review* 9(3): 36–39.

Panagariya, Arvind. 1994, March. East Asia: A New Trading Bloc? *Finance and Development*: 16–19.

Petersen, Christian E. 1992, May. Trade Conflict and Resolution Methodologies. *Conflict and Peace Economics*: 62–66.

Wu, Terry and Gaspar, Julian. 1994, February 15. North American Free Trade Agreement Implications for East Asia. Working Paper.

CHAPTER 6

The NAFTA Market and Management Training for Successful Entry

V. H. (MANEK) KIRPALANI

NAFTA's economic and market size is analyzed, and the significance of NAFTA for world trade and foreign direct investment is pointed out. The management education and training requirements for outside international managers who wish to effectively lead their firms into NAFTA are discussed in detail. Coverage extends to content, methods of delivery, location of training, and type of instructors.

NAFTA was formed primarily in response to the perceived threat that the European Union (EU) would block off exports for nations outside the EU. The EU is further ahead than North America on the road to integration. While both regions have free movement of capital, the EU has a customs union and a common external tariff, and is close to achieving a common market with EU-wide common standards and the free movement of people. It is also moving in the direction of an economic union and a harmonizing of national economic policies.

The world is trade dependent. Exports of goods and services account for over 15 percent of the world's GNP. Economic prosperity is inextricably tied to international trade and, in many cases, foreign direct investment. This chapter first looks at the prospects occasioned by NAFTA; then it focuses on management education and training for successful entry into the NAFTA markets. NAFTA will allow its member countries to achieve economies of scale in traditional exporting industries and wider scope in the new technology-driven sectors of the economy. The standard of living among the member nations should rise as they begin to use their comparative advantages and other competencies to specialize their exports and optimally allocate resources. Thus, they will likely purchase an increased level of imports. The Adam Smith adage remains gen-

Table 6.1
NAFTA Country Overview

Country	Population (Millions)	GDP ($ Billions)	GDP (Per Capita)	Export ($ Billions)	Wages ($/Hour)
United States	253	5,673	22,457	418	14.77
Canada	27	593	22,038	128	16.02
Mexico	88	285	3,017	27	1.08

Sources: Royal Bank of Canada, Statistics Canada, *Time* Magazine; reported in *The Gazette*, Montreal, Quebec, Canada, August 15, 1992, D1.

erally true today: "It is . . . as foolish for a nation as for an individual to make what can be bought cheaper" (Gray, 1988). This chapter also presents an overview of NAFTA and describes its significance for world trade and finally, discusses management training needs for successful entry by foreign, including Indian, firms.

NAFTA: AN OVERVIEW

NAFTA, with its 365 million people and GDP of some $6.5 trillion, will soon vie with the EU as the world's richest market region (see Table 6.1). With more than one-third of its people below 15 years of age, Mexico is forecast to have a population of 140 million by A.D. 2025, an increase of 63 percent. While the increase in North America will only be of the order of 20 percent over the period, this will bring the total NAFTA population close to 500 million (Lipsey, Schwanen and Wonnacott, 1994). Canada joined in response to the major forces of enhanced global competitiveness as seen, for example, through the EU. If under a solely U.S.–Mexico free trade agreement (FTA), a U.S. firm lowered its cost of production by sourcing part of its product from Mexico, then it would become more competitive than its Canadian counterpart. EU brings home the reality of trading blocs and of countries being shut out of lucrative markets. Moreover, if Canada had permitted a U.S.-Mexico FTA to form, then the United States would have become the hub and Canada and Mexico two different spokes, with resulting greater benefit to the hub than to either of the two spokes (Barker, 1992). Mexico joined for many reasons, but in this context an old saying, "Poor Mexico! So far from God and so close to the U.S., may be pertinent." Now here was a chance for Mexico to join a wealthy bloc. However, a critical contributing factor to the NAFTA agreement was the deregulation, liberalization and privatization of the Mexican economy. For example, the government sold the Banco Nacional de Mexico to Mexican entrepreneur Roberto Hernandez and his partners for $3.2 billion.

The Long-Term Strategy

The United States launched the Enterprise for the Americas Initiative (EAI) on June 27, 1990, to help the Latin American and Caribbean countries undergo economic reforms. The EAI attempts to shift the focus of economic interaction towards an economic partnership in the Americas, based on the three pillars of increased trade, increased investment and debt reduction (Nuechterlein and Birch, 1991). Specifically, these objectives strive to:

1. Expand trade, with the ultimate goal of forming a hemispheric system linking all the Americas, starting with Canada and Mexico. In the meantime, the United States is prepared to make arrangements within bilateral frameworks. It will also try to obtain deep tariff reductions, through GATT/WTO on Latin American special interest products.

2. Increase investment. The United States will work with the Inter-American Development ment Bank to create a new lending program and a new investment fund to finance market-oriented investment reforms and privatization. Europe and Japan will contribute to the fund. The help on the investment side will include reduction of the debt owed to the U.S. government (Bundy, 1991).

3. Reduce debt: The United States will sell some U.S. commercial loans to facilitate debt-for-equity and debt-for-nature swaps; environmental improvement debt-for-nature swaps are also being promoted.

The NAFTA Framework

1. NAFTA will eliminate Mexican tariffs and trade-restrictive import licensing. By the year 2008 all tariffs within NAFTA are scheduled to be ended.

2. NAFTA will strengthen regulations governing a clean environment.

3. Intellectual property rights will be protected, and laws governing such protection will be enforced more rigorously.

4. Canada has largely fulfilled its objectives in NAFTA. Canada has obtained:

   • clearer rules of origin.

   • extension of duty drawback provisions.

   • consultation and dispute settlement on customs administration.

   • strengthened "sideswipe" exemption from U.S. safeguards. If the United States institutes a protectionist regulation against other countries, Canada and Mexico are exempted.

   —the Auto Pact safeguards.

   —continued quotas to support supply management for poultry and dairy products.

   —exemption for cultural industries.

   —social and health services.

5. Accession clause: Other countries who want to join NAFTA will have to meet certain eligibility criteria, notably, a stable macroeconomic environment, an open trading system for goods and services, a multilateral trading regime and a more liberal foreign investment framework. Furthermore, other countries will have to accept the same obligations as existing members in general and in regard to specific sectors. Thus, there will be no renegotiation from scratch. No future erosion of the rights and obligations of existing numbers will occur just to accommodate the interests of new participants.

Macrobenefits of NAFTA to Members

The major macro gains are the economic benefits that will accrue from liberalized trade, namely:

- No duties will equate with lower prices.
- Lower prices should translate into higher purchasing power.
- Scale economies achieved from serving a large combined FTA market should result in lower production costs.
- Competitiveness for organizations within the FTA may be enhanced through possible increases in productivity.
- The dynamism of the national economies will improve because of increased competition between firms in the partner countries.

Since Mexico is the smallest economy and Canada is the next smallest, these benefits should be greater for them, in that order, than for the United States. Moreover, all three partners have gained by imposing the condition that at least 50 percent of the value of the product has to be added in the partner countries. Without this condition, outsiders could take advantage of NAFTA by bringing their products into the NAFTA region after crossing at the lowest tariff point.

The only exception applies to the apparel industry, which has annual quota volumes. Although rules of origin will not be a restriction up to the annual quota volumes, these quotas will be set below the current trade levels.

The Maquiladora Program

This program, created in 1965, was built on the proviso that the U.S. tariff would be charged only on the value added outside the United States on products manufactured abroad from materials and parts originating from the United States. It was mainly a subcontracting program, with the American products entering Mexico duty free. Value added took place at the Maquiladora plant. Low or no duty was levied on Maquiladora product entry into the United States due to the GATT Generalized System of Preferences (GSP) applicable to all less developed countries (LDCs), including Mexico. However, the GSP rule stipulates that only 35 percent of the value added be in the country of origin. NAFTA is stipulating that 50 percent must originate in the NAFTA member country.

The Maquiladora program has now grown to two thousand plants employing some five hundred thousand workers, a significant part of the industrial work-force in Mexico. In the last five years, the Maquiladoras have been growing at 20 percent per year. The Maquiladoras started in a free trade zone along the U.S.–Mexico border. Rapid growth led to an overburdened infrastructure and shortages of skilled human and other resources. As a result, some Maquiladoras are situated in different interior sites in Mexico. The big task now is for Mexico to contribute more in terms of added value in order to reach the 50 percent country of origin figure: in addition to labor, there has to be an increased input of Mexican raw material, parts and components. So far the components have never exceeded 2% of the added value (Schechter, 1992). The Maquiladora program will have to be adjusted under NAFTA rules of origin governing prod-uct content. But the time period allowed for such adjustment is by the year 2001.

Trade and Industry

U.S.-Mexican trade is of the order of $60 billion a year; the United States is Mexico's biggest export market, and some 50 percent of Mexico's imports come from the United States. A U.S. International Trade Commission study indicates that U.S. cement, electronics, grains and oilseeds sectors will gain, while citrus and other fruit and vegetables, cheaper household glassware and the tuna in-dustry will lose (Davies, 1991). The best U.S. export prospects appear to be oil and gas field machinery, and production plus distribution equipment for electric power. Other U.S. industries likely to benefit include avionics, capital goods, computers, financial services, machine tools, paper products, petrochemicals and telecommunications equipment (Dowd, 1991).

Canadian trade with Mexico presently is only around $4 billion a year. Ca-nadian industries likely to benefit are fabricated metal products, paper and pulp, and telecommunications (Allard, 1990). Vulnerable sectors include footwear, vegetable processors, household furniture, major appliances and wineries (Lav-elle, Barrows and Traficanta, 1988). All Mexican tariffs for NAFTA countries will be removed in 10 years, but many will be phased out sooner. Of particular interest to Canadian exporters are the faster phaseouts in some aluminum, most auto parts, agricultural, contribution and resource machinery, fertilizer, fish med-ical equipment, prefabricated housing, printed circuit boards, selected wood, pulp and paper items and telecommunications equipment. On the whole, Canada and the United States will have the opportunity to benefit from a growing Mex-ican market, but they are likely to lose ground to Mexico in low-tech and labor-intensive industries.

SIGNIFICANCE OF NAFTA FOR WORLD TRADE

Overall, NAFTA has much to commend it. It is limited to trade issues and is fully consistent with GATT requirements. It does not contain a social charter such as the one adopted by the EU because, unlike the EU, it does not seek a high degree of political and social integration. However, the three countries have affirmed their commitment to advance the rights of workers and promote high standards through mutual cooperation.

The signatories of NAFTA have constructed this comprehensive trilateral trade agreement to allow for other countries to join. NAFTA is important because of the future potential with Mexico and other Latin American countries. It is expected that most Latin American countries will ultimately link or join NAFTA. Chile has applied for NAFTA membership and is very likely to be accepted. Chile's standard tariff is only 15 percent. Today it mainly imports cars and exports agricultural goods, including wine. In August 1992 Mexico signed an agreement to establish a free trade zone by 1997 with five Central American nations: Costa Rica, El Salvador, Guatemala, Honduras and Nicaragua (*Globe and Mail*, 1992), even though less than 1 percent of Mexico's trade occurs with these markets now. The agreement will allow Central American exports free access to Mexico three years before Mexico is allowed free access to the Central American markets. Thus, NAFTA may expand. It also may extend to other South American countries, which sooner or later will do whatever is necessary to open up their borders to NAFTA members and join NAFTA.

Large trading blocs tend to do most of their growing trade within their borders. For example, the EU conducts more than 50 percent of its foreign trade among its members, and this percentage is growing. The same can be expected for NAFTA because as Mexico becomes more affluent the United States and Canada will have preferred access. The rest of the world will gain by trading with the large NAFTA bloc but not much more than it gains today by trading with the individual NAFTA countries.

For outsiders, real gains can come from entering NAFTA by investing in manufacture in NAFTA countries, in either wholly owned or joint ventures. Indian firms are very knowledgeable in leather goods, medicinal drugs and selected food processing. These firms should be welcome in Mexico, which has much leather, a population of over 85 million and a growing economy. The outsider's investment has to result in production of goods and services that meet the 50 percent member country of origin rule for such production to qualify for duty-free exports to other NAFTA countries. Outsiders should seriously consider this investment proposition due to NAFTA's potential.

MANAGEMENT TRAINING FOR SUCCESSFUL PENETRATION

International managers who wish to penetrate the NAFTA market will in many cases want to enter through Mexico or Chile because of the low labor costs. To be successful these managers must have contextual and technical competencies (Finney and Von Glinow, 1988). By contextual competency, we mean Spanish-language ability; understanding of the culture and value orientation of people in the home and host countries; recognition of the importance of religion, politics, history and culturally relevant information; and ability to operationalize managerial responsibilities to meet local foreign conditions (Taggart, Wheeler and Young, 1994). By technical we mean knowledge of the industry in the home country and in Mexico. Knowledge of the society and how it functions will also be useful. This knowledge can be obtained in a holistic way by studying a country's culture and philosophy; politics, political institutions and history; and economics. In the realm of culture and philosophy a number of questions arise:

- Are cultures coming together?
- Are there market segments within countries or cross-nationally in NAFTA?
- What significantly different consumer wants exist in the different NAFTA countries which have to be met with appropriate variations in the marketing mix?
- How do culture and philosophy manifest themselves in business negotiations and industrial relations?
- How does culture affect market structure and consumer/customer behavior?

In the area of politics, political institutions and history, it is important to learn the extent to which the system encourages concentration or diffusion of power; and the attitude to foreigners and regulations concerning inward foreign direct investment. In the economic sector, international managers need to know demographics, income distribution, structure of the economy, government fiscal and monetary policy, size of public and private sectors, information on consumption/investment/savings, balance of payments and foreign exchange reserves.

All international managers must have professional skills, managerial abilities, special personal qualities and intercultural competence (Auteri and Tesio, 1990). Professional skills are essentially technical; managerial abilities involve, among other things, good communication and leadership abilities; and special personal qualities include openness to change, management of stress and personal efficiency. Competent managers score high in these three areas. The fourth area, intercultural competence, is one in which education and training are needed for effectiveness when the managers are entering foreign markets with very different cultures.

Indian international managers who want to lead their companies effectively into the NAFTA market must receive adequate education and training. Hence, they will have to address four issues: content, methods of delivery, locations and type of instructors. In regard to *content*, in order to equip themselves appropriately, managers would do well to attend management development seminars dedicated to NAFTA on the topics mentioned above as well as on the cultural environment (ethics, environmentalism, leadership in an intercultural setting and selected business practices), negotiations, international business opportunities and research, strategies and methods of entry for international firms, and conflict areas and conflict resolution between governments and multinational enterprises. *Methods of delivery* encompass factual, analytical and experiential learning. The factual side is comprised of area briefings, lectures and articles/books. The analytical side should have case studies, culture assimilators of different kinds and sensitivity training modules. Experiential learning can be obtained through interactive language training, role-playing modules, simulations and, if possible, field trips. The *locations* of training can be in the home country, but this should be bolstered by attending seminars when going to the NAFTA countries; a variety of seminars are now being offered in the United States and Canada. As to the *type of instructors*, these should as far as possible be visiting international faculty members, since it is hard to retain permanent international faculty members in most countries.

CONCLUSIONS

NAFTA offers a market with a great deal of economic potential—in fact, more than its individual member nations would have achieved on their own. Given the fact that NAFTA members will trade with each other duty-free and that NAFTA is large enough in size, has a plethora of resources and has North American members who are technologically advanced, NAFTA will likely be a trade-creating area for its members. Such a large market is likely to grow for the foreseeable future and is well worth penetrating. However, for outsiders penetration of this market requires the surmounting of tariff barriers, since NAFTA members will have zero tariffs among themselves. Because surmounting tariff barriers will not be easy, especially with the productivity increases likely to take place within NAFTA industries, the more productive strategy for outsiders will be to make foreign direct investments within NAFTA.

As is well known in the international sphere, the message sent is not necessarily the message received for people interpret symbols and words that are encoded in different ways. Body language/gestures, written documents versus words, high-and low-context levels of cultures, attitudes toward women, time and personal space are just a few examples of the cultural differences that should be learned.

For marked effectiveness, Indian companies, whether making foreign direct investments or exporting to NAFTA, will require educated and trained international managers. Management education must cover, at a macrolevel, the philosophy, politics and economics of the NAFTA region. At the microlevel, education and training needs have been detailed in this chapter, but the concentration should be on obtaining a grasp of foreign culture and the way culture affects the doing of business. Methods of delivery of education and training, location of training and type of instructors have also been described here. These facets of international management education and training are of crucial importance.

REFERENCES

Allard, Christian. 1990, November. Mexico for Sale: Gringoes Welcome. *Canadian Business* 63: 72–76.

Auteri, E. and Tesio, V. 1990. The Internationalisation of Management at Fiat. *Journal of Management Development* 9(6): 6–16.

Barker, Tansu. 1992, June. NAFTA Prospects for Canada: Can We Afford Not to Join? Proceedings of the Administrative Sciences Association of Canada (ASAC) Annual Conference, Quebec.

Bundy, Kelly. 1991, November. Advancing the Goal of a Free Trade Hemisphere. *Global Trade* 110: 32–34.

Davies, David. 1991, April. Bentsen on Free Trade. *Business Mexico*: 49–50.

Dowd, Reilly A. 1991, June 17. Viva Free Trade with Mexico. *Fortune* 123: 97–100.

Finney, M. and Von Glinow, M. A. 1988. Integrating Academic and Organizational Approaches to Development the International manager. *Journal of Management Development* 7(2): 16–27.

Globe and Mail. 1992, August 24.

Gray, E., 1988. Free Trade Free Canada. Ontario: Canadian Speeches, 5.

Lavelle, P. J., Barrows, D. and Traficanta, F. 1988, Summer. The Ontario Government's Perspective on the Canada-U.S. Free Trade Agreement. *Business Quarterly* 53: 8–12.

Lipsey, Richard G., Schwanen, Daniel and Wonnacott, Ronald J. 1994. *The NAFTA: What's In, What's Out, What's Next.* Toronto: C.D. Howe Institute.

Nuechterlein, Donald and Birch, Ian. 1991, May. Free Trade with Mexico and South America: The Anticipated Issues and Timeframe to Be Connected. Working Paper 91-09. Kingston, Ontario: Queen's University, School of Business Research Program.

Schechter, Cheryl. 1992, March 12. The Maquiladora Industry and Free Trade. Mexico Trade Letter. Mexico City/Paris/Tijuana: Goodneth, Riqulwe/Associaelos.

Taggart, Jim, Wheeler, Colin and Young, Stephan. 1994. The Training of International Managers: The Strathclyde Perspective. *Journal of Teaching in International Business* 6(2): 1–19.

PART III

Global Investment Issues

CHAPTER 7

Economic Liberalization and Foreign Direct Investment in Developing Countries: Japanese Investments in India and China

JAIDEEP ANAND AND ANDREW DELIOS

Foreign direct investment (FDI) into developing countries has increased rapidly in recent years. Some of these investments have been motivated by the large untapped markets of these countries, while others have been motivated by access to resident assets like low-cost labor. This growth in FDI has coincided with decentralization in Japanese manufacturing. Consequently, Japanese multinational enterprises (MNEs) have become the dominant investors in the countries of South, Southeast and East Asia. We analyze patterns of Japanese FDI and MNE strategies and find that Japanese FDI into India is more frequently motivated by market access and is part of a multidomestic strategy. Japanese entries into China more frequently tend to be motivated by the desire to access location-specific resources and are part of a global strategy. We conclude that MNEs respond to country-specific and industry-specific factors, as is visible in their investment and organizational strategies.

Foreign direct investment (FDI) into developing countries grew rapidly in the late 1980s and first half of the 1990s. In 1994, FDI inflows to developing countries reached $84 billion, or 37 percent of worldwide FDI. The countries of South, Southeast and East Asia have accounted for the bulk of this increase in FDI to developing countries. Approximately 70 percent of developing country FDI ($61 billion) was invested in the countries of this region (UNCTAD, 1995). China is the largest recipient of FDI among developing countries and the second largest recipient of FDI in the world. More than half of the FDI invested in the developing countries of Asia is found in China ($34 billion). In 1995 these trends were expected to continue as developing country inflows were projected to increase to $90 billion (UNCTAD, 1995). Similarly, FDI into India, albeit from a low base, has been growing rapidly, as the following figures illustrate:

in the first year following the introduction of the new industrial policy, FDI approvals grew by 159 percent, and in the following year, this figure increased to 270 percent. Actual FDI in 1993 surpassed $3 billion and grew rapidly to $5 billion in 1994, which contributed to annual net capital inflows of $1 billion (Bhattacharyya, 1995).

Despite the impressive growth of FDI in this region in the past decade, this subject has received little research attention. FDI studies have typically examined flows of investment between the triad markets of North America, Europe and Japan (Dunning, 1993). The most extensive ongoing research project on multinational enterprises (MNEs) and FDI, the Harvard Multinational Enterprise Project, concerned MNEs in the triad markets and supported at least 17 books, 151 articles and 28 doctoral theses (Vernon, 1994). Even when the focus of FDI has shifted to the developing economies as host sites, researchers have tended to focus on investment in these countries by firms resident in North America (e.g., Beamish, 1984; Kumar, 1990, 1994; Lall and Mohammed, 1983).

Beyond the lack of intensity with which Asian-based FDI has been studied, the case of FDI in South, Southeast and East Asia is particularly interesting because it tends to be motivated by two polar objectives. Some of the investments in the region are motivated by the large untapped markets of these countries. China and India, for example, account for 40 percent of the world's population, while the countries of the ASEAN region have a population base approaching that of North America or Western Europe. Through the rapid economic growth in these regions, a large body of consumers now exists there. For example, in many popular press articles, frequent reference is made to India's middle class of 250 to 300 million people. Other investments in this region are motivated by access to low-cost labor. Skilled and semiskilled labor pools exist in abundance in these countries. For MNEs, which are shifting production in response to differences in global factor markets, the availability of a large pool of inexpensive and technically skilled textile workers in China, electronics workers in Malaysia or software engineers in India can be a compelling motive for relocating their manufacturing operations to these countries.

Meanwhile, Japan has become a dominant investor in the world. In the last 30 years, FDI outflows from Japan have increased substantially. For example, in the 1960s, the amount of Japanese FDI flowing into the United States as a share of all FDI into the United States, was negligible. But by 1990, Japan had emerged as the second largest foreign investor in the United States, with a 20 percent share of all FDI in the United States (Lipsey, 1994). Japanese industry is increasingly turning to foreign overseas affiliates for manufacturing as Japan becomes a less attractive place from which to export (Lipsey, 1993). In the countries of Asia, Japan leads North American and European firms in investment. In the 1990s, Japan was the largest foreign investor in the region, and in 1995, it possessed 1.5 times more stock of FDI in these countries than firms from either the United States or Western Europe (UNCTAD, 1995). Thus, with the increasing importance of FDI outflows from Japan and the increasing at-

tractiveness of developing Asian economies for FDI inflows, Japanese investment in this region presents a particularly interesting case for the study of FDI
and market entry strategies.

This study is descriptive; that is, we do not present hypotheses and systematically test them. Rather, we present data on Japanese subsidiaries and draw
inferences regarding the sectoral distribution, entry strategy, sourcing and marketing strategies, as well as other aspects of managing international operations.
Given the limited literature existing in this field (Aswicahyono and Hill, 1995),
the recent nature of the phenomenon and the paucity of data, such an exploratory
approach can make a valuable contribution. We limit host sites for Japanese
FDI to the two largest countries in the region: India and China. These two
countries present an interesting case for contrast because both have liberalized
what were closed economies at different times. In addition, India and China are
often concurrently evaluated by investors considering their next large investment
(Thomas, 1994), suggesting that some competition for FDI exists between these
countries. Therefore, in order to illuminate the role of country-specific factors
and industry–country interactions in determining market entry strategies and the
outcomes of Japanese FDI, we compare the strategies of Japanese MNEs operating in India and China.

METHODOLOGY

Unlike many other studies conducted at the macrolevel, we focus on information from individual subsidiaries. The data used in this study are drawn from
two editions of *Japanese Overseas Investment*, a publication of Toyo Keizai Inc.
(Toyo Keizai, 1989, 1994). These sources contain information on Japanese FDI
gathered by a large sample annual survey of Japanese foreign subsidiaries, the
most recent of which was in 1993. The survey respondents are the managers of
Japan's 15,200 foreign subsidiaries. The survey is conducted in December of
each year by Toyo Keizai, and many researchers have defended the use of
information in the Toyo Keizai survey for analyses (e.g., see Hennart, 1991;
Woodcock, 1994; Yamawaki, 1994). We selected our sample using the following criteria: the subsidiaries had to be in the manufacturing sector, Japanese
ownership had to exceed 10 percent, and the subsidiaries had to be located in
India or China. This sample includes 88 percent of the Japanese subsidiaries in
India and 66 percent of those in China in the 1994 survey. In terms of subsidiary
counts, 76 cases of Japanese FDI in India and 456 cases of Japanese FDI in
China comprise our sample.

ANALYSIS

Sectoral and Geographical Distribution

We begin by identifying some general patterns and trends in the Japanese
ventures in India and China. First, we find that Japanese FDI in China is located

Table 7.1
Comparison of FDI in India and China with the World

Industry	SIC	Industry % of Total		
		World	India	China
Food and Kindred Products	20	6.7	2.6	11.5
Textile Mill Products	22	5.0	1.3	5.7
Apparel and other Textile Products	23	3.5	1.3	17.4
Lumber and Wood Products	24	1.0	0.0	1.6
Furniture and Fixtures	25	1.2	0.0	1.4
Paper and Allied Products	26	1.1	0.0	0.7
Printing and Publishing	27	1.0	0.0	0.0
Chemicals and Allied Products	28	12.5	11.8	7.3
Petroleum and Coal Products	29	0.1	0.0	0.7
Rubber and Misc. Plastics Products	30	5.7	0.0	1.8
Leather and Leather Products	31	0.4	0.0	0.9
Stone, Clay, and Glass Products	32	2.5	5.3	2.3
Primary Metal Industries	33	4.7	2.6	2.5
Fabricated Metal Products	34	7.4	2.6	3.9
Industrial Machinery and Equipment	35	9.2	10.5	9.1
Electronic and Electrical Equipment	36	17.5	22.4	16.2
Transportation Equipment	37	11.3	34.2	5.7
Instruments and Related Products	38	4.7	3.9	6.2
Miscellaneous Manufacturing Ind.	39	4.5	1.3	5.0

Note: In each of the tables, because of rounding, column totals may not always sum to 100, and row percentages, in industries, may not be perfectly consistent between tables because of rounding.

principally in the fast growing southern and eastern coastal provinces (Hainan, Guangdong, Fujian, Zhejiang, Shanghai, Jiangsu and Shangdong) in which many of China's export-oriented special economic zones are found. In India, Japanese FDI is concentrated geographically and in a few specific sectors (see Table 7.1). In terms of two-digit SIC codes, investments in the manufacture of electronic (SIC-36) and transportation equipment (SIC-37) account for 57.6 percent of the cases in this subsample. Other prominent sectors are industrial machinery and equipment (SIC-35) and chemicals and allied industries (SIC-28), with, respectively, 10.5 percent and 11.8 percent of the cases of FDI in the subsample. Each of the remaining eight sectors does not account for more than 5 percent of FDI. This categorization demonstrates the dominance of capital-intensive manufacturing industries. Automobile, truck, motorcycle, automotive component parts and industrial equipment and machinery manufacture (all SIC-37 or 35) account for more than half of all Japanese FDI in India.

Sectorally, Japanese FDI in China displays a much more even distribution than that in India, though FDI in food, textile and clothing industries is disproportionately represented in China. Conversely, investment in these three industrial sectors is underrepresented in India. As stated earlier, investment in India is singularly concentrated in heavy manufacturing industries such as industrial machinery and transportation equipment as well as in the electronics industry. In a pattern mirroring India's underrepresentation in textile, food and clothing industries, Japanese investment in China is underrepresented in the transportation, industrial machinery and electronics sectors, in comparison to both India and the world.

We also find that Japanese FDI in India is concentrated geographically. The states of Haryana and Maharashtra accounted for almost half the cases of Japanese FDI in India as measured by the number of subsidiaries and by the equity value of each subsidiary. FDI in these two regions is concentrated in the cities of New Delhi and Bombay, which suggests the existence of industrial clusters. The other two regions with significant amounts of Japanese FDI were the states of Tamil Nadu and Karnataka, which together accounted for another 21 percent of the FDI in India. The remaining 30 percent of FDI was distributed among eight other states.

The two dominant sites, Haryana and Maharashtra, have an almost equal number of subsidiaries. Twenty-five percent of Japan's subsidiaries are located in Haryana, and 21 percent in Maharashtra. However, the amount of equity invested in Maharashtra is 1.25 times that of Haryana and more than six times that of any other state in India. In Haryana, Japanese FDI was exclusively in capital-intensive manufacturing industries such as automobiles and metals, with automotive manufacturing dominating. For example, Toyota and Suzuki's investments in the Maruti joint venture are located around New Delhi. In Maharashtra, Japanese FDI did not display any particular industrial pattern. Service industries are frequently represented here (though these are not visible from this sample)—hotels, financial and engineering, and manufacturing industries—glass, metals, chemicals and automotive. FDI in Karnataka was exclusively in electronic equipment and was concentrated in the city of Bangalore, an emerging center for electronics and computer software manufacture. In Tamil Nadu, FDI was dispersed among textile, automotive and electronic equipment manufacture.

Growth of Japanese Investment

Interestingly, the first reported case of FDI in India was in June 1957, but the next few decades saw little such activity: less than half of the investments that existed in the early 1990s had been made before 1985. The 1986–88 period was a relatively strong period of investment, for one-third of the reported investments took place during this period. The rate of investment seemed to drop in the 1989–91 period, due partly to uncertainty in India and partly to Japan's domestic problems. However, since the economic liberalization process was instituted in 1991, there has been a resurgence in Japanese FDI.

The amount of Japanese investment flowing into India, as a proportion of total Japanese overseas investment is still minor—0.44 percent of all FDI—but it is increasing at a rapid pace. Even during those recent periods in which total

FDI outflows from Japan decreased in absolute numbers, the absolute number of Japanese FDI cases in India increased. Thus, India has recently taken a larger share of Japanese investments worldwide.

In comparison to China, FDI in India is still small, and the reported number of cases of Japanese FDI in China is approximately 10 times that of India. This is consistent with the distribution of total FDI (from all countries) between India and China: China had received 10 times the investment of India (Thomas, 1994). Almost half of the investments in China were made in the period since 1992, compared with less than 20 percent of all cases of FDI formed in India in the same period. This makes the average age of ventures in China much smaller (three years less) than that in India. Although China has attracted a greater amount of Japanese FDI than India, the popularity of both counties as host countries for Japanese FDI has increased in the last few years.

Role of Chinese and Indian Subsidiaries in the MNEs

We examine the role of Indian and Chinese subsidiaries in the worldwide operations of the MNE by analyzing two variables: the extent to which these subsidiaries are dependent on sources of inputs outside of India, and the extent to which the output from these subsidiaries is exported. A global strategy involves multiple linkages among subsidiaries and between the headquarters and subsidiaries, whereas a multidomestic approach involves more self-sufficient subsidiaries with little need for transactions between subsidiaries in different countries. We use these two variables to judge the level of integration of Indian and Chinese operations in the worldwide system of Japanese MNEs.

A subsidiary can use a combination of three possible locations for the sourcing of inputs and the sale of outputs: (1) the local country in which the subsidiary is located, (2) the home country (in this case, Japan), or (3) a third country. Products that are sold in markets outside of the host country suggest that the subsidiary has adopted a global (re-exporting) strategy. Where products are sold within the country, the subsidiary can be characterized as adopting a multi-domestic (market penetration) strategy. Similarly, we distinguish between inputs sourced from the host country and those sourced from aboard. Table 7.2 presents the patterns in marketing strategies and the corresponding patterns in input strategies.

In India, products are generally sold within the country, suggesting a market penetration role for these subsidiaries. This is in contrast to China, where goods are produced for sale in China 47.6 percent of the time and for re-export in 52.4 percent of the cases. Goods are re-exported to both Japan and other countries; this is unlike the case of India in which goods, if not sold in India, are exported back to Japan. Subsidiaries in China, on this measure, appear to be more internationally integrated.

This strategy of market penetration by Japanese firms in India contrasts

Table 7.2
Patterns in Marketing Strategies, India and China

	Marketing		Sourcing	
	India	China	India	China
Region	Proportion of Respondents:		Proportion of Respondents:	
1. Japan	34.7	38.1	18.2	48.9
2. Host country	65.3	47.6	77.3	48.9
3. Third Country	0.0	14.3	4.5	2.2
Strategy				
Multi-domestic (2)	65.3	52.4	77.3	48.9
Global (1+3)	34.7	47.6	22.7	51.1

Note: The strategy items had a lower response rate in the survey (approximately 20 percent) across both countries. Respondents and nonrespondents were comparable on most organizational characteristics identified in this study.

sharply with the re-export strategy in other locations with low wages. A firm's principal motivation in locating in low-wage countries is to internalize the low cost of labor and develop a wage advantage (Kumar, 1994). This is particularly important for Japanese MNEs trying to compensate for the loss of comparative advantage in industries such as textiles and clothing (Kojima, 1978).

Similarly, the input sourcing pattern of Japanese subsidiaries in India is in contrast to that in China: Japanese subsidiaries in India show a greater reliance on local sourcing than do subsidiaries in China, for only a small percentage of inputs (22.7%) were sourced from outside the host country. Conversely, inputs for production in China came almost equally from inside and outside of the country, reflecting the more global nature of subsidiary strategy in China.

Investment Motivation

These patterns of input sourcing and sales of output are consistent with the stated objectives of the subsidiaries. Table 7.3 provides a breakdown of these objectives for the establishment of subsidiaries. The primary motives for doing FDI in India were (1) as a response to government invitation (e.g., government investment incentives) and (2) for market expansion. Subsidiaries that indicated the market expansion motive were primarily in the transportation equipment industry. The local resources were a factor in the chemicals industry, where natural resources and low-cost labor were cited as reasons for investment. Whereas market entry is the dominant motivation for FDI in India, low-cost labor is the most frequently cited motivation for investment in China (30.8%), with market expansion being of somewhat less importance (26.9%). In order to explore the relationship between the motive for subsidiary formation and the subsequent strategy, we examined these two classes of variables simultaneously

Table 7.3
Motives for Investment in India and China

| | % responding Yes | |
Motive	India	China
Access to raw materials	7.7	7.7
Abundance of natural resources	4.6	5.7
Access to low-cost labor	4.6	30.8
Response to gov't. Invitation	33.8	13.5
Expand market	41.5	26.9
Collect information	0.0	0.9
Obtain royalty	4.6	5.7
Establish export base	1.5	3.7
Counter trade friction	1.5	0.9
Raise capital	0.0	0.0
Other motive	0.0	4.8

Note: The response rate for these items was 40 percent.

(Table 7.4). Intuitively, we expect the low-cost-labor-driven investment to be more globally managed and market-entry-driven investments to exhibit more local sourcing and sales.

In India, investment as motivated by market expansion and in response to government invitation tended to focus on the domestic rather than on the export market. Inputs, however, were generally sourced in India, with the exclusion of the input strategies corresponding to the government invitation and market expansion motive. For these two motives, inputs were generally sourced evenly from Japan and India. Subsidiaries in China exhibit a somewhat contrasting pattern. Investment as motivated by access to low-cost labor and markets, and by government incentives tended to be oriented to a more global strategy. Japanese firms established ventures in China to reduce labor costs, and output from these ventures was both exported and distributed locally. In the manufacture of products in China, inputs tended to be sourced both locally and from Japan.

This picture is consistent with the sectoral distribution of the subsidiaries in the two countries: almost half of the subsidiaries established in China are in labor-intensive industries such as textiles and food and clothing manufacture. Establishment of a subsidiary in China is a factor seeking investment in which labor and other factors of production are components of a global strategy. Investment in India was more in response to government incentives and was oriented toward market entry. The existence of a large population and a growing domestic market, increasing incomes and relative political stability attracts firms to invest in longer term, market penetration strategies (Root and Ahmed, 1979; Wheeler and Moody, 1992). Hence, we observe these motives in both China and India.

Table 7.5 provides a breakdown of sourcing and market strategies by industry.

Table 7.4
Motives and Strategies for Subsidiary Formation, India and China

Motive for FDI	India				China			
	Products		Sourcing		Products		Sourcing	
	Exported	Sold Locally	Japan	Local	Exported	Sold Locally	Japan	Local
Access to raw materials	8.3	2.8		7.4	12.8	12.8	17.1	9.8
Abundance of natural resources	5.6	2.8		7.4	2.6	2.6	7.3	9.8
Access to low-cost labor		2.8			28.2	2.6	4.9	9.8
Response to local restrictions	8.3	22.2	22.2	14.8	10.2	2.6	9.8	12.2
Expand market	8.3	30.8	25.9	14.8	17.9		17.1	2.4
Collect information						2.6		4.9
Obtain royalty		2.8		3.7	2.6		2.4	
Establish export base		2.8		3.7	2.6		2.4	
Counter trade friction		2.8						
Raise capital								
Other motive								
Total	30.5	69.8	48.1	51.8	76.9	23.2	61.0	39.1

Note: All column totals represent percentage of "Yes" respondents in that motive, for the broad category.

Table 7.5
Comparison of Marketing Strategies across Industries in China and India

Industry	SIC	India Products Exported	India Products Sold Locally	India Sourcing Japan	India Sourcing Local	China Products Exported	China Products Sold Locally	China Sourcing Japan	China Sourcing Local
Food and Kindred Products	20					7.4	18.5	23.5	
Textile Mill Products	22					3.7		5.9	
Apparel and other Textile Products	23	4.8				22.2		14.7	
Lumber and Wood Products	24					3.7	3.7	5.9	2.9
Furniture and Fixtures	25						3.7	2.9	
Paper and Allied Products	26						3.7		2.9
Printing and Publishing	27								
Chemicals and Allied Products	28	9.5	14.3		13.3	3.7	3.7		2.9
Petroleum and Coal Products	29					3.7			2.9
Rubber and Misc. Plastics Products	30							2.9	
Leather and Leather Products	31								
Stone, Clay, and Glass Products	32		4.8						
Primary Metal Industries	33		4.8		6.7			2.9	2.9
Fabricated Metal Products	34		9.5	6.7	6.7			2.9	
Industrial Machinery and Equipment	35	4.8	4.8	6.7	6.7	3.7	3.7	2.9	
Electronic and Electrical Equipment	36	4.8	4.8	6.7	6.7	3.7		2.9	2.9
Transportation Equipment	37	4.8	23.8	33.3	6.7	7.4	3.7		2.9
Instruments and Related Products	38	4.8						8.9	2.9
Miscellaneous Manufacturing	39								
Total		33.5	66.8	53.4	46.8	59.2	40.7	76.3	23.2

Note: All column totals represent percentage of ''Yes'' respondents in that industrial sector, for the broad category.

Table 7.6
Subsidiary Size in India and China

Measure[1]	India	China
Sales ($)	35	7.20
Equity Investment ($)	3.90	8.96
Value added per employee ($)	0.064	0.024
Number of Employees	545	294
Labor Intensity (employee/ $ million in equity)	139	33

[1]All monetary values are reported in millions of U.S. dollars.

In India, to the extent that there were transactions with the outside world, they were in only a few fields such as the chemicals, electronics and instrumentation fields. Perhaps this is where the competitive advantage of Indian engineers and technicians lies. In China, on the other hand, the strategies in different industries vary widely. For example, the food, textile and apparel industries source exclusively in Japan. However, production from the apparel and textile industries is sold entirely in Japan, while production from the food industry is both exported and distributed in China and Japan, though local sales are greater. Similarly, input strategies are more evenly distributed across industries. Investment in India, spurred in large part by host government invitation and the desire to expand markets, is more characteristic of a multidomestic strategy. That FDI in India is not focused primarily on re-exports has been identified earlier (Kumar, 1994). To examine the issue further, we consider two sets of variables corresponding to two hypotheses: productivity in these subsidiaries and the pattern of ownership structures.

Size and Productivity

Table 7.6 presents various measures of the size of investments. On the basis of sales and employment measures, subsidiaries in India are larger. However, the average equity invested in subsidiaries in India is lower. We use two ratios to further these figures: employment to equity capital (a relative measure of labor or capital intensity), and sales per employee. Industrial production in China is more labor intensive than that in India. On average, Japanese subsidiaries in India produce double the dollar value of output per employee of the subsidiaries in China ($30,000 per employee for China versus $63,000 per employee for India).

These patterns are consistent with the distribution of investments across industries in these two countries. Japanese FDI in India is in heavier industrial industries, SIC (35,36,37), which require more skilled labor. After the United States and Russia, India has the largest reserve of technically trained labor, and, intuitively, the productivity of Indian labor should be higher. In addition, the inputs to the production process have greater value in heavier industries. For example, in the transportation equipment sector, many of the inputs to manufacture in India may consist of component parts, which already have a high value-added component. This trend is reflected in the sourcing strategy in India in SIC-37 in which inputs are sourced primarily from Japan. These are likely components that are assembled in automotive manufacture in India. Because of the greater initial value of production inputs, the sales per employee figure tends to overestimate the value added per employee.

A second aspect of the explanation of this pattern is the comparative age of the subsidiaries. Ventures in India are, on average, eight years older than those in China. Since the equity reported in the Toyo Keizai survey is the book, not market, value of the subsidiary, this measure understates the size of the ventures in India. Third, the subsidiaries in China are concentrated in textile, clothing, food and other low-tech manufacturing industries, which despite the capital employed still involve a significant labor component in product manufacture. A multinational operating with a global strategy would be expected to locate labor-intensive production, in which there is a lower value-added component per labor hour of manufacture, in low-wage countries. The labor intensity of production, or low value added per employee, is reflected in the lower sales per employee in China as compared to such sales in India.

Organizational Characteristics

Parent firms have several options when entering foreign markets. Notwithstanding local restrictions on the form of market entry, four common strategies for market entry are exporting, licensing, shared ownership ventures and sole ventures (Agarwal and Ramaswami, 1991). However, since this study is concerned with direct investment, it concentrates on the latter two forms of market entry: shared ownership ventures such as capital participation and joint ventures, and sole ventures like greenfield wholly-owned subsidiaries (WOS) and acquisitions. Local ownership restrictions precluded market entry by WOS in India and prior to 1991, generally restricted foreign equity ownership in a subsidiary to 40 percent (Ahluwalia, 1994). Not surprisingly, Japanese firms formed no WOS in this pre-July 1991 period. The mode of foreign investment was either that of joint venture or partial capital participation, with the joint venture being preferred in the majority of subsidiaries (Table 7.7). Post-July 1991 conditions allow foreign investors to freely hold up to 51 percent equity share in a joint venture, and provisions exist for foreign investors to seek a greater than 51 percent share (Ahluwalia, 1994). In the eight joint ventures formed in the 1991–93 period, the Japanese partner took at least a 35 percent ownership position, and in four of the joint ventures, at least a 50 percent equity share.

Japanese FDI in China displays greater diversity with respect to the mode of

Table 7.7
Entry Mode by Industry, India and China

Industry	SIC	India		China		
		JV	CP	JV	CP	WOS
Food and Kindred Products	20	1.3	1.3	10.9	0.7	
Textile Mill Products	22	1.3		5.5	0.23	
Apparel and other Textile Products	23	1.3		15.3	0.5	1.9
Lumber and Wood Products	24				0.23	
Furniture and Fixtures	25			1.4		
Paper and Allied Products	26			1.4		
Printing and Publishing	27			0.7		
Chemicals and Allied Products	28	9.3	2.7	7.0		
Petroleum and Coal Products	29			0.7		
Rubber and Misc. Plastics Products	30			1.9		
Leather and Leather Products	31			0.7		
Stone, Clay, and Glass Products	32	4.0	1.3	1.9	0.5	
Primary Metal Industries	33	2.7		2.1		
Fabricated Metal Products	34		1.3	3.2	0.5	0.23
Industrial Machinery and Equipment	35	9.3	1.3	6.3	2.3	0.7
Electronic and Electrical Equipment	36	18.7	4.0	13.2		3.2
Transportation Equipment	37	18.7	16.0	4.9		0.5
Instruments and Related Products	38	2.7	1.3	4.9		1.4
Miscellaneous Manufacturing	39	1.3		3.5		1.6
Total (percentage)		**70.6**	**29.2**	**85.5**	**4.5**	**9.5**

Note: JV = joint venture; CP = capital participation; WOS = wholly-owned subsidiary.

entry, perhaps reflecting the reforms in the Chinese economy in the 1970s and 1980s. Joint ventures, capital participation and WOS are evident in subsidiaries in China, although joint ventures are by far the most popular form of market entry. WOSs are the next most prominent form in China, representing 9.6 percent of all subsidiaries established in China. The Japanese partner had at least 50 percent ownership in 40 percent of the foreign subsidiaries established in China, but only 50 percent ownership in 11 percent of subsidiaries established in India.

Japanese Ownership and Control

The form of entry mode can be taken as a proxy for the desired level of control. WOS and acquisitions are higher control modes; joint ventures and capital acquisition are lower control modes. A subsidiary operating under a global mandate requires that its operations be more highly integrated with those of other subsidiaries and corporate headquarters than a subsidiary operating under a multidomestic strategy (Bartlett and Ghoshal, 1989). Entry mode is a rough measure for the desired level of control, especially in countries in which the mode of entry is restricted primarily to joint ventures. Although the desire for control tendency was not manifest in a comparison of entry mode by industry in China and India, other measures do mirror the expressed global strategy–high control relationship. A more granulated measure, which captures this relationship, is the average equity ownership by the Japanese partner.

A joint venture, for example, operating as a component of a global strategy needs to be flexible and responsive in managing activities that are coordinated globally (Harrigan, 1985; Porter and Fuller, 1986). However, there are inherent managerial difficulties in operating a joint venture (Killing, 1983), and one method of overcoming these difficulties is to increase the formal level of control by increasing the share of equity ownership (Gomes-Casseres, 1989; Stopford and Wells, 1972). Ventures in China, identified as more globally oriented in their strategy, do indeed have greater equity participation by the Japanese partner. The average Japanese ownership in China is 56 percent, which is significantly ($p < .001$) greater than the 30 percent average in India. Furthermore, within China, equity ownership by the Japanese partner increases as the subsidiaries' strategic stance moves from a local to a global orientation. Table 7.8 depicts this relationship between ownership levels and strategy. In India, there is no consistent pattern between strategies and ownership levels. In contrast, in Chinese subsidiaries of Japanese multinationals, the tendency is for higher ownership levels to be associated with more globally oriented strategies.

The number of Japanese employees in Japanese subsidiaries in Asia tends to be correlated with the level of equity ownership (Lipsey, 1994). The emergent trend for higher ownership levels to be associated with a more global strategy is corroborated by this second proximate measure for control, the number of Japanese employees in the subsidiary. Table 7.9 displays this relationship as higher Japanese employment levels are found in those subsidiaries operating under a global mandate.

The average number of Japanese employees in ventures in China is significantly greater ($p < .05$) than that in India. In 62 percent of the subsidiaries in India, there were no Japanese employees, while only 33 percent of subsidiaries in China operated without any Japanese employees. The absolute number of Japanese employees could, however, be an artifact of the size of the subsidiary. To control for subsidiary size, Japanese employment is scaled by the total employment, with the new measure being the ratio of Japanese employment to total employment. By this measure, Japanese employment in China is two times that in India (Table 7.10). Subsidiaries in China, through the use of home country employees, are better linked with the Japanese parent firm and other subsidiaries. This trend is strongest in the food, textile and apparel industries, all of which have greater than average Japanese participation in the operations of the subsidiary and each of which was identified as having a particularly strong global orientation.

Table 7.8
Strategy and Ownership, India and China

Equity Ownership by Japanese Partner	India Products Exported	India Products Sold Locally	India Sourcing Japan	India Sourcing Local	China Products Exported	China Products Sold Locally	China Sourcing Japan	China Sourcing Local
0 to 19%	5.5	11.1	6.7	13.4		3.7		2.9
20 to 29%	5.5	33.3	26.7	20.0	3.7		8.8	2.9
30 to 39%	5.5			6.7	7.4		5.9	
40 to 49%	11.1	22.2	13.3	6.7	11.1	14.8	26.5	2.9
50% or more		5.5	6.7	6.7	40.7	18.5	35.3	14.7
Total	27.6	72.1	53.4	46.8	62.9	37.0	76.5	23.4

Table 7.9
Japanese Employment and Ownership in India and China

	India Products Exported	India Products Sold Locally	India Sourcing Japan	India Sourcing Local	China Products Exported	China Products Sold Locally	China Sourcing Japan	China Sourcing Local
Number of Japanese Employees	2.13	0.29	0.60	1.53	3.71	1.33	2.80	1.00

Table 7.10

Average Number of Employees by Industry, India and China

Industry	SIC	India			China		
		Avg. # Employees	Avg. # Japanese Employees	Employees/ Japanese Employee	Avg. # Employees	Avg. # Japanese Employees	Employees/ Japanese Employee
Food and Kindred Products	20	144	1.50	96	74	1.36	54
Textile Mill Products	22				286	4.00	71
Apparel and other Textile Products	23	450	1.00	450	272	2.87	94
Lumber and Wood Products	24				115	0.40	287
Furniture and Fixtures	25				204	3.20	64
Paper and Allied Products	26				118	0.50	236
Chemicals and Allied Products	28	579	0.86	673	87	1.85	47
Petroleum and Coal Products	29				139	2.67	52
Rubber and Misc. Plastics Products	30				162	0.38	426
Leather and Leather Products	31				617	0.50	1234
Stone, Clay, and Glass Products	32	676	5.25	129	444	3.25	136
Primary Metal Industries	33	436	0.50	872	142	0.33	430
Fabricated Metal Products	34	184	0.00		154	1.31	117
Industrial Machinery and Equipment	35	467	0.17	2747	416	3.47	120
Electronic and Electrical Equipment	36	589	1.60	368	547	4.65	118
Transportation Equipment	37	617	1.62	381	545	2.31	236
Instruments and Related Products	38	239	1.00	239	318	3.30	96
Miscellaneous Manufacturing	39				109	2.07	52
Average Number of Employees		**545**	**1.48**	**368**	**295**	**2.63**	**112**

Performance

Although several differences in motives, strategies and structures of the ventures in India and China have been identified, perhaps suggesting different levels of commitment, performance between subsidiaries in the two countries is equal. Plausible arguments could be made for the partners being more committed to a venture involved in a multidomestic strategy (because of greater independence) or the Japanese partner being more committed under a global strategy (because of interdependence and close scrutiny by the parent). However, no distinct trend emerges when we compare performance across industries. We cannot draw any definite conclusions due to some of the weaknesses in the performance item (a three-point measure) and the fundamental differences in the two markets.

CONCLUSIONS

This study has empirically examined the patterns of Japanese direct investment in India and China. Investments have grown much more rapidly in China, and investments in China are distributed across a greater number of industrial sectors. Japanese FDI in India and China was motivated by different factors and involved a different strategic stance. FDI in China more frequently tended to be part of a global strategy. Subsidiaries were located in China for access to low-cost factors of production, and production was frequently in the food, textile, clothing and other such labor-intensive industries. Japanese ventures in India were a market-seeking investment spurred by government incentives and the desire to expand into a market that was protected from exports.

In comparing the outcomes of Japanese investment in these two countries, a link can be drawn between the characteristics of the host country and the strategy used by MNEs in operating in these countries. The presence of large pools of skilled and semiskilled labor in both countries was not sufficient to attract export-oriented investment. In China, where economic liberalization and initiatives such as special economic zones fostered greater economic integration with foreign economies, MNEs tended to operate with a more global strategy. This is reflected in the industries entered by Japanese MNEs and the characteristics of the established subsidiaries. Japanese MNEs established subsidiaries in labor-intensive industries such as textiles, clothing and food manufacture; the control of these subsidiaries was high; and the transfer of technology and management skills was facilitated by placing more expatriate Japanese employees in these subsidiaries. Thus, the host country (China) benefited not only from the monetary gains of increased exports but also from intangible gains such as management skills and technology transfer.

To some extent, the subsidiaries established by Japanese MNEs in India provided monetary benefits to the host country as domestic production substituted for the import of products in many of the capital-intensive, heavy industries (automotive and machinery manufacture) in which the majority of FDI occurred.

However, because investment in these industries was market-seeking and because the pre-liberalization economy of India had limited links with other economies, output from Japanese subsidiaries generally was not exported from the country. Japanese MNEs had little incentive to incorporate the most current management practices and technologies in these subsidiaries, which is reflected in the low level of ownership taken and the lack of commitment of expatriate Japanese employees to these ventures. Consequently, there was minimal transfer of management skills and technology to the host country via the subsidiary.

These differences have important implications for public policymakers in host countries and for MNEs. Reaffirmed in this study is the equivocal effect of government incentives with respect to FDI. Where incentives promote the integration of the subsidiary with other entities in its parent MNE, the links between the host country and the external economic world are tightened. The host country is more likely to benefit from the re-export of the subsidiary's product and from the transfer of intangible management skills and technology through the establishment of more modern and technologically sophisticated subsidiaries. As U.S. and European MNEs enter these two large and emerging markets with greater frequency, they will encounter their usual competitors as well the principal foreign denizens of these countries, the Japanese MNEs. An awareness of the relative presence of Japanese MNEs in these countries and an understanding of their strategies is an early and essential step in devising and implementing effective foreign market entry strategies in India and China.

NOTE

We gratefully acknowledge Shige Makino for providing access to the Toyo Keizai data. We thank Azimah Ainuddin, Shige Makino and Detlev Nitsch for their insightful and helpful comments on earlier versions of this chapter.

REFERENCES

Agarwal, Sanjeev and Ramaswami, Sridhar N. 1991. Choice of Foreign Market Entry Mode: Impact of Ownership, Location and Internalization Factors. *Journal of International Business Studies* 23(1): 1–27.

Ahluwalia, Montek S. 1994, Spring. India's Quiet Economic Revolution. *Columbia Journal of World Business*: 7–12.

Aswicahyono, H. H. and Hill, Hal. 1995. Determinants of Foreign Ownership in LDC Manufacturing: An Indonesian Case Study. *Journal of International Business Studies* 26(1): 139–158.

Bartlett, Christopher A. and Ghoshal, Sumantra 1989. *Managing across Borders: The Transnational Solution*. Boston: Harvard Business School Press.

Beamish, Paul W. 1984. Joint Venture Performance in Developing Countries. Unpublished doctoral dissertation. University of Western Ontario, London, Ontario, Canada.

Bhattacharyya, B. 1995. Recent Developments in Trade and FDI in India. Working Paper, Indian Institute of Foreign Trade.

Dunning, John H. 1993. *Multinational Enterprises and the Global Economy*. Reading, MA: Addison-Wesley.

Gomes-Casseres, Benjamin. 1989. Ownership Structure of Foreign Subsidiaries: Theory and Evidence. *Journal of Economic Behavior and Organization* 11: 1–25.

Harrigan, Kathryn R. 1985. *Strategies for Joint Ventures*. Lexington, MA: Lexington Books.

Hennart, J. F. 1991, April. The Transactions Cost Theory of Joint Ventures: An Empirical Study of Japanese Subsidiaries in the United States. *Management Science* 37: 483–497.

Killing, J. Peter. 1983. *Strategies for Joint Venture Success*. London: Croom Helm.

Kojima, Kiyoshi. 1978. *Direct Foreign Investment*. London: Croom Helm.

Kumar, N. 1990. *Multinational Enterprises in India*. London: Routledge.

Kumar, N. 1994. Determinants of Export Orientation of Foreign Production of U.S. Multinationals: An Intercountry Analysis. *Journal of International Business Studies* 25(1): 141–156.

Lall, S. and Mohammed, S. 1983. Multinationals in Indian Big Business: Industrial Characteristics of Foreign Investments in a Heavily Regulated Economy. *Journal of Development Economics* 13: 143–157.

Lipsey, Robert E. 1993. *Foreign Direct Investment in the United States: Changes over 3 Decades*. Working Paper No. 4124. National Bureau of Economic Research.

Lipsey, Robert E. 1994. *Outward Direct Investment and the U.S. Economy*. Working Paper No. 4691. National Bureau of Economic Research.

Porter, M. E. and Fuller, M. B. 1986. Coalitions and Global Strategy. In M. E. Porter (ed.), *Competition in Global Industries*. Boston: Harvard Business School Press, 315–342.

Root, Franklin R. and Ahmed, Ahmed. 1979. Empirical Determinants of Manufacturing Direct Foreign Investment in Developing Countries. *Economic Development and Cultural Change* 27(4): 751–767.

Stopford, J. M. and Wells, L. T. 1972. *Managing the Multinational Enterprise*. New York: Basic Books.

Thomas, T. 1994, Spring. Change in Climate for Foreign Investment in India. *Columbia Journal of World Business*: 33–40.

Toyo Keizai. 1989. *Japanese Overseas Investments (by Country) 1989*. Tokyo: Toyo Keizai.

Toyo Keizai. 1994. *Japanese Overseas Investments (by Country) 1994*. Tokyo: Toyo Keizai.

UNCTAD. 1995. *World Investment Report, 1995: Transnational Corporations and Competitiveness*. New York and Geneva: United Nations.

Vernon, R. 1994. Contributing to an International Business Curriculum: An Approach from the Flank. *Journal of International Business Studies* 25(2): 215–228.

Wheeler, D. and Moody, A. 1992. International Investment Location Decisions: The Case of U.S. Firms. *Journal of International Economics* 33: 57–76.

Woodcock, C. Patrick, Beamish, Paul W. and Makino, Shige. 1994. Ownership-based Entry Mode Strategies and International Performance. *Journal of International Business Studies* 25(2): 253–273.

Yamawaki, H. 1994. Patterns of Japanese Multinationals into the U.S. and European Manufacturing Industries. In Dennis Encarnation and Mark Mason (eds.), *Does Ownership Matter? Japanese Multinationals in Europe*. Oxford: Clarendon Press, pp. 11–28.

CHAPTER 8

U.S. Corporate Investments in India: A Study of Investors' Perceptions of the Risk-Return Relationship

RAKESH DUGGAL AND MIKE CUDD

This study is a test of the market reaction to U.S. corporate investments in India since 1991, when the Indian government started the process of economic liberalization to attract foreign capital. The study finds that these investments are perceived by U.S. stockholders as having zero net present values. The higher perceived risk of these investments may be the reason why these investments are not considered wealth enhancing.

INTRODUCTION

In 1991, the Indian government made it more attractive to do business in India. Among its other measures to attract foreign equity capital, the government raised the foreign ownership of business from 40 to 51 percent in many industries and even 100 percent in certain cases.[1] This and other measures since then have resulted in substantial U.S. corporate investments in India. For example, U.S. firms committed $1.1 billion in 1993 alone—more than they did in the previous 47 years.[2] According to a survey by Ernst and Young, an accounting and consulting firm, the number of U.S. corporate investments in India rose to 34 from 15 a year earlier, causing India to jump to fifth place in terms of U.S. business interests in 1993.[3]

Economic theory predicts that, ceteris paribus, capital investments in India will initially earn positive risk-adjusted abnormal returns for the simple reason that the demand for capital exceeds the supply of capital in that country at the present time. These abnormal returns should disappear with time once the flow of capital is allowed unrestricted into the country, thereby resulting in only normal returns on capital investments.

It may, therefore, be presumed that U.S. managers must have determined these investments to be positive net present value investments. However, because of heterogeneous expectations, the U.S. stock markets may well view the risk-return characteristics of these investments quite differently. In addition to offering abnormal returns, emerging markets also expose the stockholders of multinational companies to a variety of risks. A recent article in the *Wall Street Journal* described some of these risks for India: "Shifting political sands could hinder reform . . . religious, ethnic and other political passions flare easily. . . . Bureaucracy and rigid labor laws remain a drag on business. So too corruptions.' "[4] The article also mentions the Indian people's ambivalence toward foreign investment: a recent survey found that roughly half of Indians still want foreign investment restricted. Similarly, Political & Economic Risk Consultancy Ltd. of Hong Kong recently ranked India as the highest risk to foreign business-people based on the views of analysts and nearly one hundred corporate managers and bankers with regional responsibilities.[5]

Therefore, it is entirely possible that the stockholders of U.S. companies view these investments with caution and show a lack of enthusiasm or even a negative reaction to the announcements of these investments. These stock market reactions may force managers to restrict their investments in India, thus slowing the globalization process until U.S. investors perceive the investment climate as more investment friendly. Thus, the main objective of this chapter is to investigate the response of the U.S. stock markets to the announcements of corporate investments in India.

This study tests the following main null hypothesis:

H_0: Stockholders of U.S. companies investing in India earn normal stock returns in the announcement period of these investments.

The alternative hypothesis is:

H_1: Stockholders of U.S. companies investing in India do not earn normal returns in the announcement period of these investments.

The alternative hypothesis provides for both a positive and a negative reaction by stockholders.

A BRIEF REVIEW OF RELATED LITERATURE

In the last two decades, a rich body of evidence on domestic intercorporate investments has accumulated in the United States. In general, the evidence indicates that domestic acquisitions, though not wealth-enhancing for acquiring firms, cause significant increases in the wealth of target stockholders (Jarrell, Brickley and Netter, 1988; Jensen and Ruback, 1983). Furthermore, McConnell and Nantell (1985) found that joint ventures enhance the wealth of participating firms.

Lately, many studies have also explored the wealth effects of international mergers and joint ventures. For example, Kang (1993) finds that Japanese acquisitions of U.S. firms are wealth-enhancing for both acquiring and target firms. Marr, Mehta and Spivey (1993) report that the wealth effects of takeovers by foreign firms are higher than those for takeovers by domestic firms. However, Mathur et al. (1994) find significantly negative abnormal returns to foreign firms making acquisitions in the United States. Morck and Young (1992) attempt to relate the gains to foreign acquiring firms to information-related intangible assets owned by American target firms. Markides and Ittner (1994) find that international acquisitions by U.S. firms create value for the American acquiring firms.

   The present study attempts to investigate the wealth effects of U.S. investments in India.

SAMPLE AND METHODOLOGY

   A sample of U.S. firms that announced investments in India between 1990 and 1994 has been gathered from a computer search of the *Wall Street Journal* and the *New York Times*. The stock market reaction to the event is estimated using standard event study methodology (see Brown and Warner, 1985).

   The market model is used to generate benchmark returns:

$$R_{jt} = A_j + B_j R_{mt} + E_{jt} \tag{1}$$

where

$$
\begin{aligned}
R_{jt} &= \text{return on the } j\text{th stock on day } t \\
R_{mt} &= \text{return on the CRSP equally weighted portfolio} \\
A_j, B_j &= \text{ordinary least squares parameters for security } j \\
E_{jt} &= \text{the residual term for security } j \text{ on day } t
\end{aligned}
$$

   Parameters A_j and B_j are estimated for each security j by regressing the pre-event time series of daily stock returns, R_{jt} (where $t = -300$ to $t = -46$), on daily returns on the CRSP portfolio. The event day ($t = 0$) is defined as the day the first news about the investment appears in the *Wall Street Journal* or the *New York Times* (whichever appears earlier). The estimated equation for each security is then employed to generate benchmark returns for the 11-day ($t = -5$ and $t = +5$) period. The Daily Abnormal Returns (AR_{jt}) are then estimated for each firm as

$$AR_{jt} = R_{jt} - (A_j + B_j R_{mt}) \tag{2}$$

   To test whether the market response to these announcements is significantly different from zero, the announcement period returns are averaged across all firms in the sample for each of the 11 days to obtain Daily Average Abnormal Returns (AARs). *t*-Statistics associated with AARs are calculated to test the significance of these abnormal returns. The Daily Average Abnormal Returns are also cumulated over various periods to obtain Cumulative Average Abnormal Returns (CAARs).

$$\text{CAAR}_j = \sum_{t=-T}^{t=+T} AR_{jt} \tag{3}$$

The t-statistics associated with CAARs are also calculated.

FINDINGS

A computer search of the two newspapers yields a sample of 52 U.S. firms that invested in India during the 1990–94 period. However, 15 firms were dropped from the sample because either they are not listed on the New York Stock Exchange or the American Stock Exchange, or the stock price data for the firms are unavailable on the CRSP tapes.

Table 8.1 contains some important characteristics of these investments. One obvious outcome of liberalization has been a significant increase in the number of investments, the dollar value of investments and the average percentage of equity bought since 1990. The number of investments rises from 2 in 1990 to 14 in 1994, whereas the dollar commitment for the projects increases from $1.2 billion to $2.1 billion in the same period. These investment outlays represent corporate estimates over the lives of the projects and are unlikely to equal actual expenditures in specific years.[6] Furthermore, the average equity stake of the U.S. firms rises from 40 percent to 65 percent in that period. It should be noted that information on the dollar value and equity stake is not available on all investments in the sample. Therefore, it must be recognized that these values may be somewhat skewed.

U.S. investments in India are equally divided between low-technology (e.g., food, beverage, cosmetics) and high-technology (e.g., telecommunications, automobile, computers) areas. Finally, 28 of the investments used in the sample are reported by the *Wall Street Journal* and the other nine by the *New York Times*.

The market reaction to U.S. corporate investments in India is displayed in Table 8.1. The stockholders of U.S. corporations announcing investments in India gain an abnormal return of 0.43 percent on the announcement date (day 0). This gain is significant at the 0.10 level. However, neither the 2-day $(-1, 0)$ nor the 11-day $(-5, +5)$ cumulative returns are significant at the conventional confidence levels.

This study gathers observations from both the *Wall Street Journal* and the *New York Times*. This is done to generate a sample of a decent size. However, it is possible that the response of the two readerships is not identical; therefore, combining the two may yield biased findings. Most event studies have employed the *Wall Street Journal* publication dates. The *New York Times* firms are dropped

Table 8.1

Sample Characteristics of U.S. Corporate Investments in India during 1990–94, as Reported by the *Wall Street Journal* and the *New York Times*

	1990	1991	1992	1993	1994	1990–1994
Number of Investments	2	4	4	12	15	37
*Investments in Millions of Dollars (number of firms)	1,210 (2)	N.A. –	45 (2)	195 (6)	2,712 (4)	4,162 (14)
Average Percent of Equity Acquired (number of firms)	40 (1)	45 (2)	51 (2)	79 (7)	65 (9)	65 (21)
Food/Beverage/ Cosmetics	1	2	1	7	8	19
Automobile/Power Computer/ Communications	1	2	3	5	7	18
Investments Reported by <u>Wall Street Journal</u>	2	3	4	9	10	28
Investments Reported by <u>New York Times</u>	0	1	0	3	5	9

*These represent corporate estimates over the lives of the projects and are likely to be different from the actual amounts spent in specific years.

from the sample, and the event study is performed again. As Table 8.2 shows, the market reaction is still positive at the 0.10 level.

An examination of the distribution of abnormal returns between positive and negative values on day 0 reveals that only 43 percent of the firms (16 out of 37) experience positive returns. This raises the possibility that a few large values may be driving the results. A closer examination of individual abnormal returns to firms reveals a significant outlier: Bausch & Lomb stockholders earn a highly significant abnormal return of more than 15 percent on day 0. When this observation is dropped from the sample, the results displayed in Table 8.3 are obtained. The day 0 abnormal returns to U.S. firms are reduced to an insignificant 0.02 percent (see Table 8.4). It appears, therefore, that, on average, U.S. corporate investments in India do not enhance stockholder wealth.

Two possible explanations of the above finding can be advanced. The first explanation—which is also the more obvious one—is that the market is not

Table 8.2
Abnormal Returns to a Sample of 37 U.S. Firms That Invested in India during 1990–94

Event Day	Abnormal Returns (AARs) (%)	t-Statistic	Positive: Negative
-5	-0.01	-0.0	16:21
-4	-0.37	-1.7*	14:23
-3	-0.28	-1.3	12:25
-2	0.16	0.7	22:15
-1	-0.09	-0.4	17:20
0	0.43	1.9*	16:21
+1	-0.03	-0.1	18:19
+2	-0.16	-0.7	15:22
+3	0.12	0.6	18:19
+4	0.10	0.5	21:16
+5	-0.27	-1.2	18:19

*Significant at the 0.10 level in a two-tailed test.

enthused by these investments and regards them to be zero net present value projects. Alternatively, a lack of information on these investments may explain an absence of response on the announcement days. The two U.S. newspapers do not generally devote much space to U.S. corporate investments in India, perhaps because of the small size of many of these investments. Except for some large deals, such as PepsiCo's and Coca-Cola's entries into India, much of the news coverage of these investments is very brief, often omitting information about the size of the investment and percentage stake acquired in the Indian venture. In the absence of detailed information, a pronounced market response in either direction may not be expected.

Since the sample includes six U.S. investments in India from the preliberalization era (1990–91), these firms are segregated from the 30 investments in the post-liberalization period to see if the latter investments are perceived to be more wealth enhancing by stockholders. The post-liberalization investments yield a positive one-day (day 0) abnormal return of 0.17 percent as opposed to −0.25 percent return for the earlier investments. However, neither these individual returns nor the difference between the two returns is statistically significant.

The sample includes six investments that involve outright mergers with or acquisitions of indian firms. Evidence from mergers and acquisitions in the United States indicates that acquiring stockholders on average do not gain from mergers and acquisitions. The six mergers and acquisitions are separated from the 30 joint ventures to see if stockholder returns are different for the two categories. Stockholders of merging firms earn a positive abnormal return of

Table 8.3
Abnormal Returns to a Sample of 29 U.S. Firms Whose Investments in India
Were Reported by the *Wall Street Journal* during 1990–94

Event Day	Abnormal Returns (AARs) (%)	t-Statistic	Positive:Negative
-5	-0.25	-1.0	11:18
-4	-0.19	-0.8	12:17
-3	-0.26	-1.0	10:19
-2	0.19	0.8	19:10
-1	-0.24	-0.9	12:17
0	0.42	1.7*	12:17
+1	-0.16	-0.7	12:17
+2	-0.21	-0.8	10:19
+3	0.24	0.9	16:13
+4	0.22	0.9	17:12
+5	-0.20	-0.8	14:15

*Significant at the 0.10 level in a two-tailed test.

0.50 percent as compared to 0.03 percent for stockholders of firms announcing joint ventures. Once again, neither the returns nor the difference in the two returns is statistically significant.

Returns to U.S. firms announcing joint ventures are further analyzed to determine if a majority stake in a joint venture is perceived by the markets to be more wealth-enhancing, since a majority stake, by providing more control to the U.S. firm, may be perceived to be less risky in a foreign country. Firms with majority stakes in joint ventures earn a return of 0.65 percent versus -0.39 percent for those with minority stakes. Although the difference is in the predicted direction, it lacks statistical significance.

If capital flow from a capital-rich country to a capital-poor country is motivated by a higher expected return, then it is reasonable to assume a positive relationship between the size of investment and the rate of return. The event day abnormal returns to U.S. firms are regressed on the reported size of investment to test the above relationship. The regression yields the following coefficients:

Variable	Coefficient	t-Probability
Constant	-0.2190	0.50
Investment (in millions of dollars)	0.0009	0.06
n = 14 F = .22	R-square = 0.26	

Table 8.4

Abnormal Returns to a Sample of 36 U.S. Firms (excluding Bausch & Lomb, an outlier) That Invested in India during 1990–94

Event Day	Abnormal Returns (AARs) (%)	t-Statistic	Positive:Negative
−5	−0.03	−0.1	15:21
−4	−0.36	−1.6	14:22
−3	−0.25	−1.2	12:24
−2	0.16	0.8	22:14
−1	−0.09	−0.4	17:19
0	0.02	0.1	15:21
+1	−0.16	−0.7	17:19
+2	−0.17	−0.8	15:21
+3	−0.07	−0.3	17:19
+4	0.12	0.6	21:15
+5	−0.25	−1.1	18:18

These results show that larger U.S. investments in India are more wealth enhancing for stockholders.

Finally, we may argue that developing countries may be willing to yield better terms to multinational firms in such areas as telecommunications, computers and automobiles than to firms investing in food and beverage businesses, where the need is not imminent or the technological gap separating the developing countries from developed countries is not huge. Firms investing in low-tech areas are separated from those investing in high-tech areas to see if the returns are different for the two groups. The high-tech investments yield a 0.15 percent return as compared to a 0.06 percent return to low-tech investments. The difference is statistically insignificant.

SUMMARY AND CONCLUSIONS

This study investigates the announcement period wealth effects for the stockholders of U.S. corporations investing in India. After discarding an outlier, the study finds zero abnormal returns for the acquiring firms. Moreover, the abnormal returns to investing firms appear to be statistically identical for mergers and joint ventures. Cross-sectional analyses reveal a positive and significant relationship between the dollar size of investment and abnormal returns to acquiring firms.

Given an informationally efficient market, these findings indicate that U.S.

stockholders do not perceive the investment opportunities in India to be positive net present value projects. If stockholders perceive India to be a high-risk country, they may discount cash flows from these investments at a higher risk-adjusted rate, thus reducing them to mere zero net present value projects. If these risk perceptions turn out to be true, then this may have a bearing on U.S. managers' investment decisions down the line and may slow the pace of future U.S. investments in India.

NOTES

1. See "India Pins Hope for Future on Capitalism," *Wall Street Journal*, October 21, 1991, A-15.

2. See "India's Market Reform Requires Perspective," *Wall Street Journal*, June 6, 1994, A-1.

3. See "U.S. Firms Show Investment Interest in Mexico, India," *Wall Street Journal*, November 28, 1994, A-2.

4. See note 2 above.

5. See "Foreign Businessmen Face Greater Risks in India . . .", *Wall Street Journal*, June 26, 1995, C-2.

6. In the absence of detailed information on the timing of outlays, it is not possible to express these investments in terms of their present values.

REFERENCES

Brown, Stephen and Warner, Jerold B. 1985. Using Daily Stock Returns: The Case of Event Studies. *Journal of Financial Economics*. 14: 3–31.

Jarrell, G., Brickley, James A. and Netter, Jeffrey M. 1988. The Market for Corporate Control: The Empirical Evidence Since 1980. *Journal of Economics Perspectives* 2: 49–68.

Jensen, M. C. and Ruback, Richard. 1983, April. The Market for Corporate Control: The Scientific Evidence. *Journal of Financial Economics* 11: 5–50.

Kang, Jun-Koo. 1993, December. The International Market for Corporate Control: Mergers and Acquisitions of U.S. Firms by Japanese Firms. *Journal of Financial Economics* 34: 345–371.

Markides, Constantinos and Ittner, Christopher. 1994. Shareholder Benefits from Corporate International Diversification: Evidence from U.S. International Acquisitions. *Journal of International Business Studies* 25: 343–366.

Marr, Wayne, Mehta, Sanjeev and Spivey, Michael. 1993, July/August. An Analysis of Foreign Takeovers in the United States. *Managerial and Decision Economics* 14: 285–294.

Mathur, Ike, Nanda, Rangan, Chhachhi, Indudeep and Sridhar, Sundaram. 1994, March/April. International Acquisitions in the United States: Evidence from Returns to Foreign Bidders. *Managerial and Decision Economics* 15: 107–118.

McConnell, John J. and Nantell, Timothy J. 1985. Corporate Combinations and Common Stock Returns: The Case of Joint Ventures. *Journal of Finance* 60: 519–536.

Morck, Randall and Young, Bernard. 1992, August. Internationalization: An Event Study Test. *Journal of International Economics* 33: 41–56.

CHAPTER 9

An Empirical Comparison of Commercial Profitability in the Private and Public Sector in India: Identifying the Effect of Competitive Intensity

KANNAN RAMASWAMY AND WILLIAM RENFORTH

This chapter compares the relative profitability of state-owned enterprises and privately owned firms in the Indian manufacturing sector. Using a matched pair design, the results show that private sector firms clearly outperformed their public sector counterparts. However, these profitability differences seem to be accentuated when competitive intensity is high and are minimized at lower levels of competition. This suggests that competitive intensity moderates the relationship between ownership status and commercial profitability. Consequently, industry competitive market structure must be considered when evaluating the effects of ownership form on performance.

INTRODUCTION

Sweeping economic reforms are transforming the economic landscape of developing countries worldwide. Countries such as India, Pakistan, Bangladesh, Nigeria, Sudan, Chile, Argentina and Venezuela are implementing a variety of initiatives to hasten the transformation of historically regulated economies into free market systems. Privatization is one such initiative that is envisioned as a viable means of revitalizing poor performance economies. This trend builds in part on the experiences of developed countries such as the United Kingdom, Canada and Sweden that privatized substantial segments of their state-controlled industries. It also stems from general disillusion with the politicized management of state-owned enterprises (SOEs), the anemic financial performance of the public sector and significant changes in external political and economic conditions (Baer and Birch, 1992; Bhaya, 1990; Shirley, 1989; Vickers and Yarrow, 1988). Confronted with the generally disappointing performance of SOEs and the dire economic situation of many developing countries during the 1980s, privatization became a centerpiece of economic liberalization and structural reform. The transfer of ownership to private hands was expected to foster efficient production of strategic goods and services, forcing these firms to follow market signals. The result is significant momentum behind the transfer of government ownership to the private sector.

Anecdotal experiences detailing the pressures to privatize and the consequences of the painful transformation are often in stark contrast to the promises that normally accompany these programs. Economic reforms in Eastern Europe have not resulted in the dramatic gains that are needed to improve their performance. This seems to be especially true in cases where a state-run monopoly such as telephones and telecommunications has been replaced by a private monopoly run by nongovernment investors. For example, telephone subscribers in Argentina pay much higher tariffs now than they did before privatization (Bussey, 1995). Privatization has not resulted in guaranteed profits either. Venezuela's privatized telephone monopoly Cantv lost $44 million last year—just two years after it had been privatized. Mexicana and Aeromexico, Mexico's privatized airlines, are technically bankrupt. The privatized construction industry in Honduras has clearly shown that it can reduce its overall operating cost only if government subsidies continue (Burke, 1990). These are but a few instances of privatization's failure to deliver the supposedly superior benefits of market reform. Similarly, the results of systematic empirical studies that have examined the relative performance of SOEs and private firms are far from conclusive.

Although the role of privatization has been the subject of several studies (Austin, Wortzel and Coburn, 1986; Okoroafo and Kotabe, 1993; Veljanovski, 1987; Vickers and Yarrow, 1988), the results have been mixed. This chapter argues that any comprehensive evaluation of the benefits of privatization must follow from an examination of the relative merits of private versus public ownership. In keeping with that objective, this chapter reports findings from a comprehensive evaluation of comparative performance in a matched sample of public and privately owned firms in the Indian manufacturing sector. It goes beyond the static snapshot of comparisons to examine whether the intensity of competition within an industry environment influences the magnitude of performance differences between SOEs and private firms. Is private ownership always a better form of governance, or is the performance superiority of private enterprises over SOEs constrained by the characteristics of the particular markets in which they operate? Are performance differences between private firms and SOEs accentuated or suppressed depending on the nature of the market? Are such differentials invariant across various market types?

THE LITERATURE

Although there has been a proliferation of studies on privatization and its potential benefits, a middle-range theory of state-run organizations has yet to emerge. This can be traced to widespread "armchair theorizing" and a remarkable lack of well-designed empirical studies that isolate ownership effects. Much of the literature is characterized by personal preferences and opinions rather than well-reasoned explanations of external realities. Thus, the debate over the relative superiority of private forms of ownership encompasses equally persuasive perspectives that are ideologically entrenched (see Adhikari and Kirkpatrick, 1990; Aharoni, 1981; De Angelo, Zoratto and Tanabe, 1992; Funkhouser and MacAvoy, 1979; Yarrow, 1986).

Comparative Performance of SOEs and Private Organizations: Competing Views

The debate over public and private ownership has been addressed primarily from two different theoretical perspectives—the profit maximization approach and the public interest approach. A dominant school of thought holds that private firms can be expected to perform better than public firms because of the problems related to the transfer of property rights in SOEs. It is argued that the property rights associated with private ownership encourage managers to maximize profitability. The incentives created by the link between the use of private assets and the income and wealth of owners motivate managers to perform efficiently. Public sector managers allocate resources that do not belong to them; hence, they do not bear the costs of their decisions, nor do they gain from efficient behavior (De Alessi, 1980). Thus, public and private sector managers are expected to behave in entirely different ways.

Another strand of this approach builds on profit maximization motives and argues that privately owned firms tend to perform better because they offer critical managerial incentives to stimulate performance-enhancing behaviors. It is also believed that when ownership is diversified in private hands, the shareholders monitor performance more closely (Alchian, 1977; Vickers and Yarrow, 1988) and hold managers to higher performance standards. Since such incentives are not normally available in SOEs, it is expected that there will be insufficient motivation and control to optimize organizational efficiency or performance.

Presenting a competing view, public interest theory articulates a rationale that builds on the role of SOEs in maximizing social economic welfare. SOEs are often directed by social objectives that include promotion of regional development, realizing positive foreign exchange balances, facilitating access to goods and services for disadvantaged publics, combating inflation and generating employment (Adhikari and Kirkpatrick, 1990; Aharoni, 1986; Lewin, 1982; Ramamurti, 1987). Since governmental oversight agencies are themselves agents of the public, they are expected to promote public welfare or risk corrective action initiated by the electorate. It can also be argued that SOE managers have a lower propensity to engage in myopic profit-maximizing behavior in the short run because their shareholders (public) do not focus on commercial profitability to such an extent that long-run performance is compromised—a situation that is known to detract from performance in large, privately held companies. Hence, the executives of SOEs can undertake riskier projects with longer gestation periods unhampered by instantaneous payoff expectations. Moreover, some researchers have suggested that even managers of privately held firms do not necessarily focus on efficiency maximization but rather concentrate on growth (Baumol, 1959) or nonpecuniary goals such as large staffs, perquisites and prestige (Maccoby, 1976; Stano, 1975; Williamson, 1964). This argument is strengthened by the fact that no empirical study has effectively demonstrated that firms offering higher managerial incentives are more efficiently managed (Aharoni, 1986). Since the electorate can exercise control over SOEs by pressuring government to eliminate inefficiencies, SOE managers may not respond any differently than private sector managers. Thus, we should expect SOE managers to perform as well as their private sector counterparts, maximizing public welfare without unduly compromising organizational efficiency. As Whitehead (1988) observes, "there are no inherent reasons why enterprises in private ownership should operate more efficiently than those in public ownership."

Relative Performance of Private and Public Organizations: Empirical Research

The empirical validation/refutation of these competing positions is fraught with significant problems. For example, five major reviews of studies have examined the relative performance of SOEs versus private firms. Of these reviews, three found that private firms have an edge over public firms (Bennett and Johnson, 1979; Boardman and Vining, 1989; Borcherding, Pommerehne and Schneider, 1982), while the other two found no significant differences or that the public sector had an advantage (Boyd, 1986; Millward, 1982). These inconsistent findings could have resulted from inadequate conceptualization or faulty sampling methods.

Industrial organization economists have theorized that the overall profitability of an industry is a function of several factors such as the level of competitive rivalry, product differentiability and substitutability. It is axiomatic that these industry-specific attributes act in conjunction with ownership-specific factors to influence profit differences between firms and SOEs. However, very little is known about the extent to which the profitability level attributed to a particular governance structure (public versus private) is limited by the intensity of market competition. Thus, while private ownership might confer some distinct advantages that enable the firm to focus on commercial profitability, these benefits could be circumscribed by the level of competitive intensity that characterizes the industry. It is plausible that at low levels of competition the differences between public and private ownership would be insignificant because both types of firms would adopt similar rent-seeking behaviors (Vining and Boardman, 1992). Furthermore, under conditions of limited competitive intensity, there might not be any significant incentive for either organization to adapt distinct strategies that differentiate themselves in the marketplace. Consequently, one form of ownership might not enjoy a significant performance edge under such conditions.

With increasing competition, profitability differences would begin to emerge because the privately owned firms will possess the crucial competencies that favor rapid response to changes in the marketplace and a unified focus on profitability. Private ownership, as observed earlier, offers the incentives and motivation for managers to proactively adopt profit-maximizing behaviors, a crucial factor that may be absent in state-owned firms. Moreover, private firms can operate without the confining constraints of state-run bureaucracies that stifle managerial initiative. Hence, top managers of these firms are expected to develop the repertoire of skills that are critical for navigating their firms through the maze of heightened competition. Their counterparts in SOEs are less likely to develop similar skills because they are either insulated from competition given the very loose performance-monitoring systems or are directed by ambiguous ownership that places a premium on social welfare rather than commercial profits. Consequently, private firms would handle increasing competitive rivalry better than SOEs.

This contention is consistent with the findings reported by Caves and Christensen (1980: 974), who observed that state-owned railroads in Canada performed just as well as those privately held. Although they extrapolated their findings to argue that "public ownership is not inherently less efficient than private ownership" and that the "oft noted inefficiency of government enterprises stems from the isolation from effective competition rather than public ownership per se," the duopolistic nature of the Canadian railroads could have been responsible for the lack of significant performance effects. Performance differences would be smaller in duopolies or near monopolistic contexts because both public and private firms are more likely to follow similar strategies given the absence of competition. However, the performance benefits arising from ownership status will be accentuated in competitive conditions and dampened in noncompetitive (or low-competition) environments. Thus, ownership factors will act in tandem with competitive intensity to influence organizational profitability. A comparable relationship is suggested in Xu's (1994) recent review of the performance of Chinese SOEs. He noted that Chinese state enterprises are in worse condition than they were five years ago. This result was attributed to the rapid expansion of the private sector which has made the market more competitive, resulting in decreased profitability for state enterprises. Building on these theoretical arguments and the limited empirical findings originating from prior research, it can be hypothesized that competitive intensity will moderate the linkage between public or private ownership status and commercial profitability.

Despite the persuasive theoretical logic that underscores the importance of competitive intensity in determining firm performance, few studies have attempted to examine this critical area empirically. The lack of comprehensive empirical examination of market influences may stem from the severe constraints imposed by the samples that have been used in prior research. For example, the review of 54 studies by Boardman and Vining (1989) shows that a significant majority used North American "firms" involved primarily in services. Unfortunately, many of these settings are natural monopolies (e.g., water and electric utilities) or doupolies (e.g., railroads), contexts that are unique enough to stifle generalizability. Thus, the restrictive samples employed in prior research do not permit a clear examination of the influence of market forces simply because most studies are skewed toward monopolies where by definition competition is nonexistent. The developed economies that were used in most prior research settings do not have any significant state investments in manufacturing. This has resulted in samples that are biased toward service firms. In these sectors, contractual arrangements and outright privatization have often replaced government monopolies with private monopolies (Savas, 1977), thus suppressing the role of free market competition.

DATA AND METHODOLOGY

Setting and Sample

It is apparent that progress in the resolution of the private versus public governance debate requires that all these conceptual and methodological issues be addressed effectively. In doing so, this study was designed to overcome several of these shortcomings. It systematically matched each SOE with a private sector firm that was comparable on dimensions such as product range and investment in fixed assets. It also provided a context for explicitly identifying the role of competitive intensity in influencing profitability differences.

India was used as the research setting. This choice was driven by several key considerations. India has historically operated a mixed economy in which state-run enterprises and private firms operate in the same industry environments, competing in the same markets. Other than core sectors such as energy and telecommunications, the government has always fostered competition between privately owned firms and SOEs in all other industries (e.g., pharmaceutical, electronics, cotton textiles, paper and transport equipment). Hence, India offers an ideal setting for studying performance differences between public and private firm, head-to-head competitors. The relatively large number of SOEs and equivalent private sector firms ensured that a sufficiently large sample exists for statistical analysis, thereby overcoming the small-sample problems identified in earlier studies.

The sample selection methodology employed and data sources utilized were based on those developed in prior studies examining the performance of SOEs in India (Ramaswamy and Renforth, 1995). The sample was limited to manufacturing firms only. Since most prior studies have examined service contexts, it was felt that a comprehensive evaluation of manufacturing industries would complement prevailing knowledge. The sample was carefully selected so that each SOE was matched with a majority Indian-owned private sector firm that essentially manufactured the same products and had comparable investments in fixed assets. This pairing of firms was done at the four-digit industry classification code level to ensure that the two groups exhibited competitive scope similarities. Thus, for all intents and purposes the two groups were quite similar but for the difference in ownership type (public versus private). By choosing comparable groups, we were able to explicitly control the extraneous influences of factors such as size, product range and industry type that can drive profitability. This made it possible to attribute performance differences between the two groups largely to ownership factors. This process of sample selection yielded a large group of matched public and private sector firms ($N=55$ pairs) for analysis, representing roughly 25 percent of all federally controlled SOEs in India.

Data Sources and Measures

Longitudinal data covering a five-year period (1988–92) were obtained from annual reports published by the Centre for Monitoring Indian Economy (CMIE). The following measures were used in the analysis.

Commercial profitability: Profitability of commercial enterprises is often evaluated in terms of financial profits generated per unit of sales (ROS) or return on investment (ROI). The capital markets use these measures to assess the viability of alternative investments and to provide an objective estimate of the financial well-being of organizations. Although widely accepted as aggregate measures of performance and often used in research, these indicators are thought to be biased in favor of short-term time horizons. Hence, return on value added (ROVA) was used to complement ROS and ROI. ROVA has the unique advantage of remaining quasi-invariant across industries and has been identified as "the most direct measure of the contribution that an organization makes to society" (Hofer, 1983). Hence, its use in this study was considered all the more pertinent.

Competitive intensity: Competitive intensity (CINTEN) has been measured through the use of either concentration ratios (Boardman and Vining, 1989; Vining and Boardman, 1992) or a Herfindal index (Oster, 1990). In this study, we used both approaches and found that the concentration ratios were highly correlated with the corresponding Herfindal indices. Thus, in further analysis the Herfindal index (HI) was used. It was computed as $HI = 10,000\Sigma\, S_i^2$ where S_i is the market share of the ith firm in the industry. This index was computed for the top four firms in each industry represented in the sample. It can take values from 10,000 (monopolies) to 0 (perfect competition).

Control variables: The regression models used to examine the role of competitive intensity included a logarithmic function of investment in fixed assets (SIZE) as a control variable proxying firm size.

Analytical Procedure

Data relating to individual firms were averaged over the five-year period 1988–92. Since it was our objective first to examine static performance outcomes, averaging data was considered defensible. Analysis of variance (ANOVA) methodology was used to identify performance differences between the two groups. Regression analyses were used to study the influence of competitive intensity. The following equations present the linear (1) and moderated regression models (2) that were used.

$$Y_0 = \beta_0 + \beta_1 \text{ STATUS} + \beta_2 \text{ CINTEN} + \beta_3 \text{ SIZE} + e \tag{1}$$

$$y_0 = \beta_0 + \beta_1 \text{ STATUS} + \beta_2 \text{ CINTEN} + \beta_3 \text{ SIZE} + \beta_4$$
$$\text{CINTEN} \times \text{STATUS} + e \tag{2}$$

where:

y_0 = the measure of profitability (ROS, ROI, ROVA)
STATUS = the dummy variable proxying ownership (0 = private; 1 = SOE)
CINTEN = the measure of competitive intensity
SIZE = the control measure of firm size

RESULTS AND DISCUSSION

The results clearly show statistical evidence to support commonly held beliefs that SOEs are less profitable than their private sector counterparts. The moderated regression analyses show that competitive intensity moderates the linkage between ownership structure and financial performance. A discussion of these results follows.

Comparisons of Commercial Profitability

The private sector firms outperformed the SOEs on each of the three profitability measures that were examined (see Table 9.1). The results suggest two important observations. First, the SOEs actually lost money. Private firms are not merely more profitable than SOEs; they produce healthy financial returns while SOEs generate losses. Second, it provides some insight into the motives behind recent moves in India to reform or privatize SOEs. Although SOEs are created mostly to achieve social or strategic objectives rather than to maximize profits, there is evidence that policymakers rely on financial profitability to judge the overall performance of SOEs (Ramamurti, 1987) despite its shortcomings (Likierman, 1983). Therefore, financial profitability can be a fairly good proxy for how satisfied policymakers are likely to be with the performance of SOEs. Given the negative financial profitability of Indian SOEs, the rush to privatize is logical (Ramamurti, 1992). In this sense, government policymakers may be more sensitive to any level of loss than they are to low levels of profits. Losses imply the necessity to provide additional funds, oftentimes from other sources of government revenue or through deficit financing (Ahluwalia, 1994), an obviously difficult political decision.

Second, noteworthy differences exist among the measures of commercial profitability utilized. Although the private sector group outperformed the SOEs on all three indicators, the difference was highest for ROS (26.5432). Mean differences in ROI and ROVA were less extreme, but still significant. It is possible that the ROS indicator is especially sensitive to the artificial, government mandated output prices that SOEs are expected to maintain. In contrast to private sector firms. SOEs in India are expected to transfer products to other government agencies or sell their output at prices that are set by the government, normally below market prices (Bhagawati, 1993). Thus, their return on sales might be biased downward. It must also be noted that the mean difference between the two groups was lowest when ROVA was used as the measure of profitability (0.2506). This indicator also exhibited relatively lower standard deviations compared to ROI and ROS, suggesting that it might be more normally distributed. It could be argued that value added provides a firmer basis for intersectoral comparisons (Adhikari and Kirkpatrick, 1990; Bhaya, 1990; Hofer, 1983). In essence, these results support prevailing contentions that private ownership is associated with higher levels of commercial profitability (Funkhouser and MacAvoy, 1979; Kim, 1981; Millward, 1982). This comes as no surprise because SOEs are known to focus more on public interest than commercial success.

The Role of Competitive Intensity

The regression analyses suggest that competitive intensity moderates the influence of governance structure (public versus private) on commercial profitability. The moderator was significant in both the ROI and ROS models. Although it was not significant in the ROVA model, the direction of the sign was as expected. Collectively, the results show that (a) competitive intensity moderates the relationship between ownership and profitability, and that (b) the linkage becomes more negative for higher values of competitive intensity. The dummy variable proxying ownership status was also found to be negatively related to profitability in the linear model, thus further supporting the ANOVA results discussed earlier. The incremental F tests also show that in both ROI and ROS models the addition of the moderator does indeed increase the explanatory power of the model, although in small increments. The small incremental R^2s are not surprising because ownership and competitive intensity are but two factors of a very large array of elements that could potentially influence profitability. These findings consequently provide a persuasive argument for including competitive intensity as a critical, albeit indirect, determinant of profitability. While SOEs might be less profitable than private firms, the profitability differential becomes accentuated with increasing competitive intensity. The analyses also show that in the presence of the moderator, the direct effect (ownership

$\rightarrow$ profitability) becomes insignificant. This underscores the importance of competitive intensity and its role in circumscribing the influence of ownership status on profitability. Perhaps this is the reason prior studies have reached divergent conclusions. It is also possible that studies that did not find significant profitability differentials between SOEs and private firms were skewed toward monopolistic settings, while those that did uncover differences might have used more competitive settings.

Taken together, these findings support our contention that both forms of governance (public and private) achieve roughly comparable outcomes in settings where competitive rivalry is limited and that ownership becomes a critical issue only as competitive intensity increases. Simply stated, substituting a private monopoly for a public monopoly is not likely to change performance.

These results have several important implications for privatization efforts. They provide persuasive evidence that the ability of private governance to generate superior profits is constrained by the extent of market competition. Thus, privatization could be the means to realize better profitability, provided that the SOE currently operates in a competitive environment. Should the SOE find itself in a market where competitive intensity is rather low, changing its ownership structure might not bring about the profitability increases expected. By extension, this implies that efforts to develop competitive market structures, open economies and incentives for management performance are necessary, or even alternative, components of a comprehensive strategy.

This chapter represents an effort to compare the performance of SOEs and private sector firms using a relatively large sample. The sample design explicitly matched each SOE with an equivalent private sector counterpart. This is a marked improvement over previous studies that have relied on small samples of heterogeneous firms. Although our findings are more robust than some of its predecessors, some limitations must be acknowledged. First, using multiple industries might have reduced internal validity because industry-specific factors could have a significant role in driving firm performance. However, the potential pitfalls associated with such an approach were largely ameliorated since we followed the multi-industry ANOVA analyses with an explicit examination of the variations in industry context (competitive intensity) using moderated regressions. Second, performance assessment was limited to the evaluation of commercial profitability alone. This ignores other performance dimensions such as operational efficiency and social welfare. Future studies could provide additional insights by incorporating a variety of both efficiency and public interest measures. Building on the results reported here, future empirical examinations might extend the domain of the performance construct to explore whether competitive intensity plays a similar role with respect to other parameters such as efficiency. Do SOEs operating in competitive contexts perform more efficiently than others functioning under monopolistic/duopolistic conditions? Is the relationship between ownership and efficiency moderated by market competition?

Questions such as these need to be addressed as we progress toward a middle-range theory of state-owned enterprises. It is in that direction that we now turn.

REFERENCES

Adhikari, R. and Kirkpatrick, C. 1990. Public Enterprise in Less Developed Countries: An Empirical Review. In J. Heath (ed.), *Public Enterprises at the Crossroads*. London: Routledge Publishing.

Aharoni, Y. 1981. Performance Evaluation of State Owned Enterprises: A Process Perspective. *Management Science* 27: 1340–1347.

Aharoni, Y. 1986. *The Evolution and Management of State Owned Enterprises*. Cambridge, MA: Ballinger Publishing.

Ahluwalia, M. S. 1994, Spring. India's Quiet Economic Revolution. *Columbia Journal of World Business* 29: 6–12.

Alchian, A. A. 1977. *Economic Forces at Work*. Indianapolis, IN: Liberty Press.

Austin, J. E., Wortzel, L. H. and Coburn, J. F. 1986, Fall. Privatizing State Owned Enterprises: Hopes and Realities. *Columbia Journal of World Business* 21: 51–60.

Baer, W. and Birch, M. 1992, Fall. Privatization and the Changing Role of the State in Latin America. *Journal of International Law and Politics* 25: 1–25.

Baumol, W. J. 1959. *Business Behavior, Value and Growth*. New York: Macmillan Publishing.

Bennett, J. T., and Johnson, M. H. 1979. Public versus Private Provision of Collective Goods and Services: Garbage Collection Revisited. *Public Choice* 34: 55–63.

Bhagawati, J. 1993. *India in Transition: Freeing the Economy*. Oxford: Clarendon Press.

Bhaya, H. 1990. Management Efficiency in the Private and Public Sectors in India. In J. Heath (ed.), *Public Enterprise at the Crossroads*. London: Routledge Publishing, pp. 228–240.

Boardman, A. E. and Vining, A. 1989, April. Ownership and Performance in Competitive Environments: A Comparison of the Performance of Private, Mixed and State Owned Enterprises. *Journal of Law and Economics* 32: 1–33.

Borcherding, T. E., Pommerehne, W. W. and Schneider, F. (1982). Comparing the Efficiency of Private and Public Production: A Survey of the Evidence from Five Federal States. *Zeitschrift für Nationalokonomie/Journal of Economic Theory: Public Production*, Suppl. 2: 127–156.

Boyd, C. W. 1986. The Comparative Efficiency of State-Owned Enterprise. In A. R. Negandhi, H. Thomas, and K. L. K. Rao (eds.), *Multinational Corporations and State-Owned Enterprises: A New Challenge in International Business Volume 1 of Research in International Business and International Relations*. Greenwich, CT: JAI Press, 179–194.

Burke, M. 1990. Private versus Public Construction in Honduras: Issues of Economics and Ideology. In D. J. Gayle and J. N. Goodrich (eds.), *Privatization and Deregulation in Global Perspective*. Westport, CT: Quorum Books.

Bussey, J. 1995, April 10. Privatization Improves Services—At a Price. *The Miami Herald*, B-1.

Caves, D. W. and Christensen, L. R. 1980. The Relative Efficiency of Public and Private Firms in a Competitive Environment: The Case of Canadian Railroads. *Journal of Political Economy* 88: 958–976.

De Alessi, L. 1980. The Economics of Property Rights: A Review of Evidence. *Research in Law and Economics* 2: 1–47.

De Angelo, F. C., Zoratto, A. Z. and Tanabe, M. 1992. Comparative Performance of State-Owned and Private Business Firms in Brazil. In J. Rivera and X. A. Aguilar (eds.), *Integration in the Americas*. San Diego, CA: Association of Latin American Studies, 79–86.

Funkhouser, R. and MacAvoy, P. W. 1979. A Sample of Observations on Comparative Prices in Public and Private Enterprise. *Journal of Public Economics* 2: 353–368.

Hofer, C. W. 1983. ROVA: A New Measure for Assessing Organizational Performance. in *R. Lamb* (ed.), *Advances in Strategic Management*. Greenwich, CT: JAI Press, 43–55.

Kim, K. S. 1981. Enterprise Performance in the Public and Private Sectors: Tanzanian Experience, 1970–75. *Journal of Developing Areas* 15: 471–484.

Lewin, A. 1982. Public Enterprise, Purposes and Performance: A Survey of Western European Experience. In W. T. Stanbury and F. Thompson (eds.), *Managing Public Enterprises*. New York: Praeger.

Likierman, A. 1983. The Use of Profitability in Assessing the Performance of Public Enterprises. In V. V. Ramanadham (ed.), *Public Enterprise and the Developing Countries*. London: Croom Helm.

Maccoby, M. 1976. *The Gamesman*. New York: Simon and Schuster.

Millward, R. 1982. The Comparative Performance of Public and Private Ownership. In E. Roll (ed.), *The Mixed Economy*. London: Macmillan.

Okoroafo, S. and Kotabe, M. 1993, Second Quarter. The IMF's Structural Adjustment Program and Its Impact on Firm Performance: A Case of Foreign and Domestic Firms in Nigeria. *Management International Review* 33: 139–156.

Oster, S. 1990. *Modern Competitive Analysis*. New York: Oxford University Press.

Ramamurti, R. 1987, July. Performance Evaluation of State-Owned Enterprises in Theory and Practice. *Management Science* 33: 876–893.

Ramamurti, R. 1992, Second Quarter. Why Are Developing Countries Privatizing? *Journal of International Business Studies* 23: 225–249.

Ramaswamy, K. and Renforth, W. 1995. A Comparative Study of Commercial Profitability, Managerial Efficiency, and Public Interest in SOEs and Private Firms in India. In S. B. Prasad (ed.), *Advances in International Comparative Management*. Greenwich, CT: JAI Press.

Savas, E. S. 1977. *The Organization and Efficiency of Solid Waste Collection*. Lexington, MA: D. C. Heath/Lexington Books.

Shirley, M. M. 1989. *Reform of State Owned Enterprises: Lessons from Bank Lending*. Washington, DC: World Bank.

Stano, M. 1975. Executive Ownership Interests and Corporate Performance. *Southern Economic Journal* 42: 272–278.

Veljanovski, C. 1987. *Selling the State: Privatization in Britain*. London: Weidenfeld and Nicolson.

Vickers, J. and Yarrow, G. 1988. *Privatization: An Economic Analysis*. Cambridge, MA: MIT Press,

Vining, A. and Boardman, A. 1992. Ownership versus Competition: Efficiency in Public Enterprise. *Public Choice* 73: 205–239.

Whitehead, C. 1988. *Reshaping the Nationalized Industries*. New Brunswick, NJ: Transaction Books.

Williamson, O. E. 1964. *The Economics of Discretionary Behavior: Managerial Objectives in a Theory of the Firm.* Englewood Cliffs, NJ: Prentice-Hall.

Xu, L. 1994. Inefficiency of State Enterprises, Ownership, Control and Soft Budget Constraint. Unpublished doctoral dissertation, University of Chicago, Chicago, IL.

Yarrow, G. 1986, April. Privatization in Theory and Practice. *Economic Policy* 2: 323–364.

PART IV

Managerial Issues

CHAPTER 10

Managing Diverse Human Resources for Globalization

A. V. SUBBARAO

This chapter discusses the diversity of human resources in two developed countries, the United States and Canada, and in three developing countries, India, Malaysia and Sri Lanka. The public policies of these nations that are influencing management of workforce diversity are analyzed separately as equality, equity, job preference and job reservation models. A representation model is presented for managing diverse human resources in workplaces that compete in global markets.

Globalization of markets is a reality, and managing workplaces for competition in global markets is the challenge that managers face today and in the future (Pucik, Tichy and Barnett, 1993). The global workforce is recognized as an important resource for competition (Johnston, 1991), and mobility of the global workforce poses a challenge to managers to manage this important resource efficiently and effectively. Mobility of workforce from developing to developed countries (World Bank, 1995) is increasing the diversity of the workforce in industrialized nations, particularly in North America which relied on immigrants to meet the demand for knowledge workers. Increasing investment opportunities in developing nations through joint ventures are not only facilitating the transfer of knowledge, but are also increasing the diversity of knowledge workers in developing countries. The diversity of workforce in developed and developing countries has also been increasing steadily during the last three decades due to the increasing participation of women and other segments of the population in labor markets (Workforce 2000, 1987).

Human resource management policies and practices in the past were developed for a workforce that was not as diverse as it is today. In the organized sectors of the industry, they were developed jointly through negotiations between managers and unions which represented the interests of the majority of their membership. Management policies and practices in unionized workplaces and in large bureaucratic organizations were standardized and implemented uniformly regardless of the increasing diversity of the workforce (Fernandez, 1991). The "one-size-fits-all" model of management resulted in "advantaged" and "disadvantaged" groups of a diverse workforce (Jamieson and O'Mara, 1991). Managers of workplaces, now and in the future, face the challenge of managing a diverse workforce fairly so that all human resources will be utilized for competitive advantage in global markets. "Making Full Use of the Nation's Human Capital," according to the Federal Glass Ceiling Commission of the United States (1995), is "Good for Business."

Workforce diversity has been recognized in the United States, and the experience of managing diversity is expected to improve the competitive advantage of American workplaces in global markets (Fernandez, 1993). Diversity of workforce and disadvantages of groups of a diverse workforce are also recognized in Canada (Subbarao, 1994). Disadvantaged groups in the labor markets of the Asian developing countries such as India, Malaysia and Sri Lanka, too, were recognized soon after their independence (Subbarao, 1995b). Policymakers in the United States, Canada and the Asian developing countries developed policies for improving the employment opportunities of the disadvantaged groups, and those policies are expected to influence the management of workforce diversity. Managers' reactions to public policies might improve the employment opportunities of the disadvantaged groups. However, to manage diverse human resources for competitive advantage in global markets, managers have to recognize the challenge of diversity and have to become innovative agents of change for management in modern workplaces (Kanter, 1983).

This chapter presents a model for managing workforce diversity, which it is hoped will appeal to innovative managers of workplaces that compete in global markets. In order to appreciate the importance of managing workforce diversity, managers need to recognize workforce diversity. In the following section, diversity of workforce in developed countries, the United States and Canada, as well as in the developing Asian nations, India, Malaysia and Sri Lanka, is briefly described. Since the public policies for improving the employment opportunities of the disadvantaged groups in a diverse workforce might influence management of workplaces, they are analyzed briefly in the second section of this chapter as equality, equity, job preference and job reservation models of managing workforce diversity. The third and final section presents a model of managing workforce diversity in developed and developing countries.

WORKFORCE DIVERSITY IN DEVELOPED COUNTRIES

Gender, age, ability, race, ethnicity, education, skin color and language are some of the many dimensions of workforce diversity in North America. Workforce diversity in North America has been increasing since the introduction of color-blind immigration policies in the 1960s and the increasing participation of women in the labor force in the 1970s.

Women now constitute 45 percent of the workforce in both the United States and Canada, compared to only one-third in 1971. Their participation in the labor force increased to sixty percent in 1991 from 40 percent in 1971, while that of men remained the same at 76 percent during the last two decades in Canada (Subbarao, 1994). Women will comprise three-fifths of the new entrants into the workforce until the year 2000 (Workforce 2000, 1987), and they are expected to constitute half of the workforce in North America in the twenty-first century. Not only the labor force participation of women increased, but also their university level education, indicating their greater abilities and aptitudes for higher level occupations. By 1991, almost as many women held university degrees as did men, whereas in 1971 women's share of the degree holders was less than half. Both men and women in today's workforce are more mature than they were three decades ago: the median age of the workforce is currently 34 years, in spite of the decreasing labor force participation of both men and women over 55 years of age.

The share of nonwhites, like that of women, in the North American workforce has been steadily increasing during the last three decades. They will constitute 29 percent of the American workforce in the year 2000 whereas they were only 18.4 percent in 1985 (Workforce 2000, 1987). The number of nonwhites, known as visible minorities in the Canadian workforce, increased by 60 percent between the last two census periods of 1986 and 1991. In 1991, they constituted 9.1 percent of the Canadian workforce as against their share of 6.3 percent in 1986 (Subbarao, 1994). Canadians of Asian and African origin are the most highly educated in the workforce compared with any other ethnic group: 21.24 percent of Canadians of Asian and African ethnic origins have university degrees, whereas only 9.45 percent of British origin and 8.64 percent of French origin have university degrees. Only 1.78 percent of aboriginals in Canada have university degrees, and 29.36 percent of them have less than grade 9 education, the highest in comparison with any other ethnic group. Like Canadians of Asian origins, Asian Americans are also highly educated, and they are considered model minorities in the North American workforce (Federal Glass Ceiling Commission, 1995).

Religion and language enhance the cultural diversity of the Canadian workforce. While America is a secular state, Canada recognizes and protects the interests of the two majority religious groups: 45.38 percent of Canadians are Catholics and 34.21 percent are Protestants. In the province of Quebec 86 percent of the people and in Ontario 35 percent are Catholics. In both provinces, primary and secondary school level education controlled by Catholics is supported by public taxes. The U.S. Constitution, on the other hand, prohibits religious teachings in the public school system. In the United States, English is the only language in the workplace, while in Canada, English and French are the two official languages recognized in the Canadian constitution. Specifically,

67.12 percent of Canadians have knowledge of English only, while 15.27 percent have knowledge of French only; 96 percent of those who have knowledge of French only are the residents of the Province of Quebec, and the official language of Quebec is French; 16.12 percent of Canadians have knowledge of both official languages, and of those 55 percent are residents of Quebec. Language is a dimension of workforce diversity in the three Asian developing countries, too.

WORKFORCE DIVERSITY IN ASIAN DEVELOPING COUNTRIES

India is a land of languages; 14 languages were recognized in 1950 when the sovereign republic adopted its own constitution. In 1972, Sri Lanka adopted Sinhalese as the official language and Buddhism as the official religion for a country with 74 percent Sinhalese, 18.2 percent Tamils and 7.4 percent Muslims. Similarly, Malaysia adopted Malay as the official language and Islam as the official religion for its population, with 61.3 percent Bhumiputras (sons of the soil), 30 percent Chinese and 8.2 percent Indians. Unlike Sri Lanka and Malaysia, India is a secular state, even though 83.4 percent of Indians follow Hinduism, in addition, 11.19 percent of Indians are Muslims that follow the Islamic faith.

Apart from religion, the caste system among Hindus is the most important dimension of diversity in the Indian workforce. There are over three thousand caste groups among Hindus in India, and the castes have a close association with occupations. The occupational hierarchy coupled with the caste hierarchy has created a society of forward, backward and depressed classes in India. Hindu caste groups that were engaged in ''untouchable'' occupations such as cleaning services and cremation of dead bodies were categorized as the depressed class in the 1931 census. The depressed class castes were listed in the schedule of the Indian constitution, and since then they have been referred to as the scheduled castes (SCs). Similarly, the tribes that, were also identified as a depressed class were listed in the schedule of the Indian constitution, and they are called the scheduled tribes (STs). Today 15.05 percent of Indians belong to SCs and 7.51 percent to STs.

The Backward Classes Commissions in India identified other castes in 1955 and 1980 in addition to the SCs and STs, as economically and socially backward. They identified 43.70 percent of Indians of other Hindu castes and 8.4 percent of non-Hindu religious groups as backward, and they known as other backward classes (OBCs). The Second Backward Classes Commission, known as the Mandal Commission (1991), categorized 22.56 percent (SCs and STs) as backward classes, 52 percent other backward classes (OBCs) and 25.44 percent forward classes. Among the forward classes, Brahmins constitute 5.52 percent and Rajputs 3.9 percent of the Indian population. Brahmins and Rajputs, due to their priestly and ruling occupations in pre-independent India, respectively, were the most privileged among Indians. They also had access to education and wealth. After independence, Brahmins had access to higher level occupations in the civil service. The prime minister of India and chief ministers of most of the states soon after independence were Brahmins. The policymakers of independent India recognized the inequality of employment opportunities among India's diverse workforce and proclaimed the principle of equality in the country's constitution in 1950.

PUBLIC POLICIES AND DIVERSITY

Fundamental Rights (Article 15) in India's constitution provide for equal treatment of every citizen and prohibit discrimination in employment on grounds of religion, race, caste, sex, language or place of birth. Canada, too, adopted the principle of equality in its 1982 constitution. Section 15(1) of the Canadian constitution's Charter of Rights proclaims that ''every individual is equal before and under the law and has the right to equal protection and equal benefit of the law without discrimination based on race, national or ethnic origin, colour, religion, sex, age or mental or physical disability.'' However, Indian and Canadian workers could seek protection of their constitutional rights of equality only against the state encroachment, and through a lengthy and costly judicial action.

The equality policy embedded in the 1962 Human Rights Code of Ontario and the 1964 Civil Rights Act (Title VII) of the United States, on the other hand, is applicable to both public and private sector workplaces. Moreover, in both countries, administrative agencies enforce the equality policy, and they are expected to be more accessible to disadvantaged workers than the judiciary. Accessibility and wider applicability of the civil rights and human rights legislation are expected to have more influence on workplace management policies and practices than the constitution's equality principle. Hence, the effects of the human rights and civil rights legislation on human resource management policies and practices in the workplace are analyzed under the equality model.

Equality Model

Every person, according to the Ontario Human Rights Code of 1962, ''has a right to equal treatment with respect to employment without discrimination because of race, ancestry, place of origin, colour, ethnic origin, citizenship, creed, sex, sexual orientation, age, record of offences, marital status, family status or handicap.'' Separate human rights legislation is applicable in the federal and each provincial jurisdiction in Canada, and they all have more or less similar equality policy.

Title VII of the U.S. Civil Rights Act of 1964 provides that it ''shall be an unlawful employment practice for an employer'' . . . ''(1) to fail or refuse to hire or discharge any individual, or otherwise to discriminate against any individual with respect to his compensation, terms, conditions, or privileges of employment, because of such individual's race, colour, religion, sex, or national origin''; or ''(2) to limit, segregate, or classify his employees or applicants for employment in any way which would deprive or tend to deprive any individual of employment opportunities or otherwise adversely affect his status as an employee, because of such individual's race, color, religion, sex or national origin.'' The Civil Rights Act that was legislated after prolonged debates in the U.S. Congress was consolidated in 1972 in the Equal Employment Opportunities Act. The EEO Act is enforced by the Equal Employment Opportunities Commission (EEOC), and the Human Rights legislation in Canada is enforced by the Human Rights Commissions (HRCs).

The equality policy is very broad and vague in offering employment opportunities for a diverse workforce in North America. However, enforcement of the policy and its interpretations have specific implications for human resource management policies and practices. In order to initiate the enforcement process in the equality model, an individual has to complain of discrimination by an employer. The EEOC in the United States and the HRCs in Canada will process the complaints, and the process includes investigation and conciliation. In the event a complaint is not resolved, the EEOC submits it to the federal courts. In Canada, the HRCs recommend appointment of administrative tribunals, known as human rights tribunals and boards of inquiry, to adjudicate on the complaint. Adjudicators' decisions in Canada, like the federal court decisions in the United States, can be appealed all the way to the Supreme Courts of the respective countries. The Supreme Court interpretations have clarified the equality policy, and the courts have judged certain human resource management policies and practices as discriminatory.

The U.S. Supreme Court, in a landmark decision in 1971, clarified the equality policy by stating that unintentional discrimination, like the intentional, is prohibited by legislation. An unintentional discriminatory employment policy or practice that has an adverse effect on an individual or a group of workers, according to the U.S. Supreme Court, is systemic discrimination. In one case, an employment policy required a high school diploma and a specified intelligence test score for recruitment and selection of workers for semiskilled and unskilled jobs. When the employer failed to prove those requirements as bonafide occupational qualifications (BFOQs) for the jobs, they were found to be discriminatory (*Griggs v. Duke Power Company*, (1971), 401 U.S. 424).

The U.S. Supreme Court's interpretation of the BFOQ requirement has been adopted by the tribunals and courts in Canada. In 1979, a tribunal found that height and weight requirements in the recruitment of police officers were discriminatory, for they were not proven to be BFOQs (*Colfer v. Ottawa Board of Commissioners of Police, Board of Inquiry*, 1979). The Supreme Court of Canada found that an employment policy regarding the retirement of firefighters at a specified age (60 years) violated the equality policy since that age was not proven to be a BFOQ (*Ontario HRC & Hall and Grey v. Borough of Etobicoke*, (1982) 1 S.C.R. 202). The Supreme Court of Canada also found that termination of employment of workers for their inability to work on certain religious days was discriminatory since work on those specified days was not proven to be a BFOQ (*Ontario HRC & O'Malley v. Simpson-Sears Ltd.*, (1985) 2 S.C.R. 536; *Central Alberta Dairy Pool v. Alberta HRC*, (1990) 2 S.C.R. 489). The Supreme Court of Canada further clarified that the equality policy requires an employer's duty to accommodate a diverse workforce if the employment policies that are not proven as BFOQs have an adverse effect on an individual's or group's access and advancement in a workplace. The employer's duty to accommodate a diverse workforce, if necessary through special measures and programs, is an important requirement of the employment equity model.

Equity Model

Employment equity, according to the Canadian federal Employment Equity Act of 1986, means "more than treating persons in the same way but also requires special measures and accommodation of differences." Human rights legislation in Canada provides protection for employers who adopt special programs and plans to improve the employment opportunities of disadvantaged groups against the reverse discrimination complaints of advantaged groups. The Supreme Court of Canada interpreted that indeed, a human rights tribunal had the authority to impose on an employer a special program for increasing the representativeness of a disadvantaged group of workers since their representatives in the workplace was less than their share in the labor markets. An employer was required to hire one women of every four workers hired until the representatives of women among the blue-collar skilled trades in the workplace was proportionate to their share of the skilled trades in the external labor markets (*Action Travail des Femmes v. Canadian National Railway Co.*, (1987) 1 S.C.R. 114). In other words, the equity model, unlike the equality model, recognizes the importance of results of an employment program. An effective program for managing a diverse workforce is not only fair in offering employment opportunities regardless of individual differences unrelated to job performance, but also ensures diversity of workforce in a workplace proportionate with the diversity in the labor markets.

The U.S. Supreme Court has approved affirmative action programs adopted by employers for increasing the representatives of disadvantaged groups. In one case, an employer in agreement with a union developed a temporary training program of skilled trades in which half the trainees would be blacks until their representativeness among skilled trades in the workplace was proportionate to their share in the labor markets (*Kaiser Aluminium and Steel Workers Union v. Weber*, (1979) 61 L Ed 2d). In another case, an employer adopted a temporary program to promote women into supervisory positions until their representativeness in the workplace was proportionate to their share in the labor markets (*Johnson v. Transportation Agency, Santa Clara County, California*, (1987) No. 85-1129). However, affirmative action programs are being challenged, and the

U.S. Supreme Court is finding that the U.S. Constitution does not provide for such programs. The Canadian constitution, on the other hand, does protect such programs, for its Section 15(2) "does not preclude any law, program or activity that has as its object the amelioration of conditions of disadvantaged individuals or groups including those that are disadvantaged because of race, national or ethnic origin, colour, sex, age, mental or physical disability."

The Canadian federal government in 1986 and the Ontario provincial government in 1994 enacted employment equity legislation (Bill 79). This bill was repealed in 1995 soon after the Conservatives were elected and formed the Ontario government that replaced the New Democrats. In 1987, the Ontario government passed pay equity legislation, and most of the provinces in Canada have enacted such legislation since 1987. While the purpose of the pay equity legislation in Canada is to reduce and eventually to eliminate pay differences between men and women performing work of equal value, the purpose of the employment equity legislation is wider and covers more diverse groups of the workforce than women only.

Employment equity legislation requires that employers develop special measures to improve the access and advancement of women, aboriginals, persons with disabilities and racial (visible) minorities. In Canada these four groups are designated as disadvantaged in employment. According to the Ontario policymakers, as stated in the preamble of the EE Act, 1994 (Bill 79), the four groups "experience higher rates of unemployment than other people in Ontario," and they also "experience more discrimination than other people in finding employment, in retaining employment and in being promoted." As a result of the barriers of access and advancement in workplaces, the policymakers stated that "they are underrepresented in most areas of employment, especially in senior and management positions, and they are overrepresented in those areas of employment that provide low pay and limited chance of advancement."

The Canadian federal EE Act and the Ontario provincial legislation require that employers compare the representativeness of the four designated disadvantaged groups in their respective workplaces at different occupational levels with those in the labor markets. To facilitate comparison, the federal government has made available to employers statistical information based on the 1986 census data, known as "availability data," relating to the distribution of the four designated groups in different occupations in Canadian labor markets. According to those data, 2.5 percent of all men in the Canadian workforce were employed in upper level management positions, while only 0.6 percent of all women and 0.9 percent of all visible minorities were in these positions. In contrast, proportionately more women (14.6%) than men (10.0%) were employed in professional occupations, which required high levels of education and human capital investment. Since visible minorities are highly educated relative to other groups, proportionately more visible minorities (13.6%) were employed as professionals than men (10.0%) in general in Canadian labor markets. Visible minorities were, in fact, overrepresented among aerospace engineers (21.5%), chemical engineers

(16%), electrical engineers (15.4%) and pharmacists (16.5%), while the racial minorities constituted only 6.3 percent of the total Canadian workforce (Sub-barao, 1994). The distribution of women and Asian Americans in upper level management and professional occupations in American labor markets was similar to that in Canada (Federal Glass Ceiling Commission, 1995).

The availability data in Canada support the statements of the Ontario policymakers that there was less diversity in upper level management positions and skilled trades, and more concentration of women and racial minorities in lower level clerical and service operations. Proportionately more women (30.9%) than men (6.1%) were employed in clerical positions, and more visible minorities (13.2%) than men (6.8%) were in low-paying service occupations: 98.8 percent of secretaries and stenographers, 96.7 percent of typists and clerks and 93.9 percent of receptionists were women; and 29.6 percent of fabricating, 28.1 percent of sewing machine operators, 26.6 percent of knitting and 21.6 percent of laundering operators were visible minorities in Canada. In the United States, too, women were mostly in clerical occupations, and blacks and hispanics were concentrated in declining occupations with no prospects of advancement (Workforce 2000, 1987). Both in the U.S. and Canadian workplaces, access of women and of nonwhites was restricted in union-controlled skilled trades and crafts. Very few women (1.4%) and racial minorities (4.6%) in comparison with men (12.5%) were in the skilled trades and crafts in Canada.

In 1988, employers, as required under the federal EE Act, filed their first annual statistical reports of distribution of the designated groups in their respective workplaces to the enforcement agency. Employers' reports also confirmed the low representativeness of the designated groups in upper level management positions and skilled trades, and the concentration of women in clerical positions and of visible minorities in professional occupations. Only 0.1 percent of all women and 0.7 percent of visible minority men, as against 1.3 percent of men, were engaged as upper level managers in workplaces covered by the federal EE Act; 13.6 percent of visible minority men were employed as professionals, while only 5.6 percent of all men were in similar positions. If professionals were developed for decision-making occupations, proportionately more visible minorities could have advanced into upper level management positions. Only 0.4 percent of women were employed in skilled crafts and trades, while 17.4 percent of men were in those occupations. Over 60 percent of all women were concentrated in clerical occupations, which attracted only 6.9 percent of men (Subbarao, 1994).

The representativeness of designated groups in different occupations in workplaces covered by the federal EE Act was more or less similar to that in the Canadian labor markets. Employers in Ontario, just as those in the federal jurisdiction, were required to undertake analysis of their workforce and to develop employment equity plans for improving workforce diversity at different occupational levels. Each employer was also required to review workplace human resource management policies and practices, and to eliminate those that are barriers of access and advancement of diverse groups. Results of review of employment policies and practices, as well as the workforce analysis, would be included in an employer's equity plan submitted to the enforcement agency in Ontario, the Ontario Employment Equity Commission. Improvement of workforce diversity at different occupational levels will, of course, depend on the effectiveness of enforcement of the legislation.

Research evidence indicates that the federal EE Act has not been very effective in increasing the representativeness of the designated groups in different occupations (Jain and Hacket, 1989). Employment programs in the federal public service, which is also supposed to be a model employer, were not very effective. Visible minorities were appointed to only 2.4 percent of the executive positions, and women constituted only 17.6 percent of the executives. However, visible minorities constituted 13.2 percent of chemists, 13.4 percent of mathematicians and 12.8 percent of medical doctors, and 98.8 percent of stenographers and 81.3 percent of clerks were women in the federal public service (Employment Equity in the Public Service, 1994). The federal EE Act does not apply to the federal public service. However, the government developed employment equity programs for the federal public service under the Financial Administration Act. The effectiveness of the EE programs depends on employer commitment and legislation enforcement.

Enforcement of the EE Act seems to be similar to that of the human rights legislation. The Royal Commission on Equality in Employment (1984) observed that the complaint-based enforcement of equality policy "is increasingly under serious attack for its statutory inadequacy to respond to the magnitude of the problem of discrimination" in workplaces. The Commission added that the case-by-case approach of enforcing equality "is in the position of stamping out brush fires when the urgency is in the incendiary potential of the whole forest." The Ontario Human Rights Code Review Task Force (1992) also found four impediments to enforcement of equality policy: (1) unconscionable delays in handling of claims (complaints); (2) denial of hearings to all but the smallest number of claimants (complainants); (3) disempowerment of those who try to claim their rights under the Code; and (4) an enforcement approach that continues to be out of date and out of touch with present-day realities. The EEC's case-by-case approach in the United States, was as ineffective as that of the HRCs in Canada. However, the enforcement of the United States' Federal Contractors Compliance Program, and the language-based programs have been more effective than the equality or equity programs in Canada.

Job Preference Model

The Federal Contractors Compliance Program was introduced in the United States through Executive Order 11246 of 1965. This Executive Order required each contractor to submit along with the tender an affirmative action plan to hire racial minorities, women, persons with disabilities and veterans, and to implement the plan when a contract was awarded. In Philadelphia where one-third of the workforce was black, the building contractors failed to implement the plans when the construction unions refused to train blacks for skilled crafts and trades through their apprenticeship programs. The contractors could not hire blacks because their collective agreements with the construction unions required them to hire the skilled trades and crafts workers through the union "hiring halls." In 1972, the Nixon administration developed a plan, which was known as the Philadelphia plan, in which one-third of the contracts would be issued to either racial minority contractors or those who hired racial minorities (Graham, 1992a).

In the 1970s, the U.S. government found it necessary to implement an affirmative action plan with preference for hiring of blacks. Blacks in the urban ghettoes were the underclass, and the "truly disadvantaged" in the U.S. workforce needed distributive justice in employment (Wilson, 1987). The job preference plan was subsequently applied to all major contractors in other industries such as transportation, education and defense (Graham, 1992b; Williams, 1992). However, the Reagan and Bush administrations of the 1980s were not committed to either affirmative action or job preference plans, and in the absence of political commitment, the programs were ineffective.

The language-based job preference policies of Malaysia, Sri Lanka and Canada have the commitment of policymakers and the governments. In fact, the policymakers in Malaysia and Sri Lanka represented the majority of the population in their respective countries, for whose benefit the language-based employment policies were developed and implemented. The official language policy of Malay was to benefit Bhumiputras (sons of the soil) that constituted 61.3 percent of Malaysians, and the official language policy of Sinhala was to benefit Sinhalese that constituted (74 percent of Sri Lankans). The official language policy of Malaysia benefited Bhumiputras in the civil service. However, it was not as effective in the private sector as it was in the civil service. In the private sector workplaces, Bhumiputras were employed in 28.4 percent of the decision-making positions, while Chinese who constituted 30 percent of the population were in 66 percent of the decision-making positions (Wyzman, 1990). Prior to independence when the language of work in Sri Lanka's civil service was English, Tamils, who constituted 18 percent of the population, were in 30 percent of the administrative positions. By 1970, their share of the decision-making positions dropped to 6 percent (Hubbel, 1990).

The Canadian Official Languages Act of 1969 proclaimed English and French as the two official languages of Canada. As required under the legislation, a policy of institutional bilingualism was adopted for the federal civil service and for the crown corporations of the government of Canada. Institutional bilingualism required specification of proficiency in English and French for certain jobs, particularly supervisory and decision-making positions. The Royal Commission on Bilingualism and Biculturalism (B & B Commission, 1969) observed that until 1969 "bilingualism [in the workplaces] was demanded of most Francophones but not most Anglophones'' and ''in the struggle up the corporate ladder, the present work system in the large corporations gives Anglophones a built-in advantage over the Francophone colleagues.'' As a result, the Commission further observed that ''Canadians of French origin in all regions of the country participate less in the high level occupational categories (particularly those of managers, professionals and technical personnel) and more in the blue collar and unskilled occupations.'' After the bilingualism policy was implemented, the representativeness of Francophones, increased to 21 percent of management positions in 1989 from 18 percent in 1978 in the federal civil service. In 1989, they also constituted 22 percent of the scientific and professional occupations in the federal civil service. Bilingualism was specified as a job requirement for 29 percent of the civil service positions in 1989, and it was required for only 21 percent in 1974 (Treasury Board, 1989). The language-based employment policies of Canada, Malaysia and Sri Lanka, like the job preference affirmative action plans of the United States, are expected to increase the employment opportunities of disadvantaged groups in the respective countries' workforce.

Job Reservation Model

Job reservation policy in India, also was designed to improve the employment opportunities of the truly disadvantaged. In 1950, the government of India developed a results-oriented policy of employment to accommodate the backward (depressed) classes, the SCs and STs. The Indian constitution adopted the job reservation policy as a temporary 10-year program that was to be terminated once the representativeness of the backward classes in the civil service and in the public sector (government) enterprises (PSEs) was proportionate to their share in the labor markets. Article 16(4) of the constitution of India provided ''for the reservation of the appointments or posts in favour of any backward class of citizens which, in the opinion of the state, is not adequately represented in the services under the state.'' Because the representativeness of the SCs and STs in the civil service and in the PSEs, particularly in professional and decision-making positions, never reached the expected proportionate levels, the reservation policy has been extended every tenth year. Even after four decades of implementation of the reservation policy, the SCs and STs constituted only 5.68 percent of the upper level decision makers in the civil service, while they were 22.5 percent of the population. However, they constituted 24.40 percent of the cleaning and clerical workers in the civil service, and 81.93 percent of the sweepers in the PSEs were SCs and STs.

The state governments, too, developed employment reservation programs for other backward classes (OBCs), in addition to those for the SCs and STs, as was recommended by the Second Backward Classes Commission in 1980. In some states such as Karnataka, 66 percent of jobs in the state civil service and in the state PSEs were reserved for SCs, STs, and OBCs, since the three disadvantaged groups together constituted two-thirds of the state's population. The Supreme Court of India, however, found that reservation of more than 50 percent of the vacancies was unconstitutional since such a reservation would violate the constitutional requirement of maintenance of efficiency in administration (*Balaji v. State of Mysore, AIR 1963, SC 649*). India's policymakers are now contemplating an amendment to the constitution to provide for reservation of more than 50 percent of jobs in the civil service and the PSEs to accommodate SCs, STs, and OBCs. Nonetheless, the representativeness of these groups, as reported by the Commissioner of Scheduled Castes and Scheduled Tribes (1986–87), was very low in decision-making positions, and it was very high in the cleaning services in the states' civil services and PSEs.

The job reservation model, like job preference models, is results-oriented. Both are concerned with increasing the employment opportunities of specified disadvantaged groups. In countries like India and the United States, the population for whose benefit the job reservation and job preference models, respectively, were developed, were "truly disadvantaged." From a social justice perspective, the truly disadvantaged population deserved employment policies for increasing their opportunities of access and advancement in the workplace. The policies developed for specified groups were applied to workplaces in the civil service and to those that were supported by Taxpayer money. Similarly, the job preference models were also applied to civil service and government-funded workplaces. These workplaces do not compete in global markets, and their human resource management policies and practices might not be emulated by managers of workplaces that compete in global markets for survival and expansion.

The equity model, like the job preference and job reservation models, is results-oriented. It also focuses on review and refinement of human resource management policies and practices, such as recruitment, selection, development, appraisal and reward of employee performance. The purpose of review and refinement is not only to make them fair, but also to assure fairness as perceived by a diverse workforce. The equality model also requires fairness of human resource management policies and practices. However, the equality model does not provide for measures of its effectiveness in implementation. The equity model, on the other hand, focuses on the results of distribution of a diverse workforce, which is proportionate to workforce diversity in labor markets. Such a distribution of a diverse workforce at different levels in a workplace confirms employees' perceptions of equity of management policies and practices. Perceptions of fairness motivate employee performance, which, in turn, contributes to workplace effectiveness. A model of management that focuses on the equity and representation of a diverse workforce is considered appropriate for workplaces to compete in global markets.

REPRESENTATION MODEL

A representation model of management requires change, and managing change is important in workplaces that function in global markets. Along with globalization of product markets, global labor markets are also emerging with changes in the global workforce. Trends in the global workforce (Johnston, 1991) suggest that the vast majority of the new workers will join the workforce from developing countries. The global workforce is projected to grow by 600 million between 1985 and 2000, and 570 million of them will enter global labor markets from developing countries. Between 1970 and 1992, the low-and middle-income countries' share of the world's workforce rose from 79 percent to 83 percent (World Bank, 1995). The workforce in developing countries is growing at an annual rate of 3 percent, compared to less than 1 percent in the developed countries, such as the United States and Canada. Moreover, new workers entering the global labor markets from developing countries will be younger and more educated than those in developed countries. The share of total college graduates, particularly in engineering and sciences from the developing world, leaped from 23 to 49 percent between 1970 and 1985, while the share from the United States, Canada, Europe, the Soviet Union and Japan dropped to 51 percent from 77 percent (Johnston, 1991). The low-and middle-income countries' share of the world's skilled workforce with at least secondary education jumped form a third to nearly a half between 1970 and 1992 (World Bank, 1995). In both developed and developing countries, workplaces need to recruit, develop and retain skilled and professional (knowledge) workers to compete effectively in global markets.

Demand for knowledge workers and mobility of an educated workforce in global markets necessitate changes in human resource management policies and practices. In the absence of change, the diverse workforce will be distributed along functional lines in workplaces. The racial minority workforce with science and engineering skills, including those with management training, are being steered into technical occupations and away from decision-making positions in developed country workplaces (Zureik, 1983). In the developing countries, expatriates from developed countries are assigned to positions with power and financial control in joint venture and multinational corporations, whereas the local professionals are appointed to manage relations with the government, the public and workers (Dowling and Schuler, 1990; Tung, 1988). Both in developed and developing countries, women's opportunities are also limited to less powerful nondecision-making positions. Limited opportunities to advance into decision-making positions, and the distribution of women and racial (ethnic and caste) minorities along functional lines are unlikely to motivate their performance, and so they are likely to be underutilized in workplaces.

The functional distribution of a diverse workforce will also affect the access and advancement of new entrants into a workplace. Sponsorship facilitates access and advancement, and personal networks promote sponsorship (Alvarez,

1979; Ibarra, 1993a). Personal networks of women and racial minorities are more expressive than instrumental for access and advancement to decision-making positions since their networks do not cover power centers in workplaces (Ibarra, 1993b). Employees sponsor and refer candidates for positions, and the sponsored candidates are preferred in recruitment and selection. A sponsor refers a candidate from his personal networks, and networks are more homogeneous than heterogeneous. In other words, persons in decision-making positions sponsor and refer members of their personal networks for positions of power; the system unintentionally denies opportunities of access and advancement to a diverse workforce, particularly in workplaces with little diversity in management positions.

Personal networks are also important for mentoring, and mentoring is necessary for socialization, career development and advancement in a workplace. A mentor facilitates early socialization, helps the worker avoid performance pitfalls, counsels the availability of appropriate training and rewards a protégé's opportunities. A mentor–protégé relationship is more common among members of a homogeneous group than between members of diverse groups. Members of a group with little or no representation in decision-making positions are at a disadvantage, for they are unlikely to have access to instrumental networks and mentoring in a workplace. Women and racial minorities are disadvantaged in access and advancement opportunities, for they are not adequately represented in decision-making positions.

Ontario recognizes the importance of representation of diversity in its employment equity legislation. The legislation provides for representation of a diverse workforce by a bargaining agent in the process of review of workplace human resource management policies and practices, and employers are required to negotiate with their respective bargaining agents in developing employment equity and pay equity plans. However, unions have no jurisdiction over recruitment, selection, development and compensation of managers, and they are unlikely to be effective in increasing the representativeness of a diverse workforce in decision-making positions. Moreover, unions represent the interests of the majority of their membership, and the racial minority workforce is unlikely to benefit (Subbarao, 1992). The collective agreement between the University of Ottawa and the Association of Professors requires the representation of women on faculty recruitment and selection committees, but not for promotions into the university's decision-making positions. In other words, representation of diversity in human resource management committees is becoming an important component of a model of managing workforce diversity.

A diverse workforce is representation on workplace committees will offer an opportunity to understand the interests and concerns of different groups in reviewing human resource policies and practices, and in making personnel decisions. Recruitment committees with representation of diversity could search appropriate sources and recruitment methods for attracting qualified knowledge workers in diverse labor markets, instead of relying on the sponsorship of a dominant group. Diverse selection committees would be more fair in selecting from a group of diverse applicants than a committee consisting of only members of a dominant group in as much as their decisions are susceptible to stereotypes and biases. Equitable appraisal of a diverse workforce's performance is possible if the performance evaluation committees include representatives from a diverse workforce. Inequitable evaluation of knowledge workers' performance, such as in the cases of the Ontario Liquor Control Board (*Karumanchiri v. Liquor Control Board of Ontario* (1987), 8 C.H.R.R. D/4076), the National Research Council of Canada (*Grover v. NRC*, 1992) and the Canadian International Development Agency (Public Service Commission of Canada's Appeal Board Decision of the appeal of Ranjit Perera, 1994) could have been avoided, and the career development of these highly educated racial minority knowledge workers would have been possible, if the performance evaluation committees had consisted of representatives from a diverse workforce.

Representation of women in job evaluation and pay survey committees is required to conduct gender-neutral evaluation of jobs in a workplace and to undertake an unbiased survey of pay rates in labor markets for developing an equitable pay system. The decisions handed down by recruitment, selection, appraisal and pay committees that consist of diversity representatives are likely to be perceived by a diverse workforce as fair. Human resource processes that are managed by committees consisting of diversity representatives as shown in Figure 10.1, are more likely to yield more representativeness at different occupational levels than those managed traditionally by a dominant group. Representativeness is expected to influence employee perceptions of fairness, and it could also contribute to equitable employee relations. Representativeness would reinforce employee involvement in management of a workplace through representation in human resources process committees. Employee performance and export performance of a workplace would reinforce an employer's commitment to representation of a diverse workforce.

Export performance is an important incentive for managers to become agents of change. Exploration and expansion of global product markets, as well as improvements in employee performance, are important for increasing export performance. Managing workforce diversity is important on both counts. Members of a diverse workforce can be assigned to explore global markets with which they are familiar and in which they are able to function better than the members of a dominant group. In other words, globalization of product markets and the emergence of a diverse global workforce, particularly among skilled and knowledge workers, are the two most important external factors that are influencing human resources management. Public policies also influence management of human resources because employers would want to avoid litigation and damage to workplace reputation. However, the job preference policies are unlikely to be extended to cover workplaces in the private sector, particularly those that compete in global markets. The policy of equality as interpreted to include

Figure 10.1
Representation Model for Managing Workforce Diversity

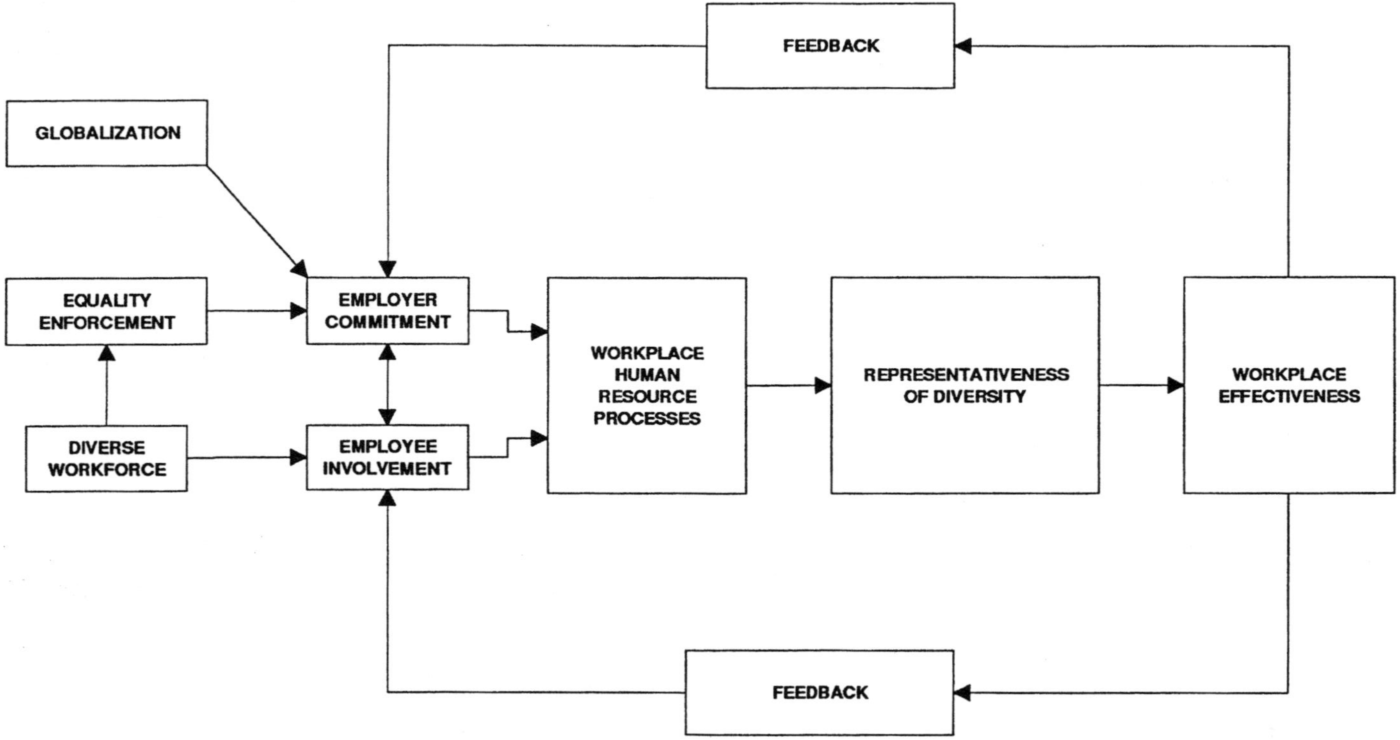

accommodation of a diverse workforce through special measures, on the other hand, is important and will influence management in workplaces of all sectors.

CONCLUSIONS

The equality principle as interpreted by the judiciary and employment equity as developed by policymakers are not significantly different. Both require fairness of human resource processes, and fair and equal treatment of a diverse workforce are required in both equality and equity models. The equity model provides for a measure of effectiveness. An effective equity model of management, the policymakers suggest, will yield representativeness of a diverse workforce in a workplace proportionate to the diversity in the labor markets. The measure of effectiveness is important for an employer functioning in diverse labor markets. Otherwise, an employer would recognize management problems only when confronted by complaints of discrimination, as employers of Japanese multinationals in the United States are facing legal challenges of discrimination of whites in the selection of decision makers (Fernandez, 1993). External enforcement of the equity model may be weak, but enforcement of the equality policy will be strengthened in as much as even those policymakers who oppose affirmative action and employment equity policies are also committed to enforcing equality policy.

Internal enforcement is better than external bureaucratic enforcement, which is not only costly but also disruptive to management. External enforcement also affects employee relations adversely when equality and equity policies are enforced only in response to employee complaints. An employer committed to human resources will develop methods of internal enforcement of equality and equity policies to motivate employee performance and promote equitable employee relations. Employee involvement in the management of human resources is a method of internal enforcement, and representation of a diverse workforce on workplace committees constituted to manage human resource processes is an efficient mechanism for improving employee perceptions of equity and equitable employee relations. Efficient internal enforcement of equity policy is likely to yield representativeness of a diverse workforce at different occupational levels. Efficient utilization of a diverse workforce not only attracts qualified knowledge workers but also improves employee performance. Employee performance and export performance are important to the survival and expansion of workplaces in competitive global markets. Managers in developed and developing countries that compete in global markets are expected to be agents of change in managing a diverse workforce.

NOTE

This chapter was presented at International Conference on Globalization and Market Economy: The Challenge of Change, December 28–30, 1995, New Delhi India.

REFERENCES

Alvarez, R. 1979. Institutional Discrimination in Organizations and Their Environments. In R. Alvarez, K. G. Lutterman and Associates (eds.), *Discrimination in Organizations*. San Francisco: Jossey-Bass Publishers, 2–49.

Backward Classes Commission. 1991. *Reservations for Backward Classes*. New Delhi: Akalank Publications.

Bilingualism and Biculturalism. 1969. *Report of the Royal Commission*. Ottawa: Queen's Printer.

Burke, R. J. 1991. Managing an Increasingly Diverse Workforce: Experiences of Minority and Professionals in Canada. *Canadian Journal of Administrative Sciences* 8: 108–120.

Dowling, P. J. and Schuler, R. S. 1990. *International Dimensions of Human Resource Management*. Boston: PWS-Kent Publishing Co.

Employment Equity in the Public Service. 1994. Annual Report, 1992–93. Treasury Board. Ottawa: Supply and Services.

Equality in Employment. 1984. *A Royal Commission Report*. Ottawa: Supply and Services.

Federal Glass Ceiling Commission. 1995. *Good for Business: Making Full Use of the Nation's Human Capital*. Washington, DC: U.S. Government Printing Office.

Fernandez, J. P. 1991. *Managing a Diverse Workforce: Regaining the Competitive Advantage*. Toronto: Lexington Books.

Fernandez, J. P. 1993. *The Diversity Advantage: How American Business Can Outperform Japanese and European Companies in the Global Market Place*. New York: Lexington Books.

Graham, H. D. 1992a. *Civil Rights and the Presidency: Race and Gender in American Politics, 1960–72*. New York: Oxford University Press.

Graham, H. D. 1992b, September. The Origins of the Affirmative Action: Civil Rights and the Regulatory State. *Annals of the American Academy of Political and Social Science* 523: 50–62.

Hubbel, L. K. 1990. Political and Economic Discrimination in Sri Lanka. In M. L. Wyzman (ed.), *The Political Economy of Ethnic Discrimination and Affirmative Action: A Comparative Perspective*. New York: Praeger, 115–139.

Ibarra, H. 1993a. Personal Networks of Women and Minorities in Management: A Conceptual Framework. *Academy of Management Review* 18: 56–87.

Ibarra, H. 1993b. Network Centrality, Power, and Innovation Involvement: Determination of Technical and Administrative Roles. *Academy of Management Journal* 36: 471–501.

Jain, H. and Hacket, R. D. 1989. Measuring Effectiveness of Employment Equity in Canada: Public Policy and Survey. *Canadian Public Policy* 15(2): 189–204.

Jamieson, D. and O'Mara, J. 1991. *Managing Workforce 2000: Gaining in Diversity Advantage*. San Francisco: Jossey-Bass.

Johnston, W. B. 1991, March–April. Global Workforce 2000: Work and Workers for the Twenty-First Century. *Harvard Business Review*: 115–127.

Kanter, R. M. 1983. *The Change Masters*. New York: Simon and Schuster.

Kram, K. E. 1988. *Mentoring at Work: Developmental Relationships in Organizational Life*. New York: University Press of America.

Morrison, A. M., White, C. W., Veslor, Van and the Center for Creative Leadership. 1987. *Breaking the Glass Ceiling: Can Women Reach the Top of America's Largest Corporations*. Don Mills, Ontario: Addison-Wesley.

Opportunity 2000: Creating Affirmative Action Strategies for a Changing Workforce. 1988. Indianapolis, IN: Hudson Institute.

Pucik, V., Tichy, N. M. and Barnett, C. K. (eds.). 1993. *Globalizing Management: Creating and Leading the Competitive Organization*. New York: John Wiley.

Rosner, J. B. 1990. Ways Women Lead. *Harvard Business Review* 6: 119–125.

Scheduled Castes and Scheduled Tribes. 1986–87. *Report of the Commission*. New Delhi: Government of India.

Status of Women in Canada: Report of the Royal Commission. 1977. Ottawa: Supply and Services.

Subbarao, A. V. 1992. Role of Labour Unions in Employment Equity Programs: A Compromise or Convenience? *Proceedings of the XXIXth Conference of the Canadian Industrial Relations Association*: 315–332.

Subbarao, A. V. 1994. Managing Workforce Diversity in Canada: Problems and Prospects. *Proceedings of the International Conference on Managing Human Resources/Labour Relations Diversity for Global Competitiveness*. Ontario: McMaster University.

Subbarao, A. V. 1995a. Managing Workforce Diversity and Enforcing Equality: Complementary or Contradictory Processes? *Proceedings of the Administrative Sciences Association of Canada*.

Subbarao, A. V. 1995b, May 31–June 4. Managing Workforce Diversity: An Innovation or an Evolution? Paper presented at the 10th World Congress of International Industrial Relations Association, Washington, DC.

Task Force, Ontario Human Rights Code Review. 1992. *Getting Human Rights Enforced Effectively: An Issue Paper*. Toronto.

Treasury Board. 1989. *Official Languages in Federal Institutions: Annual Report, 1988–89*. Ottawa: Supply and Services.

Tung, R. L. 1988. *The New Expatriates: Managing Human Resources Abroad*. Cambridge, MA: Ballinger.

Tung, R. L. 1993. Managing Cross-national and Intra-national Diversity. *Human Resources Management Journal* 23(4): 461–477.

Williams, J. B. 1992, September. Affirmative Action at Harvard. *Annals of the American Academy of Political and Social Science* 523: 207–220.

Wilson, W. J. 1987. *The Truly Disadvantaged: The Inner City, the Underclass, and the Public Policy*. Chicago: University of Chicago Press.

Workforce 2000. 1987. *Work and Workers for the Twenty-first Century*. Indianapolis, IN: Hudson Institute.

Working Toward Equality: The Discussion Paper on Employment Equity. 1991. Toronto, Ontario: Office of the Employment Equity Commissioner.

World Bank. 1995. *Workers in an Integrating World*. New York: Oxford University Press.

Wyzman, M. L. 1990. Ethnic Relations and New Economic Policy in Malaysia. In M. L. Wyzman (ed.), *The Political Economy of Ethnic Discrimination and Affirmative Action*. New York: Praeger.

Zureik, E. 1983. *The Experience of Visible Minorities in the Work World: The Case of the MBA Graduate*. Toronto, Ontario: Ontario Human Rights Commission.

CHAPTER 11

The Effects of Free Market Reforms on Market Openness, Market Attractiveness and International Marketing Strategies

MANJIT S. YADAV AND DAVID M. SZYMANSKI

This chapter examines the marketing challenges and opportunities created by the unprecedented economic transition occurring in several European, Asian and Latin American countries. The trend toward market reform or economic liberalization continues unabated and is likely to alter the economic landscapes of dozens of countries. Much has been written lately about *what* should be reformed and *how* these reforms should be implemented. However, a review of the marketing and economics literature reveals that no empirical research has been conducted on (1) factors that managers consider when evaluating the adequacy of reforms in a target market, (2) the impact of these factors on perceptions of market openness and market attractiveness, or (3) the impact of these factors on the development of firms' international marketing strategies. Research on these questions is needed not only for understanding the firm's behavior in these emerging markets, but also for formulating appropriate public policy recommendations regarding the implementation of free market reforms.

A CONCEPTUAL MODEL OF THE EFFECTS OF FREE MARKET REFORMS

Free market reforms involve changes in governmental policy aimed at bringing more freedom to the marketplace. This is generally accomplished by "reducing the role of the authorities, increasing reliance on the price mechanism rather than controls, establishing or strengthening market institutions, and integrating the country into the world economy" (Marer, 1991: 329). The conceptualization that guides our research program (see Figure 11.1) shows how free market reforms impact market openness, market attractiveness and international marketing strategies of firms. A brief overview of the rationale behind the conceptualiza-

Figure 11.1
A Conceptual Model of the Effects of Free Market Reforms

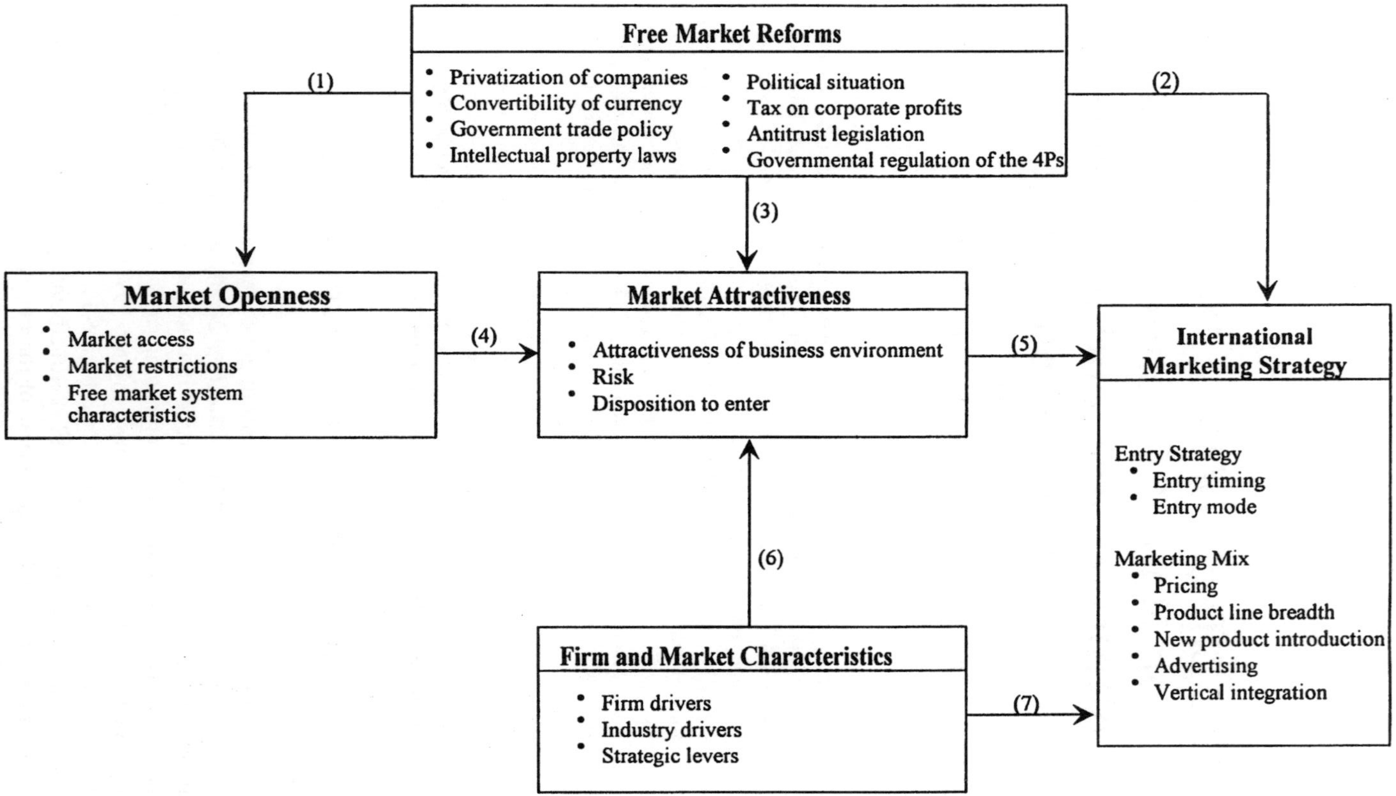

tion, and of the factors listed in the figure is provided below. (For additional details, see Szymanski and Yadav, 1995.)

Free market reforms: There is considerable agreement in the extant literature regarding the specific policy changes needed for making the transition to a free market economy. One study completed recently by the Heritage Foundation (Johnson and Sheehy, 1995) developed an Index of Economic Freedom on the basis of 10 factors considered crucial for assessing the freedom allowed in a country's marketplace. These factors are: trade policy, taxation policy, government consumption of economic output, monetary policy, capital flows and foreign investment, banking policy, wage and price controls, property rights, regulations, and the black market. The significance of these factors is reflected in the work of other advocates of free market reforms (e.g., Kornai 1990; Lipton and Sachs, 1990; McKinnon, 1991). Analytical explorations of reforms (e.g., Srinivasan, 1987), and case studies of countries that have implemented reforms (e.g., Hare, 1991) also make frequent references to these factors. The factors shown in the figure are representative of the arguments articulated in the extant literature.

The effects of free market reforms: The effects of free market reforms are shown in the proposed conceptual model (see figure). As free market reforms generally remove or reduce restrictions in the marketplace, they should enhance *market openness* (i.e., perceived market access and absence of regulatory restrictions) and *market attractiveness* (i.e., perceived attractiveness for conducting business). Market attractiveness is also influenced by two other factors: market openness and firm and market characteristics. Market openness positively influences market attractiveness—that is, all else being equal, an open market is a more attractive market from a business perspective. The characteristics of the firm (e.g., international experience) and the marketplace (e.g., market size and growth rate) also impact market attractiveness. Finally, the international marketing strategy of foreign firms is determined jointly by the effects of reforms, market attractiveness, and firm and market characteristics. Both entry strategies (e.g., when to enter and how) and the marketing mix (e.g., product and pricing decisions) are influenced by these factors. For instance, foreign firms entering a country undergoing reforms are likely to develop strategies that not only capitalize on their strategic strengths (e.g., production skills), but also match the realities of the marketplace (e.g., high rates of inflation). This reflects a contingency notion of international marketing strategy development (see, e.g., Szymanski, Bharadwaj and Varadarajan, 1993).

We are developing this research program in two stages. The objective of the first stage is to examine the effects of free market reforms on market openness, market attractiveness and marketing strategies (relationships 1, 2 and 3 in the conceptual model). Specifically, this stage will assess the relative effects of various market reforms (e.g., does convertibility of currency have a stronger effect than intellectual property laws on market attractiveness?). The second stage will focus in more detail on the role played by the firm and market characteristics in developing international marketing strategy (relationships 6 and 7 in the conceptual model). The next section presents an overview of an initial study that examined the relationships highlighted in the conceptual model.

STUDY

Design and procedure: We used a fractional factorial experimental design (Cochran and Cox, 1957) to study the hypothesized effects of free market reforms. The following eight reforms were manipulated: privatization of companies, convertibility of currency, government trade policy, intellectual property laws, political stability, tax on corporate profits, antitrust legislation and government regulation of marketing mix decisions. Each factor was manipulated over two levels (favorable, unfavorable). To estimate the main effects of these eight factors, we used a ⅛ replicate of the 2^8 design (32 cells; see Cochran and Cox, 1957: 286). The stimuli in each cell consisted of a hypothetical market opportunity described in the eight factors, manipulated according to the experimental design. Respondents were asked to examine the scenario and to answer a series of questions pertaining to the perceived openness of the market, perceived attractiveness of the market and marketing mix decisions.

Respondents were contacted by mail and completed the self-administered task as part of a short survey. Sixty-three percent of the respondents and 77 percent of their respective firms had five or more years of experience in international marketing. Sixty-seven percent of the firms sold their products in 10 or more countries. Overall, these statistics reflect the active involvement of respondents and their firms in international marketing.

Highlights of findings: Government trade policy had the strongest influence on managers' perceptions of market openness ($t = 5.07, p < .01$), followed by privatization of companies ($t = 3.74, p < .01$) and government regulation of marketing activities ($t = 2.09, p < .05$), respectively. Other factors were not statistically significant at $p < .05$. Perceived market attractiveness was impacted most strongly by government trade policy ($t = 2.81, p < .05$) and tax on corporate profits ($t = 1.36, p < .10$). Other factors were not significant at $p < .05$.

We also estimated the cumulative effects (effect size eta²s) of free market reforms on entry timing, formation of strategic alliances and marketing mix decisions. Free market reforms impacted entry timing more strongly (0.36) than strategic alliance formation (0.28). Of the marketing mix decisions, advertising decisions (0.27) and downward integration (0.16) were influenced the most.

These results indicate that while free market reforms strongly influence perceptions of market openness and attractiveness, the direct impact on marketing strategies is not as pronounced. This perhaps suggests a hierarchical mode of managerial decision making. Once perceptions of openness and attractiveness have been formed, the formulation of specific marketing strategies may depend on marketplace conditions.

REFERENCES

Cochran, William G. and Cox, Gertrude M. 1957. *Experimental Designs*. 2nd ed. New York: John Wiley and Sons.

Hare, Paul G. 1991, Fall. Hungary: In Transition to a Market Economy. *Journal of Economic Perspectives* 5: 195–201.

Johnson, Bryan and Sheehy, Thomas. 1995. *Index of Economic Freedom*. Washington, DC: Heritage Foundation.

Kornai, Janos. 1990. *The Road to a Free Economy*. New York: W. W. Norton.

Lipton, D. and Sachs, J. 1990. Creating a Market in Eastern Europe. *Brookings Papers on Economic Activity*, No. 1.

Marer, Paul. 1991, May. Foreign Economic Liberalization in Hungary and Poland. *AEA Proceedings and Papers* 81: 329–333.

McKinnon, Ronald I. 1991, Fall. Financial Control in the Transition from Classical Socialism to a Market Economy. *Journal of Economic Perspectives* 5: 107–122.

Srinivasan, T. N. 1987, September. Economic Liberalization in China and India: Issues and an Analytical Framework. *Journal of Comparative Economics* 11: 427–443.

Szymanski, David M., Bharadwaj, Sundar G. and Varadarajan, P. Rajan 1993. Standardization versus Adaptation of International Marketing Strategy: An Empirical Investigation. *Journal of Marketing*: 1–17.

Szymanski, David M. and Yadav, Manjit S. 1995. Market Openness: The Construct, Implications for Entry Strategies, and Research Agenda. Working paper, Texas A&M University.

CHAPTER 12

Equity Joint Ventures by Firms Seeking Technology from MNCs

SUNIL VENAIK

As economies become increasingly market-based, and as international trade and investment barriers get pulled down with bilateral agreements and multilateral agreements such as GATT, the foundations of domestic competition become international in character. In order to improve their competitive position, it is essential that local firms acquire technology from MNCs so that they can effectively compete against new local and foreign firms. This chapter uses the transaction cost framework to explain that, under a given set of product–market conditions, it is more advantageous for firms in developing countries to choose the joint venture mode rather than the licensing mode for seeking technology from MNCs. The chapter therefore contributes to our understanding of the international joint venture phenomenon from the perspective of the local partner.

INTRODUCTION

This chapter discusses two issues in firm strategy. First, under the new competitive patterns that are emerging as a result of changes in economic policy, how should existing local firms respond in order to retain their competitiveness? As economies become increasingly market-based, and countries reduce international trade and investment barriers, new local firms and foreign firms (multinational corporations—MNCs) intensify competition in the domestic market. In this highly complex competitive environment, it becomes increasingly difficult for existing firms with old technology to sustain their survival and growth. To retain competitiveness and successfully respond to these challenges, it is imperative for these firms to acquire new technology from MNCs. Here, the term *technology* is used broadly, and includes manufacturing, marketing and management skills and knowledge required to operate a business efficiently.

Second, what organizational governance mechanism (license or equity joint venture) should a firm choose to acquire the new technology? According to transaction cost economics (Williamson, 1975, 1985), factors such as uncertainty/complexity, opportunism and asset specificity increase the cost of monitoring the performance of parties in a contract, resulting in inefficiency and failure of the contract. To overcome the cost/inefficiency of transacting with external agents, firms internalize the transaction within the organization by using more efficient hierarchical mechanisms such as equity joint ventures. This chapter uses the transaction cost framework to explain why an equity joint venture is more efficient than a license in overcoming Williamson's transaction costs associated with the acquisition of technology by local firms from MNCs.

The chapter is divided into three sections. The first section discusses the competitive and consumer forces that impel firms to seek new technology from MNCs; the second uses the transaction cost framework to explain why local firms use international joint ventures (IJVs) to acquire the new technology; and the third concludes with a summary of the chapter, setting forth its limitations and future research issues.

Although the transaction cost theory has been used in the literature to explain the use of IJVs by MNCs for direct foreign investment (DFI) (Beamish and Banks, 1987; Kogut, 1988; Stuckey, 1983), the perspective is usually one-sided since it largely discusses only the MNCs viewpoint, with only a casual reference to the needs, requirements and preferences of the local firm. This chapter contributes to our understanding of IJVs from the perspective of the local partner. It uses transaction cost theory to explain why local firms use IJVs to obtain technology from MNCs.

Understanding the rationale of local firms for a joint venture is important for two reasons. First, as the number of alternative technologies and its suppliers (MNCs) increases, there is likely to be increasing competition among MNCs to form joint ventures with good local firms. Adoption of a customer-oriented marketing approach, with an emphasis on understanding the prospective customers' (local firms') technology needs, and tailoring the technology package to effectively fulfill those needs, would increase the MNC's chances of forming a successful joint venture with a local firm. Second, any one perspective offers only a partial account of a complex phenomenon. According to Van De Ven and Poole (1995–), "juxtaposition of different perspectives brings into focus contrasting worldviews of social change and development." Since an IJV is a complex organizational arrangement, seeing it from the perspective of both partners will enhance our understanding of the factors that determine the formation, performance and long-term success of the joint venture relationship.

THE IMPERATIVE TO ACQUIRE TECHNOLOGY FROM MNCs

In the last few years, the economies of several developing countries, including India, China and many Asia-Pacific and East European countries, have under-

Figure 12.1
New Competitive Patterns

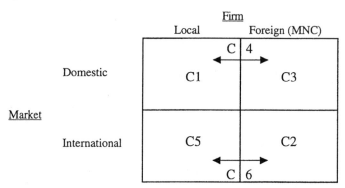

gone significant structural reforms. These changes, which are in two broad directions, are resulting in the emergence of new competitive patterns, shown as C1, C2 and so on, in Figure 12.1. In this figure, market is defined with reference to the local firm. Thus, domestic market is the national market in the country of the local firm, whereas international market is the market in countries outside that of the local firm. These centrally planned economies are undergoing rapid transformation toward market-based economies. This has spawned a new breed of entrepreneurial and aggressive local firms, and has created a new level of competition, shown as C1 in Figure 12.1. This competition either did not exist in centrally planned economies or had a low level of competitive intensity before the market reforms were introduced. While competition of type C1 is an important issue for local firms, it is not very difficult to manage since it is symmetric in character. Symmetry implies that the factors on which the local firms compete (i.e., their sources of sustainable competitive advantage), are similar. This competition poses only a small threat, since at this stage of transformation of the economy, the local firms are largely immune from the intense competition among foreign firms (MNCs) in the international market, as represented by C2 in Figure 12.1.

These countries are opening their borders to international trade and investment flows, due partly to bilateral agreements and to multilateral agreements such as GATT. The reduction in barriers to the inflow of foreign goods and capital is attracting multinational firms into these large and apparently profitable markets. The entry of foreign multinationals, with large capital resources and better technology, has added a new dimension to competition in the domestic market. Not only are these multinationals competing among themselves in the domestic market, as represented by C3 in Figure 12.1, but the local firms are also confronted with large, formidable, foreign multinationals as competitors.

The competition between local firms and foreign MNCs in the domestic market, represented by C4 in Figure 12.1, poses the greatest threat as well as a challenge to local firms since it is not only more intense and complex, but also asymmetric. Asymmetry implies that the factors on which local and foreign firms compete (i.e., their respective sources of sustainable competitive advantage) are significantly different, both in number and characteristics. The threat that this competition poses to the survival of local firms, together with the most efficient means of overcoming the threat, is the key focus of this chapter.

To complete the picture, it may be stated that a few strong and internationally competitive local firms, spurred by the growth opportunities offered by unshackling the economy, are growing overseas and competing among themselves as well as with foreign multinationals in the international market (shown as C5 and C6, respectively, in Figure 12.1).

In addition to competitive forces, the change/decline in domestic competitive position of local firms is also triggered from the consumer end. While industrial product buyers in different countries generally demand globally standardized products, there is evidence of an increasing trend toward homogenization of preferences across countries even for consumer products. Ohmae (1986), for instance, considers North American, Western European and Japanese consumers to be increasingly homogeneous in their preferences. According to Levitt (1993), the increasing obliteration of national differences among consumers provides good opportunities for firms to produce standard products for global markets. Faster and frequent travel and communication are also informing and encouraging consumers to expect, seek and get the best products and services from local firms.

The two forces—namely, the use of world-competitive technology by new local and foreign firms, combined with world-standard consumer preferences in the domestic market—are driving the technology foundations of domestic competition to become increasingly international. In the new competitive and consumer environment, it is imperative that local firms—both large and small—view their product–market technology from a broad international perspective rather than a narrow national perspective. Existing firms, with old technology from a competition-free era, are likely to find it increasingly difficult to survive and grow in the new environment created by a free economy. This does not imply that existing local firms do not possess any competitive advantage. Although plausible, such an assumption seems unreasonable, especially since many of these firms have survived and grown successfully over a long period of time. What this implies, rather, is that under the new competitive scenario, these firms' existing competitive advantage in some areas is inadequate for survival and growth in the future. To sustain and strengthen their competitive position in the face of these changes, and to avoid the risk of failure and even extinction, local firms must acquire new technology to overcome their weaknesses in manufacturing, marketing or general management. The next section discusses the mechanisms by which a local firm can acquire technology from MNCs, and uses the transaction cost theory to explain why the firm may prefer IJV over license for this purpose.

Figure 12.2
Typology of a Joint Venture

Venture location

Partners'		National	International
	Same	1	2
Nationality	Different	4	3

TRANSACTION COST EXPLANATION OF EQUITY JOINT VENTURES

Typology of Equity Joint Ventures

Since the literature on strategic alliances and joint ventures (JVs) encompasses a wide range of interfirm relationships, we should delineate the boundaries of the type of JV discussed in this chapter. Although JVs can be classified along several dimensions, a typology is shown in Figure 12.2, wherein a joint venture is classified along two dimensions: (1) venture location—national or international, and (2) partners' nationality—the same or different.[1] In a type 1 JV, both partners have the same nationality as the joint venture, whereas in a type 2 JV, the same-country partners set up a joint venture in another country. In a type 3 JV, on the other hand, different country partners create a joint venture in a third country, whereas in a type 4 JV, different country partners form a joint venture in the country of one of the partners, and thus are located internationally for the other partner. Although Geringer and Hebert (1989) consider ventures of all the three types (2, 3, 4) as IJVs, what distinguishes IJVs, and makes them an interesting and important topic of study, is the international/different nationality of the partners (as in types 3 and 4) rather than merely the international location of the venture (as in type 2).

These IJVs (types 3 and 4) are interesting because they involve a strategic alliance between partners from two different nationalities or cultures. In addition to the issues of managing an overseas venture, these IJVs have the complexity of sharing coordination and control between firms from diverse cultures. Despite their apparent complexity, they are preferred by current and prospective MNCs as a means of entering new markets as well as for acquiring new technology. The Australian Bureau of Industry Economics (BIE) report, extracts from which were published in the *Australian Financial Review* (1995), provides evidence of increasing DFI by Australian firms in the developing economies of Asia. Although it does not indicate the form of investment (wholly-owned subsidiary or a joint venture), anecdotal evidence suggests that a large proportion of this investment is in the form of IJVs. Thus, Australian firms are creating IJVs in increasing numbers and size, and across a diversity of countries, and we can expect this trend to be reflected by firms in other industrialized countries as

Figure 12.3
Mechanism for Transaction Cost Theory

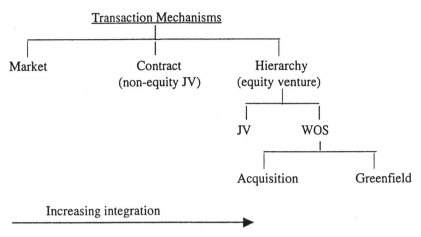

well. Type 4 IJVs, which bring together firms from two (rarely more) countries, to form a joint venture located in the country of one of the partners (and thus located internationally for the other partner), are most common, and these IJVs are the focus of discussion in this chapter.

Transaction Cost Theory

This section briefly discusses the transaction cost theory, which will explain the governance mechanism (market, contract or hierarchy) chosen by firms for pursuing internationalization strategy. As shown in Figure 12.3, firms can carry out transactions for inputs and outputs using three broad types of institutional mechanisms—market, contract and hierarchy. Markets, in the classical economics sense, are considered to be a frictionless institution characterized by perfect competition—that is, with a large number of buyers and sellers transacting at prices and quantities in perfect equilibrium. Failure of markets under certain conditions, such as the increasing need, difficulty and cost associated with policing the behavior of parties involved in a transaction, impels firms either to write complex contracts or to partially or fully internalize transactions within the firm's hierarchy.[2]

Contracts are nonequity JVs and can be of several types, such as supply and distribution contract; technical assistance and management contract; licensing and franchising; and cooperative R&D arrangement. Thus, depending on the type of contract, it has characteristics that are close either to market mechanisms at one end or to hierarchies at the other end. Williamson's transaction cost (1975, 1983, 1985) associated with a contract can therefore vary over a wide range, depending on the nature of the transaction. For example, a purchase/sale transaction, with low transaction cost, can be effectively governed by a simple supply agreement close to a market mechanism. On the other hand, a franchise or a cooperative R&D arrangement involves high transaction cost and requires a complex, contingent claim, sequential contract close to a hierarchical mechanism for effective governance. Thus, the boundaries of a contract cannot be easily delineated within the markets versus hierarchies debate. Although markets and contracts are classified separately to help explain their distinction, in the following sections, the term *market failure* is used to refer to the failure of both the market and contract mechanisms.

When the cost of writing, administering and enforcing complex, contingent claims contracts becomes excessive, firms prefer to internalize the transaction to reduce the cost (increase the efficiency) of the transaction process. Internalization implies that the transaction is carried out internally within the organizational hierarchy rather than externally with parties outside the organization. Depending on the nature/degree of internalization, the equity form can be of three types—joint venture (JV), acquisition and greenfield, with the last two combined into a single category called wholly-owned subsidiary (WOS).

To reduce the cost associated with monitoring the performance of parties in a transaction in imperfect markets, firms internalize the transaction, either partially through a JV or wholly through a WOS (acquisition or greenfield). Furthermore, the higher the cost of market failure, the greater the benefit from internalizing transactions. This economic rationale impels firms to establish hierarchical operations instead of transacting through market mechanisms.

According to Williamson (1985, in Kogut, 1988), firms choose the level of integration that minimizes the sum of production and transaction costs. Although production costs differ between firms owing to the scale of operations, learning or proprietary knowledge (Kogut, 1988), transaction costs arise due to market imperfections that are caused by seven factors. These factors can be classified into three groups (Beamish and Banks, 1987; Williamson and Ouchi, 1981): (1) the three environment factors of uncertainty/complexity, commitment/small numbers and asset specificity and intensity; (2) the two human factors of bounded rationality and opportunism; and (3) the two derivative factors of transaction frequency and information impactedness. Drawing from Beamish and Banks (1987) and Kogut (1988), we may briefly explain these factors as follows.

1. *Uncertainty/complexity.* According to this factor, the higher the uncertainty/complexity of a transaction, the more difficult it is to write, administer and enforce a complete, contingent claims contract, resulting in market failure for such a transaction.

2. *Commitment/small numbers.* If there are only a small number of buyers and/or sellers in the market, this factor results in a situation of bilateral monopoly/oligopoly. It gives rise to a greater degree of interdependence between transacting parties and an increased need for fulfillment of reciprocal commitments. It may also involve costly haggling and bargaining over contract terms and sharing of profits. In a situation of small numbers, since it is difficult to align incentives for both parties to perform

efficiently, it can be a potential cause of market failure, especially when accompanied by opportunism.

3. *Asset specificity and intensity.* This implies that when transactions involve specialized assets of high value, switching costs are high, especially if accompanied by a small number of alternatives for the utilization of these assets. When accompanied by uncertainty and opportunism, market for the deployment of such assets is very likely to fail.

4. *Bounded rationality.* This factor implies that human beings have limited ability to comprehend complexity and are unable to anticipate and include all present and future contingencies in a contract.

5. *Opportunism.* This is another human condition that involves strategic manipulation of information and seeking self-interest with guile. It encourages firms to cheat in their commercial dealings if it is in their long-term interest to do so. Both bounded rationality and opportunism are human conditions that result in increased market inefficiency and failure.

6. *High transaction frequency.* According to this factor, if the transactions associated with market-failing factors are executed frequently, the result is greater haggling and bargaining, as well as increased exploitation of the weaker party in the contract, accelerating market failure.

7. *Information impactedness.* This factor is associated with asymmetry of information between the parties to the transaction. This, combined with opportunism and uncertainty/complexity, can be a strong determinant of market failure.

In summary, the seven transaction cost factors, rarely individually but more often in combination, create market imperfections. These imperfections result in inefficiency (high cost) and failure of markets for tangible and intangible goods, although the specific combination that causes failure depends on the product–market context of the transaction.

As stated earlier, there is a large body of literature on the application of transaction cost theory for explaining the formation of international equity joint ventures by MNCs. Detailed explanations are provided by Hennart (1988) for scale and link JVs; Stuckey (1983) and Stuckey and White (1993) for vertical integration IJVs; and Beamish and Banks (1987) and Kogut (1988) for horizontal integration IJVs. Since the arguments for international equity joint ventures by MNCs are extensively discussed in the literature, these are not reproduced here. The next section provides a plausible transaction cost explanation for equity joint ventures by local firms seeking technology from MNCs.

Transaction Cost Explanation of Equity Joint Ventures by Firms Seeking Technology from MNCs

Based on the transaction cost framework, this section explains why local firms use equity joint ventures to acquire technology from foreign MNCs. As stated before, the term *technology* is used broadly and encompasses manufacturing, marketing and management skills and knowledge required to efficiently operate a business. First, a WOS is usually infeasible since local firms may not possess all the technological capabilities required to compete successfully with new local and foreign firms. Second, efficient markets may not exist for intangible assets such as brand name and technology, which a local firm seeks in order to improve its competitive position. In such a situation, the only comparison required is between an equity joint venture and a long-term contract such as licensing.

Local firms usually need and seek complex, difficult-to-learn technologies for growth, diversification or simply survival. Theoretically, the technology supplier and the technology receiver can be either from the same country or from different countries, and these countries can be either industrialized or developing. In this chapter since the focus is on newly industrializing country/developing country firms seeking technology, it is assumed that the technology is not available locally even if there are a few local MNCs. It is more likely to be available from foreign rather than local multinationals, since the foreign, owing to their relatively greater size and resources, are likely to have larger R&D budgets for developing new technologies. Hence, the technology transfer process inevitably becomes international in scope, in which technology is supplied by a foreign firm (MNC) in an industrialized country to a local firm in a developing country. In the following paragraphs, it is argued that since an equity joint venture economizes on the seven transaction cost factors discussed earlier, local firms use it as the preferred mode for obtaining technology from foreign firms.

Many technologies (such as marketing and management) required by local firms embody tacit knowledge (Polanyi, 1967, in Culpan, 1993) which is embedded in organizational routines, and difficult to express, evaluate and transfer. Although manufacturing technology can be transmitted through designs and drawings, substantial managerial/organizational knowledge is required to overcome the uncertainty associated with adapting the product/process design to the local firm environment. Because of the inherent uncertainties and complexities of technology, it is difficult to write, administer and enforce a license for its transfer, resulting in inefficiency and failure of a technology transfer license. In contrast, an equity JV overcomes this problem since the local firm does not need to resolve all uncertainties a priori. The foreign MNC's ongoing interest in the JV provides the incentive to share technology and information to overcome the uncertainty and complexity associated with technology transfer to the local JV. Thus, the local firm prefers an equity JV to a license to overcome the transaction cost associated with this uncertainty/complexity.

Although the number of foreign suppliers that have the appropriate technology depends on the product–market of the local firm, it can be reasonably assumed that few satisfy the local firm's choice criteria in terms of price and quality of technology, and the capability and reputation of the technology supplier. A small number of suitable technology suppliers results in the local firm's greater degree of dependence on the foreign MNC, both for adapting the technology to the local environment, and for ensuring its future development. The MNC's real/

perceived failure to fulfill its commitment under the license would result in costly haggling and bargaining over contract terms. With the local firm having no or few alternative sources for the supply of technology, the situation of small numbers potentially threatens failure of a technology transfer contract. However, the local firm's dependence on the MNC can be alleviated by structuring a JV that offers incentives to the foreign partner to voluntarily fulfill its commitments. This convergence of incentives of local and foreign partners for JV success is achieved through mutual investment in JV assets and through rules for sharing JV costs and benefits (Beamish and Banks, 1987; Kogut; 1988). The alignment of incentives ensures that JV problems are resolved for mutual benefit and in a spirit of cooperation rather than conflict. Thus, an equity JV can overcome the transaction cost due to small numbers more efficiently, and is preferred over license as a means of obtaining technology from MNCs.

Since local partners usually seek technology for growth and diversification, it involves the commitment of a large amount of financial and managerial resources. These investments are largely in assets in the form of plant and machinery and learning, which are specialized and dedicated to a specific process or product. If the foreign technology licensing firm acts opportunistically, and the local firm has no alternative use of these assets, especially when there are only a small number of alternative technology suppliers, the technology transfer license is likely to fail. In the case of a JV, since both partners have a mutual commitment in dedicated assets, it is in their interest to ensure its success. This reduces the likelihood of opportunism, and alleviates the potential problem associated with asset specificity and intensity. According to Kogut (1988), ''it is by *mutual hostage positions* through joint commitment of financial or real assets that superior alignment of incentives is achieved, and the agreement on the division of profits or costs is stabilised'' (italics in original). A JV is therefore more efficient in overcoming the transaction cost associated with *asset specificity and intensity*, and is the preferred mode for obtaining technology from foreign MNCs as compared with licensing.

When a local firm licenses technology from an MNC, it faces the risk of opportunistic behavior by the foreign technology supplier: such a supplier might supply outdated technology, refuse to provide managerial support to ensure successful technology transfer or grant entry into a local market either directly or through another licensee in contravention of the license agreement. Such actions could create problems in the administration and enforcement of license terms, resulting in failure in the form of license renegotiation or termination. According to Beamish and Banks (1987), ''if a JV is established in a spirit of mutual trust and commitment to its long-term commercial success, opportunistic behavior is unlikely to emerge.'' Similarly, according to Williamson (1983, in Beamish and Banks, 1987), if these positive attitudes are reinforced with mechanisms for an equitable division of JV costs, benefits, planning and decision making, the partners will be able to pursue self-interest without guile. In such a situation, the local firm would use a JV instead of a license for obtaining technology, since it is more efficient in overcoming the transaction cost due to the MNC's opportunistic behavior.

When a local firm imports a new technology, it inevitably experiences a number of teething problems during its introduction, as well as with the lower-than-expected level of subsequent performance, because of inadequate adaptation. Due to bounded rationality, not all contingencies can be foreseen and included in the license agreement. The technology supplier may refuse assistance to overcome unanticipated problems unless the license terms are renegotiated. Frequent bickering and renegotiation signals failure of the technology transfer license, even if it is not terminated. In contrast, bounded rationality is not a serious problem in a JV, since both partners are interested in and committed to the JV's success. The foreign partner monitors JV performance and provides the needed technological support to ensure that it remains competitive in the face of changing internal and external environments, such as firm capabilities, competitive conditions, consumer tastes and preferences, and government regulations. A JV is therefore a superior option to a license to overcome the transaction cost associated with bounded rationality.

To adapt a new technology to the local environment, the local firm needs frequent assistance from the technology supplier. In addition, the local firm needs the MNC's support to improve the technology for successfully responding to changes in the competitive and consumer environments. The local firm may also seek help from the MNC to develop its technology for export to world markets. These technological adaptations and improvements require frequent transactions between the local firm and MNC; this may not be agreeable to the technology supplier because of the high cost of transactions, as well as the risk of loss of proprietary knowledge. These transactions cannot be planned and included in the license agreement, owing to the dynamic nature of the environment that drives these exchanges. The MNC may therefore seek frequent renegotiation of the license terms, indicating failure of the license agreement. On the other hand, since both partners will benefit from the superior performance of the JV, frequent transactions of the foreign partner with the JV to monitor and enhance its performance may be perceived as a functional rather than a dysfunctional activity. Thus, a JV is more efficient than a license in reducing the cost associated with high transaction frequency, and is preferred by the local firm as a means of obtaining technology from MNCs.

Information impactedness refers to the failure of markets due to the asymmetry of information available to the parties to the transaction. In the licensing mode, the technology supplier may not reveal information that is critical for successfully exploiting the new technology. For example, the MNC may refuse to disclose full information about the limitations of and opportunities associated with using the new technology. It may also share only the know-how and not the know-why of the new technology. The "know-why" may enable the local firm to develop the technology for other applications, resulting in a potential loss to the MNC in appropriating returns from these new applications. Because of these limitations, a local firm may prefer not to use the licensing mode for obtaining technology, causing the market for such transactions to fail. In a JV, however, mutual trust, investment in dedicated assets and the rules for sharing costs and benefits result in alignment of interests, and ensure the commitment of both partners to the JV's long-term success. The foreign partner perceives a lower risk of misappropriation of technology and is more open to revealing the technological know-how and know-why, as well as providing state-of-the-art technology to the local JV. In such a situation, a JV is more efficient than a license in reducing the costs associated with information impactedness, and so local firms prefer it for obtaining technology from MNCs.

In summary, a joint venture is more efficient than a license in overcoming Williamson's transactions costs associated with the local firm's acquisition of technology from foreign MNCs. Since a joint venture is perceived to be more efficient in fulfilling the short-term and long-term needs of the local firm, it is preferred over the license for obtaining a new technology.

CONCLUSIONS

This chapter discusses the changing pattern of competition in the domestic market that is evolving in many developing countries in response to two major structural reforms—rapid transformation of centrally planned economies to market-based economies, and removal of barriers to international trade and investment flows. This change has generated new and complex dimensions of competition between local and foreign firms, with the technology foundations of these new competitive forces becoming increasingly international. In addition, there is evidence of increasing homogeneity of buyer behavior (both consumer and industrial) across countries. To sustain a competitive position in the new environment, existing local firms are forced to acquire new technology from foreign MNCs. Although firms can obtain technology through a license or a JV, it is argued that under a given set of conditions, a JV is more efficient than a license in overcoming Williamson's transaction costs associated with acquiring a new technology. The model in Figure 12.4 summarizes the discussion in this chapter about the process that drives the imperative for new technology acquisition by local firms through equity JVs.[3] It is possible to empirically test either the complete model or some parts of it.

Although the transaction cost theory has been used in the literature to explain the use of IJVs from the perspective of foreign MNCs, this chapter contributes to our understanding of IJVs by explaining its rationale from a new perspective of the local partner. Since IJV is a complex organizational arrangement, seeing it from the perspective of both partners will enable firms to better understand and successfully create and manage the IJV relationship.

The chapter also has several limitations. First, the higher efficiency of IJVs under certain conditions does not imply that the IJV is the best choice for all firms under all conditions. When the transaction cost is not significantly high,

Figure 12.4
New Technology Acquisition Model

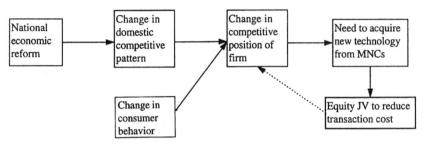

or when the transaction is simple and not repetitive, firms may use the licensing mode to obtain technology from foreign MNCs. For example, if a firm is interested in solving a specific problem, such as the redesign of a standard component or a subassembly for an automobile, it may be more efficient to acquire the technology through a one-shot license instead of forming a joint venture. Thus, if the technology is simple, static and inexpensive, a license may be adequate, but if it is complex, costly and dynamic/adaptive requiring continuous improvements, a JV may be preferable. The choice of whether to obtain technology through a license or a JV, therefore, has to be evaluated on a case-by-case basis, and is contingent on factors such as the local firm's short-term and long-term goals, firm needs and capabilities, the availability of technology suppliers and their preferences, the product–market in which the firm is operating, as well as consumer, competitive and regulatory environments. Future research may use the transaction cost theory to provide a detailed explanation of the conditions under which a license, rather than a joint venture, is more efficient (transaction cost economizing), and should therefore be used as the preferred mode by local firms to acquire technology from MNCs.

Second, the transaction cost theory is static and does not explain the inherently dynamic characteristics of the JV process. According to Hennart (1988), "one way to make it dynamic would be to focus on the speed and predictability of the rate of decay of some of the advantages traded in JVs, particularly knowledge."

Third, since opportunism is an unobservable construct (Godfrey and Hill, 1995), it cannot be easily operationalized and measured. The empirical validation of transaction cost theory therefore becomes difficult. Furthermore, as opportunism can only be realized *ex post* (and in certain ambiguous situations not realized at all), the transaction cost framework can only be used for *ex post* rationalization, and not for *ex ante* prediction of entry mode choice (Godfrey and Hill, 1995).

Finally, firms may have considerations other than efficiency for choosing a specific mode for acquiring technology from the MNC. For example, a local firm may have a strategic/competitive objective of creating entry barriers and eliminating competition through arrangements such as exclusive rights to new technology in a country or a region, (Bain, 1956, in Teece, 1985; Hymn, 1976, in Kogut, 1988; Kogut, 1988). Future research may be directed towards empirically testing the ability of transaction cost theory not only to explain the use of IJVs by local firms, but also to provide explanations beyond that offered by strategic/competitive considerations.

NOTES

1. I would like to thank Tom Vonk for his suggestions on typology in an earlier draft of the chapter.

2. I would like to thank Timothy Devinney for his suggestions on transaction cost theory in an earlier draft of the chapter.

3. I would like to thank David Midgley for suggesting the summary model in an earlier draft of the chapter.

REFERENCES

Bain, J. S. 1956. *Barriers to New Competition*. Cambridge, MA: Harvard University Press. In Teece (1985).

Beamish, P. W. and Banks, J. C. 1987, summer. Equity Joint Ventures and the Theory of the Multinational Enterprise. *Journal of International Business Studies* 18(2): 1–16.

Culpan, R. (ed.). 1993. *Multinational Strategic Alliances*. New York: International Business Press.

Dunning, J. H. and Rugman, A. M. 1985, May. The Influence of Hymer's Dissertation on the Theory of Foreign Direct Investment. *American Economic Review* 75(2): 228–232.

Ellis, S. and Shires, D. 1995, October. All the World's Now Our Stage. *The Australian Financial Review*: 1, 31.

Geringer, J. M. and Hebert, L. 1989. Control and Performance of International Joint Ventures. *Journal of International Business Studies* 20(2): 235–254.

Godfrey, P. C. and Hill, C. W. L. 1995, October. The Problem of Unobservables in Strategic Management Research. *Strategic Management Journal* 16(7): 519–533.

Hennart, J. F. 1988, July–August. A Transaction Cost Theory of Equity Joint Ventures. *Strategic Management Journal* 9(4): 361–374.

Hymer, S. 1976. *The International Operations of National Firms: A Study of Direct Foreign Investment*. Cambridge, MA: MIT Press. In Dunning and Rugman (1985).

Kogut, B. 1988, July–August. Joint Ventures: Theoretical and Empirical Perspectives. *Strategic Management Journal* 9(4): 319–332.

Levitt, T. 1983, May–June. The Globalisation of Markets. *Harvard Business Review* 61: 92–102.

Ohmae, K. 1986. Becoming a Triad Power: The New Global Corporation. *International Marketing Review* 3(3): 7–20.

Polanyi, M. 1967. *The Tacit Dimension*. New York: Doubleday. In Culpan (1993).

Stuckey, J. and White, D. 1993. When and When *Not* to Vertically Integrate. *Sloan Management Review* 34(3): 71–83.

Stuckey, J. A. 1983. *Vertical Integration and Joint Ventures in the Aluminium Industry*. Cambridge, MA: Harvard University Press.

Teece, D. J. 1985, May. Multinational Enterprise, Internal Governance, and Industrial Organisation. *American Economic Review*. 75(2): 233–238.

Van De Ven, A. H. and Joyce, W. F. (eds.) 1981. *Perspectives on Organisation Design and Behaviour*. New York: John Wiley and Sons.

Van De Ven, A. H. and Poole, M. S. 1995. Explaining Development and Change in Organisations. *Academy of Management Review* 20(3): 510–540.

Williamson, O. E. 1975. *Markets and Hierarchies: Analysis and Antitrust Implications— A Study in the Economics of Internal Organisations*. New York: Free Press. In Beamish and Banks (1987).

Williamson, O. E. 1983, September. Credible Commitments: Using Hostages to Support Exchange. *American Economic Review* 73(4): 519–540. In Beamish and Banks (1987).

Williamson, O. E. 1985. *The Economic Institutions of Capitalism*. New York: Free Press. In Kogut (1988).

Williamson, O. E. and Ouchi, W. G. 1981. *The Markets and Hierarchies and Visible Hand Perspectives*. In Van De Ven and Joyce (1981).

PART V

Country-Specific Experiences

CHAPTER 13

Perfecting Globalization in India: Blending Western Technology with the Indian Ethos

UMESH C. GULATI

Culture, like other economic resources, is necessary for the economic growth of any nation. But only a few countries, such as Japan and the four Asian Tigers, South Korea, Taiwan, Singapore and Hong Kong, have effectively harnessed this resource for rapid economic development. These countries have used their cultural resources by optimally combining the Confucian ethic with Western technology. This chapter advocates a similar blending of the Hindu ethic based on the ancient Indian culture with the market model based on Western technology. The chapter discusses the salient features of the Indian culture and the Hindu ethic which can be cultivated through every level of education, from high school to college and university, and through periodic workshops and retreats for both government and corporate workers. Through a proper blending of Western technology with the Indian ethos, India can also match the rate of economic growth achieved by the rapidly growing Asian Tigers. A hopeful sign has become evident in the West, too: an increasing emphasis on blending Eastern spiritual values with Western market values.

INTRODUCTION

The 1991 economic reforms brought about by Prime Minister Narasimha Rao and Finance Minister Manmohan Singh (R&S reforms) were a major turning point in the history of economic policy-making in India since its independence from the British rule. Faced by a severe economic crisis reflected in stagnant economic growth, high inflation and unemployment, enormous accumulation of foreign debt and plummeting foreign exchange reserves, the Congress party leadership was convinced that it must abandon its failed strategy of economic management geared to the establishment of a socialist pattern of society and a self-reliant closed economy.

Industrial Regulation

To achieve a socialist pattern of society, successive Indian governments from Nehru to Gandhi created a network of licensing, direct control and a quota system. This was done for the express purpose of attaining rapid economic growth, expanding employment opportunities, reducing poverty and decreasing inequalities in income and wealth in the country. However, little thought was given to the effect of the control mechanism on the allocative efficiency of the economic system (Gulati, 1993). As a result, the system of licensing and control created a society in which Indian industry became highly monopolistic with all the characteristics of inefficiency and lack of will to compete. Bureaucrats, who were responsible for implementing the regulation, control and licensing mechanism became enormously powerful and corrupt. Thus was formed an ''iron triangle of business, bureaucrats, and politicians'' around the regime (Bhagwati, 1988).

New Industrial Policy Statement

The Congress government under Prime Minister Narasimha Rao issued a New Industrial Policy Statement (NIP) on July 24, 1991 relating to (1) industrial licensing, (2) foreign investment, (3) foreign technology agreements, (4) public sector policy and (5) Monopoly and Restrictive Trade Practices Act (Government of India, 1991). Accordingly, industrial licensing was abolished for all industries except those specified, regardless of investment level. Foreign investment was welcomed, and the government offered automatic approval for direct investment for up to 51 percent foreign equity in 34 industries. By the same token, automatic approval would also be granted to technological agreements between foreign investors and the Indian industry. In order to encourage domestic investment in R&D, the government abolished the requirement for hiring foreign technicians and foreign testing of indigenously developed technologies. The Monopolies and Restrictive Trade Practices Act (MRTP Act), which previously regulated industrial expansion, establishment of new industrial units, merger, amalgamation and takeover, was stripped of these powers and instead would focus on controlling unfair or restrictive business practices. Finally, the reforms package called for the privatization of nonviable state-owned enterprises or ''sick industrial units,'' which had losses of $1.5 billion in 1993.

CULTURE: ITS MEANING AND SIGNIFICANCE

The R&S reforms have introduced a major cultural revolution in the Indian politico-economic system. Culture is essentially a human capacity for adapting to changing circumstances and transmitting this coping skill and knowledge to subsequent generations. It gives people "a *sense* of who they are, of belonging, of how they should behave, and of what they should be doing" (Harris and Moran, 1991: 12). One of the greatest statesmen-philosophers of twentieth-century India, C. Rajagopalachari, defines culture as "the sum-total of the way of living built up by groups of human beings and transmitted from one generation to another" (1963: 9). American cultural anthropologist, Gary Ferraro defines culture as "everything that people have, think, and do as members of their society" (1994: 17). The culture of a given society thus refers to the prevailing economic, educational and political systems, ideas, values, customs, beliefs and socially acceptable conduct and behavior of a specific group. In other words, culture, is a "collective programming of the mind" and refers to a set of unique solutions to common human problems facing people in that country (Hofstede, 1991).

The primary source for transmitting a culture from one generation to another is through the educational process, which takes place within individual families, schools and colleges. In other words, far from being genetically transmitted, culture is learned. A corollary of this statement is that culture cannot be transmitted through a government's fiat or legislation. Without a proper educational system for the transmittal of society's culture, government legislation will degenerate into a counterculture that may be completely opposed to what the government intended to achieve in the first place. This does not, however, mean that a society does not need any laws and other mechanisms of social control that keep citizens from infringing on the rights of other people.

Cultural Change

As Ferraro reminds us, any anthropological account of any society is a snapshot view of one particular time (1994: 26). Thus, no culture is static but is in the process of change. This cultural change (that is, the introduction of new ideas, thoughts, values or material objects) occurs as a result of both internal and external pressures. Cultural anthropologists call the first type of cultural change discovery or invention, while they speak of the second type as the cultural diffusion, spreading or borrowing of cultural items from one society to another. Indeed, most of the cultural change that occurs in all societies is the result of this cultural borrowing, for it is far easier to borrow someone else's invention or discovery (solution, that is) than to rediscover the solution to the common human problems by themselves.

Although this cultural borrowing is a continuing process in all societies, it is a *selective* process. If not for this selective cultural diffusion, today there would be just one culture throughout the world, a sort of cultural uniformity and stagnation. Marketing experts will attest to this selective cultural borrowing because they are always conscious of how and to what extent specific products are likely to become accepted in different cultures. All economic progress has resulted from the optimum combination of economic resources. According to Harris and Moran, culture, too, is a resource. "By combining the best in varied cultures . . . , multiple effects and complex solutions can result. Synergy is separate parts functioning together to create a greater whole and to achieve a common goal" (1991: 11). One objective of this chapter is to investigate how India must absorb and face the challenge of a new global culture with borderless markets.

CULTURAL INTERPRETATION OF THE 1991 REFORMS

Prime Minister Jawaharlal Nehru launched the first cultural revolution in India in the late 1940s after the country achieved its independence from the British rule. The basic aim of this revolution was to establish a Fabian-style socialist pattern of society, which would be informed less by considerations of one's caste, class and position in society than by the spirit of cooperation. Nehru thought that government could be an instrument of bringing about a humane society. Toward that end, all government policies were geared to owning and controlling a vast sector of the Indian economy. India was set on the road toward cultural transformation from a predominantly agricultural economy to a more industrial society, and the motivation for transformation was provided not by private profit but by social gain.

It should also be noted that in the late 1950s and early 1960s, while the United States was drawing Taiwan and South Korea into its market-type cultural orbit, providing free access to its vast market for their exports, and targeting a large share of American economic and military aid for those countries (Gulati, 1992), India was framing its development plans in the image of an highly autarchic Russian model. Understandably, while South Korean and Taiwanese plans were aimed at helping private businesses make investments, expand production in strategic industries and export, Indian plans were increasingly directed toward the expansion of the public sector and restricting that of the private sector. The socialist culture in which private business was always suspected of maximizing profits at the expense of consumers and workers came to permeate the whole Indian society and guided government decisions. Contrary to government intentions for speeding growth through cooperation rather than competition, the slow growth of production and markets created conditions in which everyone—bureaucrats, businesses, unions and politicians alike—distrusted everyone else and were driven to serve only their own selfish interests.

Second Cultural Revolution

The modus operandi of such a system was the "grease money" (i.e., corruption). Without this grease money, no government decision could be carried out. While the government had effective control over the economy through its network of license and quota mechanism, anyone could get out of this net if they were willing to pay a proper "rent" to the rent-seeking bureaucrats and politicians acting as facilitators. Thus, corruption, was a saving grace in an otherwise stagnant economy, at least for a tiny minority of people. Thanks to the collapse of the Soviet communism and the disintegration of the Soviet system on which India relied for its export markets—trading its own poor quality products for their poor quality products—and for military support, the R&S economic policy change in 1991 inaugurated the second cultural revolution in India and accepted the market culture. It rejected Nehru's thesis that socialism was inherently superior to capitalism in producing economic development in a country like India, or the government was better equipped to control inherent greed and acquisitiveness to make profits than the market. The 1991 cultural revolution accepted the principle of businesses making their decisions based on the market forces. Like the governments in Southeast Asian countries, Japan and South Korea, henceforth India too would actively support private business, promote education, develop infrastructure and seek foreign capital investment. Within a short five years, market opening initiatives changed the whole business environment and yielded excellent results: the GDP growth rate reached 6 percent, industrial production was growing at the double-digit rate, foreign exchange reserves were at a comfortable level of around $20 billion and foreign investors were forging alliances with Indian businesses at a steady pace. Whether these reforms will succeed in lifting India's growth rate to the Southeast Asian level will, however, depend on its ability to blend this new market culture and legitimization of private profit with the traditional Indian ethos of selfless work for the benefit of all.

CULTURAL TRANSFORMATION OF JAPAN AND THE FOUR ASIAN TIGERS

During the first and second cultural revolutions affecting India's economic policy-making, the choice of instrument of change was between government and market; the instrument of culture was not even an issue in the debate. Since Indian business was never an idol of the Indian masses, they successively elected Congress governments because they seemed to serve the interest of the little guy. Besides, culture acts through family training, tradition, religious belief, literature and education. Culture uses the internal force, or what Stephen Covey calls the "inside-out" approach (1989), to curb overindulgence, as compared to governmental force which works from the outside. Perhaps for that reason, too, the activist Nehru relied on the governmental instrument.

This, however, does not explain why no one in the country at that time, Nehru aside, considered culture an effective instrument of economic and social change in India. This could be attributed to a general belief that India was a backward country, that its religion was "otherworldly" and, in fact, was the cause of India's economic backwardness and political weakness, and that religion itself needed a heavy dose of reformation. In addition, the prevailing view among the economists was to follow the Marxian thesis that ethics and ideology were no more than reflections of underlying material conditions—in particular economic conditions—and therefore had no part to play in economic change within a society. In contrast, Max Weber's view that the "Protestant Ethic" was the primary cause of growth and development of capitalism in England was largely rejected because either he oversimplified Calvinism or his theory could not explain the equally robust growth of non-Protestant societies like Germany and France. This discounting of culture and the cultural ethos was the accepted paradigm in almost all economic development discussions until at least the late 1970s. Even the free marketers who rejected the Marxian approach to economic development have paid little attention to the role of culture in economic change. During the last 15 years, this view has changed in response to the unexpectedly spectacular rates of economic growth in Japan and the East and Southeast Asian countries. Although the economics establishment dominated by the United States and England continues to maintain that such rapid rates of growth in these countries are the result of market-oriented policies, strong disclaimers have come from equally renowned scholars (see, for instance, Deyo, 1987 and Johnson, 1982). This author, too, had joined the disclaimers of the antiestablishment (Gulati, 1989, 1992). However, the whole debate tended to be over the question of whether the development experience of the successful Asian countries could only be explained by free market policies, and to what extent strong government guidance and creative intervention played a major role in the rapid transformation of these economies.

The Japanese Ethos and the Confucian Ethic

Hofstede and Bond (1988) wondered why, during 1965 and 1985, the per capita GNP growth rates of the four Asian Tigers and Japan varied between 4.7 and 7.6 percent, while it remained below 4 percent for most other countries for the same period. It should be noted that all these countries have a collectivist culture in contrast to the Western individualist culture. Moreover, these countries share common Confucian roots and their thinking style is synthetic, whereas Western thinking is analytical. Thus, Hofstede and Bond believe that the success of these countries could be at least partially due to their cultural preferences.

Earlier, economics professor Michio Morishima (1982), had asserted that the secret of Japanese success that transformed a poor, war-ravaged country after its defeat in 1945 lay in combining Western technology and the Japanese ethos. It is this ethos that was at the heart of the harmonious relationship among government, business and labor working together for the country, company and the people in general. At the top of this combination was the government bureaucracy headed by the MITI and the Ministry of Finance. Together these ministries provided what Johnson (1982) calls the "administrative guidance," which selected strategic industries and sectors that needed special government support and promotion. At the microlevel, both company managers and workers regarded "unlimited dedication to the enterprise" as the highest virtue. Young nonowner managers who came to manage companies after the breakup of Zaibatsu were driven more by improving the enterprises' national and international position than by increasing their profits or their own salaries. "The attitude of such managers was comparable to that of true scholars who believe that the achievement of academic results is more important than the accumulation of wealth'' (Morishima, 1982: 169).

Confucius advocated what Morishima calls the principle of virtuous government, a government that would strengthen the people by means of morality and serve naturally to bring about order in society by raising the level of virtue among them. Missing in this list of virtues is loyalty, which according to Morishima is common to both Japan and Korea. Loyalty (*chung*) in Japan essentially means sincerity aimed at total devotion to one's lord. According to Morishima, loyalty along with "filial piety and duty to one's seniors formed a trinity of values which regulated within society the hierarchic relationships based on authority, blood ties and age respectively'' (1982).

Confucius' greatest achievement lay in throwing open to a great number of people the culture and education that had hitherto been the monopoly of the aristocracy. This secularization of education in Japan began in the Tokugawa era (1603–1867), but accelerated as the Meiji government spread Confucianism through compulsory education. It was every young man's dream to become a Samurai because he received the highest esteem because of his education.

Notice that in the Confucian ethic there is no implication for downgrading the importance of accumulating wealth. Nor is the need for making profit deprecated for business expansion. What *is* downgraded is the accumulation of wealth for its own sake (Tu Weiming et al., 1992). Thus, an apparent distinction was made between means and ends. In Confucian societies, the hero-merchant must be motivated not by a desire for personal profit, but by a desire to ease the living conditions of the people, on the one hand, and to keep the state strong and independent on the other. In other words, you can pursue profit but only for the love of humanity and the nation.

Purpose of Education

It also follows that the basic aim of education in a Confucian society is different from that in the West. As Dore points out (Tu Weiming et al., (1992), and individual's level of education determines his or her station and position in the Confucian society. In turn, individuals who rise in society by means of a tough examination system, an important feature of the educational system in East Asia, can derive legitimacy for their position and delight in being a meritocratic elite rather than a hereditary property elite. Moreover, unlike Europe and American where the schools emphasize the transmission of culture and skills, leaving the transmission of moral values to churches, in Japan and the East Asian societies, schools have served all three functions. The role of the

ethics classes in Japanese schools has been identified as extremely important in
the diffusion of the elite norms to the Japanese populace over the last century.

Fundamental to this ethical education is the need to provide a holistic vision
of linking the self, family, community and state. This requires inseparability of
moral character on the one hand and political leadership on the other. So, the
emphasis is on self-cultivation and on developing empathy for the concerns of
the family, community, corporation and the nation. Harris and Moran note that
in the work environment, the greatest motivation for workers is not the size of
their raise or the position they attain, but the development of what they call
"internal excellence" (1991: 37). In the wake of the American occupation after
World War II, Thomas Rohlen (1978) has shown that Japanese businessmen
were afraid of losing their "spirit." Thus it was that the Japanese corporations
developed a system of military-style training and Zen meditation practices
among the entry-level executives or management trainees to sustain and expand
their consciousness and cultivate their sense of service to the corporation in
which they worked.

BASIC VALUES OF INDIAN CULTURE

At the surface it appears that the Confucian ethic is quite different from the
Western or Protestant ethic in that while in the Confucian an individual must
serve the larger interest of the group, family, company or state, the individual's
interest is superior to any other interest in the West. Despite this contrast of
values between the two cultures, they share one common element. Both cultures
pertain to the sociopolitical dimension of their respective societies. In the West,
political democracy and market economy provide maximum economic welfare
for the individual, and what is good for the individual is good for the society
as a whole. In the Confucian societies of China, Japan and the Four Tigers the
market economy and administrative guidance lead to the greatest welfare of a
group or nation, and what is good for the group is good for the individual.
Either way, then, the pursuit of the Protestant and Confucian ethics leads to the
strengthening of society as a whole.

Spiritual Dimension

The basic feature of the Indian culture which at once distinguishes it from
both the Protestant ethic and the Confucian ethic is the spiritual dimension that
is added to the sociopolitical dimension in the other two cultures (Ranganathananda, 1987). There is not the least downgrading of the sociopolitical aspect
in the Indian culture. Because of nearly one thousand years of foreign rule,
spiritual, moral, economic and social degradation no doubt pervaded The whole
Indian society. It was wrongly associated both in India and abroad with the view
that the Hindus of India were "otherworldly," that Indians were interested only
in their personal salvation or emancipation (*moksha*) by retiring into forests or

mountain caves, and were not concerned about social ethics. This view is contrary to Hindu scriptures and the intuitive knowledge of every Hindu, even though they may not understand their true significance. Instead of promoting or emphasizing the negative virtue of otherworldliness, the Indian culture has a more positive flavor. The Indian culture accepts four legitimate and basic human desires: *dharma* or righteousness, *artha* or wealth, *kama* or sense pleasure, and *moksha* or freedom (from the cycle of birth and death) through direct communion with God or the Infinite. Of these, the first three belong to the realm of worldly values; the fourth is called the supreme value. The fulfillment of the first three paves the way for the fourth, moksha. Enjoyment, if properly guided, can be sublimated into spiritual experience.

It is this synthesis of sociopolitical and spiritual dimensions that is capable of generating total "human excellence" (Ranganathananda, 1990) or the so-called cultural synergy. Western technology and the market organization are essential for unleashing human energies for material progress and accumulation of wealth. But by themselves they soon begin to degenerate into excessive materialism in which corruption, crime, violence, social and political unrest become the order of the day. Even in a country like the United States, which is culturally quite exposed to the market system and materialism, globalization—the stretching of the market system to its limits—has generated a great deal of "economic anxiety" (*Business Week*, March 11, 1996) among every segment of society. To avoid the trauma of the new cultural revolution and to create a stable business, social and political environment, India must cultivate its spiritual dimension and maximize the benefits of technological revolution and globalization. As was noted earlier, such a cultural synergy has promoted the rapid economic growth and transformation of Japan and the four Tiger countries, and is capable of doing the same or even better for India.

Indian Individualism

Implied in the foregoing discussion is the individual and his ultimate goal in life in India. The individual is at the center of Indian culture whose welfare is supreme. But it is not the same kind of individualism as it is understood in the Protestant ethic or Western culture. In the West the emphasis is on social ethics or the so-called the sociopolitical dimension of a culture; in India the emphasis is on personal ethics and the spiritual dimension—what Ranganathananda (1987) calls the "character excellence" or the Hindu ethic. Hindu sages and Rishis argued that since society consisted of individuals, social welfare would follow as a matter of course if individuals themselves were virtuous (Nikhilananda, 1982:82). Another reason why the Rishis did not emphasize social ethics was that ancient Aryans had set up within the caste, or better, the *Jaati* system, a very fine mechanism of rendering help to the needy. Under this system everyone in his own Jaati was expected to perform his assigned duties, which included, among other things, sharing his prosperity and influence with one's less fortunate beings. According to Rajagopalachari (1963: 30), "This element of our culture, if disentangled from the need for purity in public administration and restricted to personal assistance and private sacrifice, can be looked upon as a loose form of trusteeship governing conduct in one's group." It is from this idea of the individual's responsibility of helping others in a community that Mahatma Gandhi developed his principle of the trusteeship form of socialism. Finally, the Hindu Rishis believed that more important than an organized charity to less fortunate people was the need for the Brahmins to provide knowledge (*vidya*), both secular and spiritual, to the rest of the community. For social charity cannot permanently eradicate suffering, but education can. The Brahmins acquired the top position in the caste hierarchy precisely for their love for knowledge and sharing it with other castes below.

Basic Values

The basic elements of the Hindu ethic essential for human excellence or self-perfection are austerity or *tapas*, self-control, renunciation, nonattachment and concentration. Tapas is the voluntary act of experiencing privation in order to achieve something higher in life. The discipline of tapas involves pain and enables a person to curb his or her impulses for self-indulgence and for the acquisition of political power. Tapas in the Upanishads meant intense thinking, the same sort of thinking that precedes creative work, making a person indifferent to his or her comforts or discomforts. These scriptures regarded tapas as a supreme value that tranquilizes the outer and inner sense organs and helps concentrate the energies of the mind and the senses. According to Ranganathananda, tapas is at the root of every human creative act or achievement, be it literary or artistic, scientific or spiritual (1990b: 379).

Along with tapas, self-control is the quintessence of the Indian culture. The sense organs that are ordinarily inclined toward enjoying material objects and seek the pleasant should be restrained and instead be directed to achieving internal peace and fulfillment, and seeking the noble. The Indian Rishis believed that self-control was essential to calm the nerves without which no spiritual truths or secular knowledge could be grasped. Self-control does not mean the deprivation and torture of the body. An optimum level of self-control is achieved by using an appropriate mix of will-power and discrimination. The Bhagvad Gita and the Buddhist scriptures recommend a middle path which requires that a person be "temperate in his food and recreation, temperate in his exertion in work, temperate in sleep and waking" (Nikhilananda, 1982: 86).

Renunciation is one of the cherished values in the Indian culture for achieving perfection in life. The idea behind this value is not to leave this world for another world, but to renounce "worldliness," which includes self-indulgence, conceit, greed, egotism and attachment. In fact, India's saint-patriot Vivekananda (1863–1902), urged Indians to enjoy life with zest, but to direct that zest toward serving the Lord in man. In other words, work must be performed because it is a means to serve some higher purpose rather than make money for its own sake. Work performed in this spirit or out of love is more productive and effective than that performed out of compulsion of some duty.

Karma Yoga

Two other values extolled by the Indian sages are nonattachment and concentration. These values fortify the individual's onward march toward achieving perfection and human excellence. The virtue of nonattachment is the essence of the Bhagvad Gita, the most popular scripture of the Hindus. Work done in the spirit of detachment and without regard to any reward is called Karma Yoga, or the discipline of work. Thus, it is not renunciation of action itself, but renunciation of the longing for the fruit that is the secret of Karma Yoga. In the Hindu tradition, work done without regard to its fruit is considered worship (Nikhilananda, 1982: 101).

Raja Yoga

The Indian Rishis consider concentration or meditation the supreme (Raja) method of experiencing the higher reality by direct perception. It is the most effective way of achieving character excellence or perfection. Concentration is an instrument by which one can sharpen the penetrating power of the mind and learn the secrets not only of the world outside but also of the world within. All great achievements of human civilization, from the Taj Mahal to Michelangelo's statue of Moses to Einstein's theory of relativity, were first conceived in the mind. Indian Rishis have recognized that achieving character excellence through concentration is very difficult, but is nevertheless achievable by practice and nonattachment.

Economic Implications of the Hindu Ethic

The five elements that form the Hindu ethic—*tapas*, self-control, renunciation, nonattachment, and concentration—provide a strong and sustained basis for rapid economic growth in India. The virtues of austerity and self-control are the necessary forces that encourage people to save and discourage them from conspicuous consumption. An economy's rate of growth is directly proportional to its rate of saving. An important economic variable that is common to all four Asian Tigers and the other fast growing countries of Southeast Asia is their very high saving rate of 30 percent or more. India's rate of saving is around 25 percent, but it has the potential of matching the savings rates of these fast growing countries given the esteem in which people leading a simple and austere life are held. The same virtues of austerity and self-control also place a high premium on patience and forbearance for the results of their strivings. In other words, like their Southeast Asian neighbors, the Indians, too, are capable of developing and nurturing long-term relationships rather than simply making the "fast buck."

Renunciation exhorts the owners of wealth to consider themselves as trustees for the welfare of their employees rather than as wielders of economic and political power. Unlike Confucius' benevolence which projects the power of the ruler or the employer, the principle of trusteeship that follows from renunciation projects the sense of humility. Selfless work and detachment can induce both greater quantity and quality of work effort, while the virtues of austerity, detachment and concentration provide the bases for analytical and creative thinking and knowledge. This is in sharp contrast to the Confucian ethic, which places so much emphasis on loyalty and obedience and hence leads to conformity and uniformity. The Hindu tradition reflects an extraordinary tolerance for diversity and debate for finding the ultimate truth and knowledge.

Education for Human Excellence

As we have seen, both Western and Confucian societies have adequate means of transmitting their respective cultures through their educational system. In both cultures, the principle of universal education is an accepted fact. The emphasis in the West, however, has been on positivist philosophy, rational thinking and physical and natural sciences. Predictably, the West is technologically the most advanced society. Through technological progress, it has lessened the incidence of poverty, checked disease, eliminated much human suffering, and improved the life expectancy. Confucian societies have been late in adopting Western technology, but their educational system is superior to that of the West. In Confucian societies education is the creed; they are fanatic about educating their children. In addition to teaching Western science and technology, they stress the moral values of filial piety, loyalty and harmony. But, as pointed out earlier, both systems concentrate on the sociopolitical aspect of culture, and both leave out the spiritual dimension or the character-excellence aspect of culture, and therefore are potentially destabilizing.

Unfortunately, education has not received as much emphasis in India as it should. Nearly one thousand years of foreign rule had demoralized the elite of India by the nineteenth century. The foreign rulers' main objective was to impose the culture that they had brought with them. Ancient Indian centers of learning were destroyed or made useless. Ironically, some of the ancient scriptures were translated into English by none other than Governor-general Warren Hastings, who was also responsible for laying the foundation for British rule in India. During the nineteenth century, even some of India's brilliant minds, like Raja Rammohan Roy, had thought that India's religion, instead of being the solution for its backwardness, was the problem for many of the country's ills. So they went on to propose legislative solutions for the country's social problems, and encouraged English and Western education among the Indian masses. They were partially right. But their neglect of mass education, both secular and spiritual, led to the creation of a divided society, one elite, educated in Western education and mimicking their English masters, and the other, the illiterate masses, steeped in tradition, superstition, with little hope for the future or the will to better their lives.

After independence, India's economic policy of self-reliance and building a socialist society depleted the treasury, leaving almost nothing for education. Thus, after nearly five decades of independence, one out of every two people in India is illiterate; illiteracy among women is much higher. The insufficient space in schools and colleges is clearly reflected in the intense competition among people belonging to different castes for admission to good schools. An uneducated mother can hardly learn about India's vast cultural tradition; much less can she be a role model for her children. In addition to science, math and the arts which Indian school curricula emphasize, the study of Indian religion and culture should be made compulsory. It is surprising that a culture which prides itself on its catholicity and universality, a culture that teaches that "the Truth is one but sages call it by various names," to quote a verse from Rig Veda, should not do more to make Indian children liberal in outlook, risk taking in commerce, and daring in experimenting with new ideas. In other words, the Indian educational system should be based on the synthesis of two energies, one emanating from developing sociopolitical aspects, making the people socially and economically efficient; and the other emanating from developing the individual's spiritual dimension, thereby enabling one's character efficiency to emerge. Only by fusing these two efficiencies can Ranganathananda's so-called human excellence be developed.

The development of one's spiritual dimension must not however, end with the high school diploma. It must continue throughout postsecondary education into the workplace. In Japan, too, following World War II, Japanese corporate executives were very anxious to continue imparting Confucian values to their managers lest the new Western culture dampen their loyalty to company and country. Today American management is discovering through Zen and transcendental meditation an effective means of bringing harmony and enhancing productivity in their workers, although the workers have exhibited equally great resistance (Austin, 1995). In contrast, in India spirituality and spiritual education are natural, as we can judge from the popularity of telecasts of the Ramayana and Maha Bharat series. Nonetheless, the scope and purpose of such education should be expanded. Specifically, companies should provide facilities to their employees for meditation and offering prayers, and conduct intensive workshops for their managers on India's cultural heritage at least once a year. Government departments also need occasional cultural retreats. These cultural activities at the workplace are the key to developing management's sensitivity toward their employees, creating in them a feeling of trusteeship, harmony between labor and management, love of labor without caring for the reward, and most of all, generating in everyone the zeal to realize their fullest potential or perfection. In this way, cultural synergy can be created for rapidly increasing output, better product quality, and most of all, unleash people's potential for continued material and spiritual progress.

SUMMARY AND CONCLUDING REMARKS

Globalization of markets and market reforms in India have brought about a cultural revolution in the country which is expected to unleash its sociopolitical energy for rapid economic growth. To match the growth rates of other successful Asian countries, however, India must harness its traditional cultural resource and fuse it with the capitalistic-technological culture to create cultural synergy. This chapter discusses the principles underlying Karma Yoga and Raja Yoga that would bring about such a cultural synergy.

Japan and the Four Tiger nations have experienced much higher rates of saving and investment than India. Together with Western technology and outward-looking policies, these higher savings and investment rates have led to higher than usual rates of economic growth in these countries. For example, Rosovsky (in Tu Weiming et al., 1992: 79) has noted that more than a century ago the Japanese government used the country's cultural treasures to accelerate its economic development. In the West, too, a great deal of emphasis is being placed on harnessing spiritual treasures for the individual's all-round development. For example, Covey (1989) has advocated maintaining a proper balance between what he calls production and production capacity (or the P/PC balance). The Indian cultural resource is much wider, deeper and inexhaustible. Regretfully, it remains unexploited, but it must be harnessed. Unless that is done, real globalization will remain a dream.

REFERENCES

Austin, Nancy K. 1995, March. Does Spirituality at Work Work? *Working Women* 88: 26–27.

Bhagwati, Jagdish. 1988, May. Poverty and Public Policy. *World Development*.

Covey, Stephen R. 1989. *The Seven Habits of Highly Effective People*. New York: Simon and Schuster.

Deo, Frederick. 1987. *The Political Economy of the New Asian Industrialism*. Ithaca, NY: Cornell University Press.

Ferraro, Gary P. 1994. *The Cultural Environment of International Business*. Englewood Cliffs, NJ: Prentice-Hall.

Government of India. *Statement of Industrial Policy*. New Delhi: Ministry of Industry, 1991.

Gulati, Umesh C. 1989, April–June. Dynamics of Economic Restructuring in a Small NIC. *The Indian Economic Journal* 37: 40–56.

Gulati, Umesh C. 1992, April. The Foundations of Rapid Economic Growth: The Case of the Four Tigers. *American Journal of Economics and Sociology* 51: 161–172.

Gulati, Umesh C. 1993. Privatization in the Third World: The Case of India. *Proceedings of the 1993 Conference: Selected Papers and Abstracts*. N.P.: Association of Global Business, 262–269.

Harris, Philip and Moran, Robert. 1991. *Managing Cultural Differences*. Houston, TX: Gulf Publishing Co.

Hofstede, G. 1991. *Cultures and Organizations: Software of the Mind*. London: McGraw-Hill.

Hofstede, G. and Bond, M. H. 1988, October. The Confucius Connection: From Cultural Roots to Economic Growth. *Organizational Dynamics* 16: 4–21.

Johnson, Chalmers. 1982. *MITI and the Japanese Miracle: The Growth of Industrial Policy, 1925–1975*. Stanford, CA: Stanford University Press.

Morishima, Michio. 1982. *Why Has Japan Succeeded?* London: Cambridge University Press.

Nikhilananda, Swami. 1982. *Hinduism: Its Meaning for the Liberation of the Spirit*. 2nd ed. Mylapore, India: Sri Ramakrishna Math Printing Press.

Rajagopalachari, C. 1963. *Our Culture*. Bombay: Bhartiya Vidya Bhavan.

Ranganathananda, Swimi. 1987. *Eternal Values for a Changing Society*. Vol. 1. Bombay: Bhartiya Vidya Bhavan.

Ranganathananda, Swami. 1990a. *Swami Vivekananda and Human Excellence*. Harvard University Lecture, Advaita Ashrama, Calcutta.

Ranganathananda, Swami. 1990b. *The Message of the Upanishads*. Bombay: Bhartiya Vidya Bhavan.

Rohlen, Thomas. 1978. The Education of the Japanese Banker. In Daniel I. Okimoto and Thomas P. Rohlen (eds.), *Inside the Japanese System*. Stanford, CA: Stanford University Press, 129–134.

Tu Weiming, et al. (eds.). 1992. *The Confucian World Observed*. Honolulu, HI: East-West Center.

CHAPTER 14

Issues in Economic Liberalization Policies and Globalization: A Case Study of Bangladesh

MOHAMMED ABDUR RAZZAQUE

Since the late 1980s, the People's Republic of Bangladesh has taken several steps to liberalize its protected economy in response to global forces. It has replaced its antiquated pro-socialist economic policies with modern pro-market policies. The adoption of these steps—long opposed by many of the country's policymakers on ideological and other sociopolitical grounds—is indicative of the government's boldness, pragmatism and economic wisdom. Undoubtedly, it has been driven largely by the need to upgrade the country's impoverished economy. No doubt, too, the economic success achieved by its Asia-Pacific neighbors has also played an important role in this respect.

Government sources tend to inflate the success of these policies in the media. However, their claims are not supported by the statistics. Indications abound that these policies have failed to achieve any significant success. Based on a recent exploratory study, this chapter evaluates these policies, identifies some of the reasons for their apparent dismal results and makes some suggestions to policymakers in Bangladesh.

INTRODUCTION

Economically backward nations of the world tend to share a desire to break the poverty circle prevalent in their societies and to achieve economic independence as quickly as possible. However, history will, testify that gaining economic independence is far more difficult than achieving political independence since political autonomy can be negotiated, legislated or won by force through war, whereas economic independence cannot. During the last three decades, the political leaders in many newly independent nations have attempted to induce economic growth and development through quick industrialization, pinning their economic aspirations on the industrial sector. This sector has been viewed as the avenue to fast and accelerated growth in income, leading to surplus instruments in further stimulating development. It is widely believed that successful industrialization enables product diversification, export promotion and import substitution, and creates new jobs. Furthermore, successful industrialization triggers an economic chain reaction resulting in other economic benefits that raise the standard of living and quality of life. The leaders in many economically impoverished nations have now accepted these expected benefits as a matter of faith.

Recent developments indicate that establishment of a free market economy is a prerequisite for the fast-paced industrialization that many less developed nations would like to have. The process of industrialization is basically driven by private sector enterprise, which can operate most efficiently in liberal economic environments. The economic success of the four Asian Tigers and, in recent times, that of other newly emerging economies such as Malaysia, Thailand and Indonesia, exemplify the virtues of liberalization and globalization.

In addition, the global failure of the socialist doctrine in the last decade led most socialist nations to dump the centrally planned system in favor of the open capitalistic system. This action has been instrumental in establishing the market economy as the only means of achieving economic emancipation. As a result, many other countries in the Asia-Pacific region have been motivated to open up and globalize their economies. Furthermore, the expectation that the Asia-Pacific region will continue to be the growth area for a long time to come (Devan, 1994; Kraar, 1992), has generated a growing economic awareness in many nations in the region, prompting them to liberalize their economies. Nations such as Bangladesh, Cambodia, India, Myanmar, Pakistan and Vietnam have followed suit and joined the bandwagon in opening up their economies.

It is too early to evaluate the success of these policies in many of these nations. However, in Bangladesh, there are ominous signs that the policies are not doing very well. The objectives of this chapter are to discuss some of the important issues pertaining to the Bangladesh experience, and to suggest some ways and means to overcome them.

EVOLUTION OF THE CURRENT ECONOMIC POLICY

The People's Republic of Bangladesh has a population of 120 million in an area of 143,998 square kilometers. It has very limited resources and one of the lowest per capita incomes in the world (Nominal—U.S. $224.00, PPP—US$1350). On the eve of Bangladesh's independence from Pakistan in 1971, 36 percent of Bangladesh's total industrial assets was under public ownership (Report of the Expert Committee Report, 1977). However, in March 1972, a little over three months after independence, this sector was substantially enlarged through the large-scale nationalization of industrial units abandoned by the Pakistani industrialists. As a result, the private sector was reduced both in size (Rahman, 1984) and in importance.

First Industrial Policy of Bangladesh, 1972

The First Industrial (Private) Investment Policy of Bangladesh announced in 1972 was heavily influenced by the ideology of freedom from "imperialistic domination." Criticizing the inadequacies of the market economy and private enterprise in facing the challenges of a densely populated, poor agrarian country such as Bangladesh, many influential left-leaning economists and opinion leaders made a strong case for adopting development planning in the country. Furthermore, to be compatible with the government's constitutional commitment to the creation of a socialist economy, this policy set various limits on private investment, which were demotivating for any rational foreign investors. In this policy statement, foreign investment was allowed only in collaboration with the public sector corporations and with a minority equity participation of up to 49 percent. Although full freedom was guaranteed for the transfer of annual profits (net of taxes) and for the repatriation of capital (spread over a number of years), nationalization in some future time (if the asset exceeded a specified limit) loomed large as a major threat. The general maladministration of the state by the ruling party coupled with its mismanagement of the economy completely shattered the morale of the entrepreneurs and destroyed their faith in the government and its institutions. The environment was not at all conducive to overseas investment.

Foreign Private Investment (Promotion and Protection) Act, 1980

The assassination of Bangladesh's founder-president Sheikh Mujibur Rahman in a military coup in 1974 also resulted in the abandonment of his government's socialist economic policies. The new president General Ziaur Rahman represented the son-of-the-soil hardiness of the small landowner and the tenaciousness of the peasant-farmer, combined with the flare of an officer. His economic philosophy was a concoction of a traditional rural-agricultural orientation and a modern urban-industrial orientation (Novak, 1993). In line with this philosophy, the government adopted policies to rejuvenate the rural economy through development of the agricultural sector and introduced an economic agenda geared toward developing a self-sufficient national economy. In 1978, the government announced its general disinclination toward a nationalization policy. It was announced that if exigencies demanded nationalization of any industrial undertaking in the future, just and fair compensation would be paid to the investor in the currency of his or her country of origin. The Foreign Private Investment (Promotion and Protection) Act, 1980, passed by the Bangladesh Parliament, provided legal backing to this commitment. Private enterprise was actively encouraged, and a new generation of domestic entrepreneurs emerged. Almost a decade after ceasing its operations in 1971, the Dhaka Stock Exchange reopened its doors. There were visible signs that the irretrievable economy left behind by the Mujib regime had started to change course for the better.

But the assassination of General Ziaur Rahman in 1981 and subsequent ouster of his democratically elected successor by a military coup in April 1982 pushed the country into yet another state of political instability. A long nine-year rule by the military dictator Lieutenant General Hossain Mohammed Ershad, who staged the 1982 coup, ensued. General Ershad's government has been accused of abuse and misuse of power, lack of accountability, nepotism, mass-scale corruption, expropriation of scarce internal resources as well as foreign aid and other vices (Khan, 1995). These allegations notwithstanding, one cannot deny that some of the visible infrastructure development in Bangladesh and the initiation of liberalized economic and trade policies took place during this period. General Ershad actively pursued privatization and the restructuring of public sector enterprises. A Board of Investment (BOI) was established in 1989 to oversee both local and foreign investments and was placed under the direct supervision of the prime minister. This period also witnessed a gradual restructuring of the economy through a shift in emphasis from the agricultural to other sectors, including industry and service. The share of agriculture in Bangladesh's GDP fell to 36 percent from 55 percent in 1970.

The democratically elected government of Begum Khaleda Zia assumed power in September 1991 by deposing General Ershad. With some cosmetic changes, its government adopted the economic and trade policies of General Ershad and his predecessor General Zia. The emergence of Asia as a center of attraction for investors prompted Bangladesh, like many other countries in the region, to open its economy to global investors, allowing them one more option. To attract foreign investment and to encourage domestic entrepreneurship, the government announced a number of policy reforms commonly referred to as the New Industrial Policy (NIP).

THE NEW INDUSTRIAL POLICY

Incentives

The first of these changes is the implementation of the new industrial policy supported by an open import regime. This provides facilities and other incentives, including duty-free import of capital machinery and raw materials for 100 percent export-oriented industries. In addition, it provides a tax holiday of up to 12 years, exemption of tax on interest on foreign loans, royalty and technical fees, and avoidance of double taxation. Avoidance of double taxation agreements has been signed with Canada, the United Kingdom, Japan, Italy, Sweden, Malaysia, Singapore and South Korea.

It is envisaged that the private sector will play a relatively more important role in Bangladesh than the public sector, which is expected to concentrate primarily on basic infrastructure and human resource development. The large-scale divestiture of state-owned enterprises has been initiated with a view to give credence to the government's commitment to liberalization and to create opportunities for existing as well as new entrepreneurs. Except for five reserved sectors, private funds for establishing independent as well as joint ventures are being sought in all areas of the economy. Potential areas of investment include composite textiles, leather, frozen food, jute goods sector, energy and power generation, minerals and gas/oil exploration, transport and communication, electronics, light industries, tourism, agriculture, agro-based industries and agro-support industries. Bangladesh is one of the three Asian countries (People's Republic of China and Sri Lanka are the other two) that offers unconditional 100 percent foreign equity or ownership in industrial investments.

In addition to enjoying Most Favored Nation (MFN) treatment from a number of countries including the United States, Bangladesh enjoys General System of Preference (GSP) facilities for exports to the United States. Bangladesh has signed bilateral trade and investment agreements with the United States, the United Kingdom, Germany, France, Italy, Belgium, Turkey, Rumania, South Korea and Thailand.

To enable prospective foreign investors to employ non-Bangladeshi employees, issuance of work permits to foreign nationals has been liberalized. Even the granting of permanent resident status and citizenship to foreigners has been simplified. While only U.S.$75,000 nonrepatriable investment in an industrial project is required for granting permanent residentship, the requirement for citizenship is a minimum nonrepatriable investment of U.S.$500,000 or a deposit of US$1 million in any recognized financial institution of Bangladesh.

Protection of Foreign Investors

The Foreign Private Investment (Promotion and Protection) Act of 1980 ensures legal protection to foreign investors against nationalization and expropriation. In addition to guaranteeing repatriation of capital and returns from it, this act also aims at ensuring equitable treatment of foreign investors with local investors with regard to indemnification, compensation, and so on, in the event of loss due to civil commotion and other unforeseen events. Adequate protection is also available for intellectual property rights, such as patents, designs, copyrights and trademarks.

Bangladesh is a signatory to the Multilateral Investment Guarantee Agency (MIGA), International Centre for Settlement of Investment Dispute (ICSID) and Overseas Private Investment Corporation (OPIC). Through MIGA, noncommercial risks of investment in Bangladesh caused by losses arising from currency transfers, expropriation, civil disturbances and war are insured. ICSID is an international organization established to settle investment disputes between states and nationals of different countries. It seeks to encourage greater flow of international investment by providing facilities for the arbitration and conciliation of disputes between host country governments and investors. OPIC, on the other hand, is the most important U.S. government agency and provides greater investment insurance to investors from the United States. In April 1994, Bangladesh accepted IMF Article VIII, which involves an agreement not to restrict payments and transfers for international transactions or to engage in discriminatory currency arrangements (International Trade Finance, 1995).

Trade Liberalization

The government of Bangladesh has also initiated major trade policy reforms by liberalizing imports, rationalizing taxation rules and making the Bangladesh currency taka (È) convertible in the current account. Since 1992, the government has made progress in reducing nontariff restrictions on trade by rationalizing tariff rates and improving export incentives. In addition, a phased program aimed at replacing direct control over trade through the imposition of tariffs is in the final stage now. Except for 93 items (in terms of the Harmonized Systems Classification) classified as restricted on health, security, social and religious grounds, the government has progressively reduced the number of products subject to ban.

A National Tariff Commission established in November 1992 has been working to streamline the customs duty structure. Plans have also been undertaken to rationalize tariffs with a view to curb anti-export bias and sort out various anomalous customs practices. Along with removing nontariff restrictions on imports, simplification of procedures has also been undertaken. Low rates of duty on imports of primary raw materials, moderate rates on intermediate products and high rates on luxury products have been imposed. In the area of exports, the government has allowed many new incentives and improved the existing ones. In order to boost and coordinate export development over the medium term, the government has adopted the Bangladesh Export Development Strategy, 1992–2000. The present structure of tariffs and the import policy are regularly being monitored and reviewed by the government to identify areas requiring further actions.

ACHIEVEMENTS OF THE MEASURES

Any attempt to assess the achievement of the new policy in concrete terms is perhaps premature at this point in time. Government routinely publicizes the success of these economic liberalization policies but has not yet published any statistics to highlight the achievements made. However, prospective investors and experts on Bangladesh give the impression that so far, the responses from foreign investors have not been very encouraging. The large-scale divestiture of state-owned enterprises has perhaps created economic opportunities for a select group of local entrepreneurs, but has done nothing significant to attract foreign investors. In reality, a few of the MNCs operating in Bangladesh since the Pakistan days, have left the country in the last couple of years.

Commitment versus Actual Investment

It has been reported that Bangladesh's fledgling capital market has attracted US$ 200 million in foreign investment (Hossain, 1995). By the end of 1995, the government of Bangladesh expected foreign investment to exceed U.S.$2 billion, which is more than the total amount invested in the country since its independence. Prospective inv tors and their expected investments, according to government sources, are as follows.

Japan	U.S.$ 358 million
Malaysia	276
United Kingdom	192
Hong Kong	117
United States	34

These commitments are for textile, chemical, light industry, electronics and service sectors. However, the latest figures available on direct investment into Bangladesh from overseas tend to give a completely contrary view. In the first half of the 1994–95 fiscal year, investment in the country dropped to a meager U.S.$5 million from U.S.$9 million for the same period the year preceding (*Asiaweek*, 1995).

EVALUATION OF POLICY ACHIEVEMENTS: AN INFORMAL STUDY

To obtain some understanding of the underlying reasons for this discouraging result, a series of informal interviews were held with a cross section of people who might shed some light on the issue. The interviewees included three groups of people. The first included prospective investors from Australia, Canada, Denmark, Great Britain, Japan, Malaysia, Singapore and the United States whose preferred place of investment was the Asia-Pacific region. The second group consisted of Bangladeshi entrepreneurs, managers, civil servants and journalists. The third included academics, economists and professionals in various fields within and outside Bangladesh. The study was carried out during the period between January 1994 and June 1995 and sought information on the following three specific issues:

• If the participant was aware of the economic liberalization policies in Bangladesh.

• If yes, what was his or her opinion about its success.

• What, in his or her opinion, were the reasons for success or failure.

The responses of these diverse groups of people provide ample food for thought for policymakers and other concerned people in Bangladesh. Most of the respondents seemed to be aware of the policies but felt that the policies were largely unsuccessful in attracting foreign investment to the country. Their various reasons for failure can be collapsed into six broad categories:

1. Too ambitious policies
2. Image problem
3. Rise of religious fundamentalism
4. Inadequate infrastructure
5. Wide-scale corruption
6. Poor selling due to bureaucratic wrangling and lack of support and information

Too Ambitious Policies

A large number of the respondents believed that the policies announced by the Bangladesh government are overambitious. Despite their apparent attractiveness, many of the policies appear to emulate the practices of some other nations in the region. The policies have not only failed to capitalize on the strengths of Bangladesh, but have also inadequately "marketed" it to the "target audiences." In addition, some of the so-called incentives lack pragmatism or rational thinking. For example, it is difficult to understand why someone would be interested in paying a million U.S. dollars to become a Bangladesh citizen. The question of attracting Hong Kong Chinese entrepreneurs does not arise since by investing almost half of this amount they can go to advanced countries such as Canada, Australia or Singapore.

Image Problem

Bangladesh's generally poor image in the international arena appears to be one of the unanimously expressed views of the interviewees. Bangladesh's ever-increasing level of poverty and dependence on the international community in the postindependence years, and the ruling government's mismanagement of the economy prompted U.S. Secretary of State Henry Kissinger to dub Bangladesh a "basket case." Although Bangladesh has come a long way in the last 25 years, that poor image of the country persists. Continued political instability, squabbles between political parties and frequent military intervention in the civil administration have all damaged the world's view of Bangladesh. Corruption by political leaders and civil servants, the indecisiveness of decision makers and maladministration of law and order have only added to its poor image. According to a recent report, the "political skepticism" prevailing in Bangladesh since early 1994 is responsible for causing uncertainty regarding the future course of reform actions and affecting Bangladesh's image as a potential host country for foreign direct investment. It is widely believed that a policy reversal such as abandoning the move toward privatization and the market economy is highly unlikely. However, no one is certain how the pace, timing and magnitude of further reform actions in economic, trade and fiscal areas will be affected if there is a change in government.

In Bangladesh, any incoming government customarily changes any policy adopted or initiated by the outgoing government. This has happened time and again, resulting in inconsistencies and a lack of continuity and credibility of policies. Such a phenomenon drastically reduces any investor's confidence in the system. Not only must a consistent set of policies be undertaken but also the governmental policies must have credibility for potential investors. Investors must believe beyond any doubt that the policies of a host government will be of sufficiently long duration that investment will be worthwhile and can be undertaken with adequate reliance on their stability. The attitudes of Bangladesh's leading opposition leaders, as reflected in their various actions, speeches and policy statements, fail to provide a foreign investor with any assurance of permanency of reform measures undertaken by the ruling government.

Rise of Religious Fundamentalism

The rise of religious fanaticism (or what the western press commonly refers to as Islamic fundamentalism) and the government's apparent unwillingness (or inability?) to contain it were also mentioned in the interviews as a demotivator to potential investors. The substitution of Thursday and Friday, respectively, in Bangladesh for the international weekly rest days of Saturday and Sunday was viewed as an economically irrational and imprudent decision by many of the interviewees, regardless of their religious beliefs. Because of this arrangement, an investor's ability to communicate with other nations of the world is effectively reduced to a mere four days. Incidentally, Indonesia and Malaysia, the largest and most developed Muslim countries, respectively, observe the traditional Saturday and Sunday as the rest days.

Inadequate Infrastructure

Poor and inadequate infrastructure has been cited as an important negative factor in attracting foreign investors. Shortage of power and absence of a reliable telecommunications system are strong disincentives for any investor. Other inadequacies related to infrastructure include a poor national transport system and rather outmoded and inadequate port facilities restricting mobility and distribution efficiency. These inadequacies might offset the lure of "cheap land." According to one estimate, U.S.$100 million is needed in the next five years to build and upgrade existing infrastructure in Bangladesh. Any investor would view such a dismal prediction as a strong demotivator.

Wide-scale Corruption

The wide-spread corruption of people in positions of power (e.g., ministers, political leaders, civil servants, bankers) has been viewed as a very strong disincentive toward investing in Bangladesh. Some potential investors experienced solicitation of bribes and kickbacks in the initial stages of launching fact-finding missions. Cutting into deals appears to be a common occurrence. Hossain (1995) reports that an investment plan by a group of Singaporean, Malaysian and Taiwanese investors to relocate a cigarette-lighter manufacturing plant from Taiwan to Bangladesh had to be abandoned when government-backed politicians wanted to cut into the deal. Corruption of political leaders and civil servants acts as a barrier to entry as the demanded kickbacks increase the effective cost of entry into the country. It has been alleged that in many negotiations, Bangladeshi negotiators are more concerned about their personal benefits than about the national interest.

Many interviewees also identified political interference as a stumbling block to investment in Bangladesh. According to some, use of undue influence by people in positions of power (and their family members) is an even worse type of corruption. Because of this, the law and order situation cannot be improved. An investor would think carefully before investing in a society with no law and order. With the current style of politicking that is prevalent in the country, it is impossible to curb such corruption.

Poor Selling: Lack of Support and Information

The study revealed that getting relevant information about Bangladesh is a frustrating experience. A large number of people reported that most of the designated officials in the Bangladesh embassies or high commissions are not only unaware of many government policies and initiatives, but they are also ignorant of facts and figures regarding the country. In addition, many of these officials are indifferent, unfriendly and unwilling to help. In narrating his experience with one of Bangladesh's most important foreign missions in an industrially developed nation, an interviewee commented that

I was appalled to see how people in charge of promoting [a nation] can do just the opposite. It is simply unbelievable! Some of them did not even know what they were supposed to know—forget about doing. (With this kind of people) your country needs a lot of luck.

The issue of the bureaucrats' unhelpful attitude and bureaucratic red-tapism also surfaced quite prominently. It was further alleged that very few of them have knowledge about the real Bangladesh. Because the system of government and organization in the country is essentially based on the philosophy of mutual mistrust, red-tapism is inevitable. However, it is difficult to explain why the bureaucrats are so unhelpful. Perhaps it is their ignorance of the importance of service orientation; or perhaps it is their status consciousness—a legacy of the colonial past. Whatever the reason may be, it is not good for the nation. Some participants believed that most of these civil servants tend to consider themselves a specially privileged, superior category of people comprising a class of their own that takes pride in alienating it from the rest of the society. A large cross section of interviewees revealed that meeting a Bangladesh bureaucrat is, in most cases, a very unpleasant experience. In the words of one respondent:

In more than one way, you are reminded that the man [the bureaucrat] sitting in front of you is wasting his time by granting you an audience. If he is able to help you solve your problem, you are obliged to please him and serve him in whatever way he wants to be served!

A good number of the potential investors interviewed reported that they found the officials of many other regional countries such as Vietnam, China and India to be more knowledgeable, friendly and helpful than their Bangladesh counterparts.

POINTS TO PONDER

If in a given geographical region a number of developing nations with comparable socioeconomic and politico-legal systems compete for the same type of foreign investments through progressive economic policies, reforms and incentives, the net effect of the incentives for any of the nations will perhaps be zero as the largesse of one nation cancels out that of another. In such cases, the investors base their investment decisions on criteria other than the incentives (Hughes and Dorrance, 1987). It is, then, logical to argue that successfully presenting a nation by focusing on and subsequently selling its relative competitive advantages to the investors becomes very important. In attracting funds from abroad, Bangladesh faces competition from countries such as Thailand, India and Pakistan, all of which can boast of having better image and infrastructure and more efficient officials to promote their respective nations. Competition from Vietnam and Myanmar, which have been able to earn the confidence of their ASEAN partners by entering into some form of strategic alliance with many of them, is also to be reckoned with. Hence, foreign investors are unlikely to have a more favorable view of Bangladesh as a host country than its regional competitors. Even a Bangladesh-born international investor who was actively looking for investment in the Asia-Pacific region dismissed the idea of investing in Bangladesh by saying: "That will be the worst decision for any rational investor."

The Cheap Labor Slogan

Policymakers must realize that the slogan "Bangladesh offers one of the cheapest labor in the world" is not necessarily true and does not constitute a strong selling point. This bald statement is utterly misleading for several reasons. First, in modern production, technology has substantially reduced dependence on labor, and labor cost in technology-intensive industries is too insignificant to provide any economic leverage. Second, most of Bangladesh's "cheap labor" is unskilled and hence less productive; they would need to be trained by the investor. This will increase their effective cost. Bangladesh is not reputed for its training facilities or education system: training its workforce would therefore not be easy. Furthermore, its laborers are pawns in the hands of the unions managed by rival political parties. Strikes and other forms of industrial actions by strong rival unions are very common. It is estimated that in 1993–94, Bangladesh lost almost U.S.$241 million due to strikes (*Asiaweek*, 1995). Hence, while government tries to present cheap labor as an incentive, an investor may not look at it that way.

Focus on Comparative Advantage

The NIEs have been successful in their policies because they were able to capitalize on their comparative advantages. The comparative advantage of a country such as Bangladesh with an abundant labor force but scarce resources lies primarily in the development of its agriculture and agriculture-related sectors. Development of the agribusiness and agro-support industry aimed at raising the level of agricultural production and export is more important for Bangladesh's economy. Labor-intensive manufacture and its exports, on the basis of small-scale production, should come next. This implies that a country rich in labor has to face the difficult organizational problem of catering to the economic needs of a large number of small-scale agriculture or informal sector units by providing them with a more cost-effective and efficient network of transport, communication and marketing. At the same time, infrastructure development, particularly in the areas of generation of power, education and training, and transport and communication, is to be given priority.

Improvements in the domestic economic organization enables a developing country to take advantage of several external economic opportunities, including foreign investment, technology transfer and adaptation, adoption of innovative ideas from abroad and international trade. The mutual interaction between economic policies and economic institutions supplements and complements any forward-looking policy. An economy is poor not only because of its vicious circle of poverty, but because of many other factors. Some of these include poor domestic policies, lack of a law and order situation, and a poor education, health and communication system. Inappropriate domestic policies explain why some countries fail to attract external economic opportunities.

One of the most important aspects of Bangladesh is that it is a growth market that can be viewed as a staging point for more mature and more saturated regional markets. Furthermore, the country's relatively undeveloped domestic market could become an attraction for investors in consumer product manufacturing.

Blind Emulation Is Bound to Fail

The policies adopted by the countries that achieved success through liberalization of their economies cannot be transferred or blindly emulated by other countries. The elements of incentives inherent in a policy may work in environment A but not in environment B since many of these elements are situation specific. To be successful, policies must be compatible with the needs as well as the realities of a specific country. They should be adapted to suit the environment of the adapting country by the creation of a socioeconomic and politico-legal framework, institution and mechanisms that promote the mobilization of resources, their efficient allocation and growth in total factor productivity.

Reevaluate the Disincentives in Disguise

A nation's desire for investment control must be taken into consideration in formulating strategies for promoting foreign investment. The policy of saddling investment with performance requirements that exclude foreign investment from some sectors often raises questions about the host country's real development policy intentions and can be viewed as a disincentive in disguise. Incentives are important, but the balance between incentives and disincentives that are not necessarily measured in money terms alone is of greater interest to foreign investors. Subjective interpretation of any restrictive measure, no matter how non-significant it is from the host country's viewpoint, also plays an important role. A study of 10 developed and developing countries (Guisinger, 1985) found 19 incentive and disincentive instruments.

ADOPTION OF A MARKETING CONCEPT

Attracting investors to Bangladesh requires special effort. Economic liberalization policies may be likened to "products" designed to attract foreign investors who are the "consumers" of the product. Countries that are trying to attract these "consumers" are competitors in a limited market. Hence, attracting foreign investors is essentially a marketing exercise—albeit a very complex one. In order to be able to sell the product successfully, the marketing mix must be right. Developing the right product, asking the right price and positioning it at the right segment of the market through the right kind of promotion is the name of the game.

In order to succeed in attracting foreign funds to Bangladesh, policymakers should adopt the marketing concept and implement it. This concept holds that key to achieving organizational goals are the tasks of determining the needs and wants of target markets and delivering the desired satisfactions more effectively and efficiently than competitors (Kotler, 1994). The success of the NIEs has proven the appropriateness of this philosophy. Implementation of this concept requires the formulation of strategies consisting of selecting a segment of the market as the target market and designing the product, price, promotion and distribution system to meet the consumers' needs within the market. All of these functions require a complete reassessment of the existing policy package, its redesign and re-launch, with a marketing—not bureaucratic—orientation. Government must show total commitment to what it publicizes; it must remove the inconsistencies in the overall policy framework.

A Separate Agency

It is prudent to give an agency such as Singapore's Economic Development Board (EDB) sole responsibility for promoting the policies designed to attract foreign funds. It should be staffed by visionary, knowledgeable, imaginative and innovative professionals with a service orientation and a dedication to their work. The government should give them total support. The structure, composition and modus operandi of the existing agency, BOI, are not conducive to attracting foreign funds.

CONCLUDING COMMENTS

For Bangladesh, the most important need of the hour is to restore the country's political stability. The opposition leaders' dangerous game of destabilizing the democratic system has virtually crippled its economy. Salman Rahman, one of the country's leading industrialists, believes that Bangladesh could have become the fastest growing economy in South Asia. He condemns the political instability in the country as ''a ridiculous state of affairs'' (Hossain, 1995). If any meaningful outcome is to be expected from any measure whatsoever, political stability is a necessity. Once that is achieved, Bangladesh's policymakers urgently need to look into the negative aspects outlined in this chapter if they want some positive results from this exercise of opening up their economy.

The leaders and the policymakers must reevaluate their strengths and weaknesses and rethink their development alternatives. It might also be worthwhile to reposition Bangladesh to attract foreign investors. One hundred percent equity, a large consumer market, a homogeneous population speaking the same language, and a hardworking and innovative labor force with the ability to face all odds are some of the real strengths of the country which need to be promoted as real incentives along with the existing ones. Other strengths that need to be encouraged include an independent judiciary, freedom of speech and expression and a free press. In addition, new sectors for foreign investment must be sought.

For example, electronic data processing is a very lucrative area that may be promoted by the government. Market share may be activated with a view to rejuvenating the capital market.

Despite so many problems, Bangladesh's macroeconomic picture is surprisingly strong. According to Nigel Ash (1995), its inflation is showing a declining trend, its gold and foreign currency reserves in early February 1995 stood at $3.1 billion equaling an eight-month import cover and the exchange rate fixed by the central bank remained relatively stable.

Transforming the economy of a Third World country through economic reform is not an easy task, for both internal and external problems must be satisfactorily addressed. This is a competitive world where globalization is a sought-after goal for many countries. To succeed in this venture, policymakers must change their bureaucratic mentality and view the whole exercise in the light of new realities.

NOTE

An earlier version of this chapter was presented at the International Conference on Globalization and the Market Economy: The Challenges of Change, held in New Delhi, December 28–30, 1995.

REFERENCES

Ash, Nigel. 1995, March. *Euromoney* 311: 157–159.

Asiaweek. 1995, May.

Bangladesh: Recent Economic Developments and Priority Reform Agenda for Rapid Growth. 1995, March 16. Report No. 13875-BD, Washington, DC: World Bank, Country Department 1: 9.

Devan, Janadas (ed.). 1994. *Southeast Asia: Challenges of the 21st Century.* Singapore: Institute of Southeast Asian Studies.

Encarnation, D. and Wells, Louis T., Jr. 1986. Competitive Strategies in Global Industries: A View from Host Governments. In Michael Porter (ed.), *Competition in Global Industries* Cambridge, MA: Harvard Business School Press.

Guisinger, Stephen 1985. A Comparative Study of Country Policies. In Stephen Guisinger and Associates (eds.), *Investment Incentives and Performance Requirements.* New York: Praeger.

Hossain, Ishtiaque. 1995, June. Bangladesh: A Nation Adrift. *Asian Journal of Political Science* 3(1): 32–48.

Hughes, H. and Dorrance, G. 1987. Foreign Investment in East Asia. In Vincent and Bishnodat Persaud (eds.), *Developing with Foreign Investment.* London: Croom Helm.

International Trade Finance. 1995, March. 233: 9–10.

Khan, Enayetullah. 1995, January. Hurdles of Democracy. *Far Eastern Economic Review* 10: 20.

Kotler, Philip. 1994. *Marketing Management: Analysis, Planning, Implementation and Control.* 8th ed. Englewood Cliffs, NJ: Prentice-Hall.

Kraar, Louis. 1992, October 5. The World's Growth Centre Is Shifting Across the Pacific. *Fortune*: 111–113.

Novak, James. 1993. *Bangladesh: Reflections on the Water*. Bloomington: Indiana University Press, 182.

Rahman, M. Zubaidur. 1984, June 14, 16. Multinational Enterprises in a Peripheral Economy: The Case of Bangladesh. In Tan Chin Tiong and Duane Kujawa (eds.), *Proceedings of the Academy of International Business International Meeting*, Singapore, 914–932.

Report of the Expert Committee on Drugs and Pharmaceutical Factories of Bangladesh, 1975–1976. 1977. Department of Industries, Government of Bangladesh.

CHAPTER 15

Profiles and Innovative Tendency of Malay Entrepreneurs: Inheritors versus Initiators

NIK RAHIMAH NIK-YACOB

This chapter addresses the issue of whether inheritors are any less entrepreneurial than initiators of businesses among the Malays of Peninsular Malaysia. Similarities and differences between these two types of entrepreneurs were examined in terms of their background profile and their innovative tendency. Based on the survey data of 488 Malay entrepreneurs, it was found that inheritors and initiators tend to have many aspects in common, especially their individual profiles, innovative tendency and business perception. However, they differ sufficiently from others in their work experience, amount of paid-up capital and net profits that a separate classification of entrepreneurship is merited for inheritors and initiators.

INTRODUCTION

Entrepreneurship is widely defined as "the process of starting and/or growing a new profit-making business" (Bird, 1989: 4). Based on this definition, entrepreneurial talent is assumed to be manifested in the ability to initiate a new profit-making business. However, many businesspersons do not start a new business but sometimes inherit an existing one and are able to turn the business around to a new height of glory. Are these inheritors any less entrepreneurial than the initiators?

This chapter examines the similarities and differences in the background profile of inheritors and initiators. The similarities and differences are indicative of the challenges and entrepreneurial events and processes that each group faces as entrepreneurs. This chapter also examines the innovative tendency of the inheritors in comparison with the initiators to determine whether the inheritors have indeed displayed this important facet of entrepreneurial behavior.

STUDY BACKGROUND

Bird (1989: 5) states that "entrepreneurial behaviour is opportunistic, value-driven, value adding, risk-accepting, creative activity where ideas take the form of organizational birth, growth, or transformation." By this definition, an inheritor is very much an entrepreneur because he or she can instigate change by bringing growth and transformation to the organization. Unlike initiators who begin life as entrepreneurs by resulting in organizational births, an inheritor may have to put right the existing business before bringing about organizational births. An initiator selects the market opportunity that he or she would like to be involved in, while an inheritor, at the beginning, has to accept the market opportunity that others have defined until he or she decides to take a different direction.

The literature is replete with discussions of the different types of entrepreneurs. Gartner (1986) states that eight distinct types of entrepreneurship have been identified: namely, escaping to something new, networking or "putting the deal together," rolling over skills or contacts, purchasing a firm, leveraging expertise, aggressively providing service, pursuing the unique idea and organizing methodically. Vesper (1980), on the other hand, has grouped the different types of entrepreneurs into those who are solo self-employed, team builders, independent innovators, pattern multipliers, economy of scale exploiters, capital aggregators, acquires, buy-sell artists, conglomerators, speculators and apparent value manipulators. Bird (1989) further suggests that we can differentiate the different types of entrepreneurship by breaking down the entrepreneurial event; specifically, we can look at the goals that the entrepreneurs seek to achieve, the entry process, the industrial and technological context, and structure or ownership of the organization. The different typologies of entrepreneurship resulted from utilizing different sets of criteria for grouping.

Regardless of the typologies of entrepreneurship, we can safely assume that different types of entrepreneurs will undergo a different set of entrepreneurial events and processes. Entrepreneurs encounter unique challenges and experiences, and they are stimulated by different events to bring about change. For example, Levinson (1971) emphasized the necessity for entrepreneurs in family businesses to manage conflicts between family members so as not to cripple the organization. For craftsmen or technical entrepreneurs, the opportunity for business entry may be realized from the specialized technical expertise, while for some other entrepreneurs, business entry is strategically planned to enhance the business's market position.

The entrepreneurs' experiences or background profile in the form of work performed, education, and age contribute to the development of skills, abilities and competencies important in entrepreneurship. The background profile of inheritors and initiators is bound to differ in some aspects because of their different entry positions into entrepreneurship. Inheritors would most likely secure some work experience in the business itself prior to leading the organization. Initiators, on the other hand, would most likely display some successes and failures in some other ventures before settling on the current business.

An inheritor is not an entrepreneur if he or she decides to keep things as they were in the organization. Hull, Bosley and Udel (1980) have emphasized that an individual who inherits an existing business is not an entrepreneur unless he or she has the intention of expanding it and makes an effort toward that end. Business expansion requires creative energy or an innovative tendency on the part of the inheritor to identify, analyze and invest in new business opportunities in the form of new products/services, new markets, new marketing strategy, new businesses and so forth. The constant need to deal with change in order to remain competitive will require that both inheritors and initiators display an innovative tendency in their entrepreneurial activity.

STUDY METHODS

To examine the similarities and differences in the background profile and innovative tendency of inheritors and initiators, a survey was conducted among Malay entrepreneurs in several areas in Peninsular Malaysia based on a structured questionnaire. The questionnaire was administered through personal interviews by trained student enumerators or was self-administered by the entrepreneurs, depending on the entrepreneur's choice. For the purpose of study sampling, and entrepreneur is defined as an individual who owns fully or partly the business that he or she is running.

A total sample of 488 Malay entrepreneurs was obtained, with 122 in manufacturing, 156 in retailing, 173 in services and the remaining in other types of businesses. A majority of the businesses were sole proprietorships, partnerships and private-limited companies, with an average existence of 8.2 years and an average number of full-time employees of 10.

Inheritors and initiators were determined through a question that asked whether the business was inherited. A ''yes'' to this question would signify that the respondent was an inheritor, while a ''no'' answer would mean that the respondent would be classified as an initiator. A total of 107 inheritors and 381 initiators was identified in the study. The entrepreneurs' background profile was measured by using several itemized rating scales, while their innovative tendency was measured based on three items in the five-point Likert Scale format.

RESULTS AND DISCUSSION

Table 15.1 presents the similarities and differences between inheritors and initiators in terms of the business and entrepreneurial profile. In terms of the business profile, three out of eight items were significantly different between inheritors and initiators. Inheritors tended to be in retailing, while a majority of the initiators were in services. In other words, among those who inherited a business, a majority of them acquired a retail business, while those who initiated a business would tend to go into a service business rather than a manufacturing or retail business.

Pattern of ownership structure, number of partners in the business, composition of partners and source of capital did not differ significantly between inheritors and initiators. A majority of inheritors and initiators were sole proprietors. Among those who operated under a partnership arrangement, the modal number of partners was two. Although there is an insignificant difference in composition of partners between inheritors and initiators, it is interesting to note that inheritors tended to have family members as partners while initiators tended to have friends as partners. The main source of capital for inheritors and initiators was their own funds rather than monies borrowed from family members, banks or financial institutions. However, the amount of paid-up capital tended to differ between inheritors and initiators. Inheritors registered a lower paid-up capital than initiators.

Not surprisingly, inheritors tended to have businesses that were longer established than initiators. Inheritors, on the average, had reported that their business had been around for 13.63 years, while initiators tended to report a significantly shorter duration of time that averaged to 6.66 years. However, initiators had, on the average, experienced almost double the net profits of inheritors. The difference in profit performance could not be attributed simply to whether the business was inherited or initiated, but it could also stem from many other different factors such as nature of the business. This point should be further investigated in future studies.

The entrepreneurial profile in terms of training, educational background, age, marital status and gender did not differ significantly between inheritors and initiators. A majority of the sampled entrepreneurs had not attended any training programs in entrepreneurship. Most of the inheritors and initiators had formal schooling up to the MCE/SPM level or high school. Most of them were male, married and between the ages of 21 and 40 years.

The only significant difference between inheritors and initiators was in their work experience. A majority of the inheritors had no other work experience besides their current job, while the opposite was true for the initiators. With regard to involvement in other businesses prior to inheriting or setting up the current business, both inheritors and initiators displayed a similar pattern in which a majority of them stated that they had no such involvement. Those who had prior experience in business cited the main reason for getting out of the other business as seeing better opportunities in other areas rather than experience of a loss, insufficient capital or poor returns.

Inheritors and initiators were similarly motivated to be involved in business. Both cited their strong liking for business as the main reason for their involvement. Similarly, when asked to identify the key success factor in their business,

Table 15.1
Profile of Inheritors and Initiators

Item	Inheritors			Initiators			Chi-sq./t	
	Freq	%	Mean	Freq	%	Mean	p	w/d
A. About the business								
1. Type of business							0.001	.20
Manufacturing	32	29.9		90	23.6			
Retailing	45	42.1		110	28.9			
Service	19	17.8		154	40.4			
2. Ownership structure							N.S	
Sole proprietorship	72	67.3		222	58.3			
Partnership	13	12.1		65	17.1			
Private limited	21	19.6		79	20.7			
Limited	1	0.9		1	0.3			
3. Number of partners							N.S	
1	1	7.1		8	10.3			
2	7	50.0		39	50.0			
3	4	28.6		19	24.4			
4	1	7.1		8	10.3			
5	-	-		-	-			
6	1	7.1		1	1.3			
7	-	-		1	1.3			
8	-	-		2	2.6			
3b. Who are the partners?							N.S	
Own family members	11	10.3		29	7.6			

	n	%	n	%	Sig.	
Spouse's family members	3	2.8	6	1.6		
Friends	1	0.9	48	12.6		
Friends of own family	–	–	–	–		
Friends of spouse's family	–	–	1	0.3		
Neighbors	–	–	–	–		
4. Source of capital					N.S	
Own funds	75	70.1	309	81.1		
Family funds	40	37.4	92	24.1		
Banks/financial institutions	26	24.3	83	21.8		
MARA	9	8.4	31	8.1		
5. Amount of paid-up capital					.023	.19
< RM5,000	25	23.8	48	12.8		
RM5,001–RM15,000	23	21.9	94	25.1		
RM15,001–RM30,000	14	13.3	61	16.3		
RM30,001–RM50,000	6	5.7	44	11.8		
RM50,001–RM100,000	15	14.3	51	13.6		
RM100,001–RM250,000	14	13.3	43	11.5		
RM250,001–RM500,000	7	6.7	11	2.9		
RM500,001–RM1 million	1	1.0	14	3.7		
> RM 1 million	–		8	2.1		
6. Number of years business was established	13.63		6.66		.000	5.40
7. Net profits last year, RM	37,385.53		64,626.05		.078	1.77
B. About the entrepreneur						
1. Training in entrepreneurship					N.S	
Nil	57	53.3	152	39.9		
Diploma/degree	8	7.5	62	16.3		

Table 15.1 (continued)

Item	Inheritors			Initiators			Chi-sq./t	
	Freq	%	Mean	Freq	%	Mean	p	w/d
MARA courses	14	13.1		60	15.7			
Courses held by govt. org.	11	10.3		61	16.0			
Courses held by private org.	5	4.7		51	13.4			
Courses held by others	8	7.5		30	7.9			
Work-in-training	12	11.2		52	14.6			
2. Educational background							N.S	
No formal schooling	2	1.9		5	1.3			
Primary school	15	14.0		30	7.9			
LCE/SRP/PMR	17	15.9		50	13.2			
MCE/SPM	46	43.0		114	30.1			
STP/HSC	3	2.8		26	6.9			
Certificate/diploma	15	14.0		77	20.3			
Bachelor's degree	6	5.6		65	17.2			
Postgraduate degree	3	2.8		12	3.2			
3. Age							N.S	
Below 21 years	3	2.8		-	-			
21 to 30 years	29	27.4		78	20.5			
31 to 40 years	28	26.4		174	45.8			
41 to 50 years	24	22.6		84	22.1			
51 to 60 years	17	16.0		34	8.9			
Above 60 years	5	4.7		10	2.6			

	n	%	n	%	Sig.
4. Marital status					N.S
Single	11	10.4	48	12.6	
Married	95	89.6	327	86.1	
Widow/widower	-	-	1	0.3	
Divorced	-	-	4	1.1	
5. Gender					N.S
Male	81	75.7	279	73.2	
Female	26	24.3	102	26.8	
6. Work experience					.025
No other work experience	54	52.9	144	39.9	
Have other work experience	48	47.1	217	60.1	
7a. Involvement in other businesses					N.S
Have been involved in other businesses	27	27.0	108	29.2	
Have not been involved in other businesses	73	73.0	262	70.8	
7b. Reasons for getting out of other businesses					N.S
Experience a loss	-	-	7	10.3	
Better opportunities in other businesses	6	31.6	26	38.2	
Problems with partners	1	5.3	1	1.5	
Insufficient capital	3	15.8	1	1.5	
Too many problems	2	10.5	7	10.3	
Poor returns	2	10.5	7	10.3	
Too competitive	3	15.8	4	5.9	

Table 15.1 (continued)

Item		Inheritors			Initiators			Chi-sq/t	
		Freq	%	Mean	Freq	%	Mean	p	w/d
8. Motivation to involve in business								N.S	
Strong liking for business		81	75.7		278	73.0			
No other career choice		10	9.3		20	5.2			
Influenced by friends/family		20	18.7		75	19.7			
Good profits		26	33.6		202	53.0			
9. Key success factor								N.S	
Diligence		19	17.8		93	24.4			
Sufficient capital		1	0.9		6	1.6			
Follow market needs		7	6.5		26	6.8			
Good management		3	2.8		7	1.8			
Focus on quality		3	2.8		20	5.2			
Good info. management		-	-		4	1.0			
Expertise/experience		4	3.7		12	3.1			
Good marketing		1	0.9		8	2.1			
10. Perceived success								N.S	
Very successsful 7		15	20.0		19	7.7			
6		24	32.0		86	34.7			
5		24	32.0		85	34.3			
Neutral 4		9	12.0		37	14.9			
3		2	2.7		10	4.0			
2		1	1.3		5	2.0			
Very unsuccessful 1		-	-		6	2.4			

11. Satisfaction with current performance						
Very satisfied	7	19	18.1	83	22.2	N.S
	6	32	30.5	103	27.5	
	5	25	23.8	90	24.1	
Neutral	4	16	15.2	49	13.1	
	3	7	6.7	26	7.0	
	2	5	4.8	14	3.7	
Very unsuccessful	1	1	1.0	9	2.4	
12a. Business prospects in the next ten years						
Very good		29	27.6	151	39.8	N.S
Good		58	55.2	177	46.7	
Not certain		14	13.3	46	12.1	
Not good		3	2.9	5	1.3	
Not very good		1	1.0	-	-	
12b. Steps to overcome poor business						
Nil		3	13.0	10	14.9	N.S
Enter a new field		5	21.7	12	17.9	
Retire		-	-	1	1.5	
Look for new things		15	65.2	44	65.7	

both inheritors and initiators attributed the success to their own diligence rather than to a particular management strategy or tools.

Both sets of entrepreneurs tended to rate their business a success. They were not only satisfied with the current performance of the business, but they also perceived good prospects for the business in the next 10 years. Some of the strategies identified for overcoming poor business prospects in the future include looking for new things and entering a new business. However, some entrepreneurs responded that they had not thought about what steps needed to be taken to overcome a decline in business prospects. This response was prevalent among both inheritors and initiators.

Do inheritors display the same innovative tendency as initiators? Results of the MANOVA analysis are shown in Table 15.2. As expected, these two groups are not significantly different in their innovative tendency. Both the multivariate test and the set of univariate tests indicate that inheritors and initiators are similar on this dimension. Based on the response mean, both groups seemed to display a high innovative tendency.

To help understand the entrepreneurs' innovative tendency, their responses on two questions pertaining to the last time a change was made and the changes brought about in the last two years were tabulated and analyzed. The result of the analysis is given in Table 15.3. As is evident from the table, a majority of the inheritors and initiators introduced changes into the business in the last year. In the last two years, the changes comprised a whole spectrum, including introducing new product/service, modifying the production process and introducing a new selling process to that of changing the store layout. From the results in Table 15.3, we can observe that the innovative tendency of the two groups of entrepreneurs does indeed translate into actual changes in the business.

CONCLUSIONS

Are inheritors any less entrepreneurial than initiators? The empirical finding seems to negate this contention. Inheritors are very much like initiators, with only some differences. However, as a whole they are more alike than different.

Ironically, inheritors and initiators tend to have similar individual profiles. They differ in work experience only in that initiators, unlike inheritors, tend to have other work experience prior to being involved in the business. They share the same motivating factor for being involved in business, and they attribute success to the factor of diligence. They have also displayed similar patterns of innovative tendency.

Inheritors and initiators differ in their type of business, amount of paid-up capital, number of years business was established and net profits. If not for these differences and the difference in work experience, inheritors and initiators could be classified in one category.

Table 15.2
Innovative Tendency Among Inheritors and Initiators

	MV F	P	UV F	P	Inheritors' Mean	Initiators' Mean
Innovative Tendency	.01	.28				
1. I prefer to introduce new features on my product/service offering.			1.37	.242	4.24	4.11
2. In operating this business I prefer to follow what other businesses are doing rather than to introduce new and untested things.			2.51	.114	2.48	2.61
3. I want my business to be known as one that is innovative.			.01	.926	4.18	4.19

Note: The three items were measured on a five-point scale where 1 represents strong disagreement and 5 represents strong agreement with the statements.

Table 15.3
Changes in the Business

	Inheritors		Initiators		p	w
	Freq	%	Freq	%		
1. The last time a change was introduced into the business					N.S	
No changes	18	17.6	69	18.9		
In the last month	13	12.7	30	8.2		
1 to 3 months ago	12	11.8	57	15.6		
4 to 6 months ago	16	15.7	54	14.8		
7 to 12 months ago	15	14.7	64	17.5		
More than a year ago	28	27.5	92	25.1		
2. Change brought about in the last two years					N.S	
New product/service	31	29.0	152	39.9		
Modification of the production process	20	18.7	60	15.7		
New office equipment	19	17.8	71	18.6		
New selling process	12	11.2	54	14.2		
Entering a new market	18	16.8	94	24.7		
Broadening the business scope	35	32.7	141	37.0		
Modification of job divisions	23	21.5	87	22.8		
New accounting system	23	21.5	66	17.3		
Usage of computer in operations	8	7.5	71	18.6		
New store layout	34	31.8	133	34.9		

REFERENCES

Bird, Barbara J. 1989. *Entrepreneurial Behaviour.* Glenview, IL: Scott, Foresman and
    Co.
Gartner, W. B. 1986. Entrepreneurial Work. Working paper, Georgetown University.
Hull, D. L., Bosley, J. J. and Udel, G. G. 1980. Renewing the Hunt for the Heffalump:
    Identifying Potential Entrepreneurs by Personality Characteristics. *Journal of
    Small Business Management* 18: 11–18.
Levinson, H. 1971, March–April. Conflicts That Plague Family Businesses. *Harvard
    Business Review*: 90–98.
Vesper, K. 1980. *New Venture Strategies.* Englewood Cliffs, NJ: Prentice-Hall.

PART VI

Sectoral and Industry-Specific Issues

CHAPTER 16

Service Quality by International Relationships: Service Firms in the Global Market

ANDERS MAJKGÅRD AND D. DEO SHARMA

Professional business services are experience goods characterized by intangibility, heterogeneity and inseparability, rendered by an expert toward problem solving. Service quality is determined by the perceptions of individuals and is sometimes impossible to evaluate, even after purchase. Consequently, the content in the relationship between the service provider and the client is important. In this chapter, we base our discussion on service quality on two interrelated fields, namely, the service marketing literature and the industrial marketing literature. Trust, commitment and adaptation are identified as constituents of service quality. This chapter is based on face-to-face interviews with the decision makers in two international Swedish service firms.

INTRODUCTION

The international marketing of services is a neglected area of research. In the last decade, however, the crucial importance of services to the economy has been increasingly recognized, partly in response to the growing international trade in services. We are also witnessing the development of a new paradigm within service marketing, which focuses on value and value creation, opening up a marriage between service quality and relationship quality (Norman and Ramirez, 1994). Service quality plays an important role by increasing benefits and delivering value to customers. It has recently been accepted that service quality not only is important for profitability, but also is a precondition for the very survival of firms. The opening of the global market in services and the increasing importance of foreign investments in them have further highlighted the importance of service quality for the survival and profitability of firms.

Value creation depends on the firm's relationship quality with its customers, suppliers, business partners and the like. Building relationships and developing service quality are complex and long-term processes. Research on the marketing of services revealed the importance of relationships between buyers and sellers (Berry, 1995; Bitner, 1995; Czepiel, 1990; Grönroos, 1991; Gummesson, 1991). These relationships are all the more important in international service marketing. Thus, it is the relationships that are crucial for gaining an understanding of the service quality. Then what constitutes quality in a service offering? How is service quality generated, improved and maintained? What is the connection between the buyer and seller relationships and the quality of the services supplied by the seller to the buyer? The purpose of this chapter is to analyze the processes that constitute service quality in business services. How is service quality affected by relationships between buyers and sellers? Based on the above analysis, a few hypotheses are proposed.

We base our discussion on two interrelated fields in marketing: service quality literature and industrial marketing and network literature. The relevance of the first needs no further comment. Research on industrial marketing is relevant because it covers the topic of interfirm exchange and the development of interfirm relationships. Concepts such as trust, commitment and adaptation are discussed in this literature. These concepts are equally important in explaining issues related to the international marketing of services (Crosby et al., 1990). The network approach has only been applied to industrial markets. A secondary purpose of this chapter is to apply the network approach to analyze the quality of service. Thus, this chapter broadens the scope of the network approach to analyze service quality issues.

We begin by defining service quality. The next section discusses relationships in business services. Then we discuss trust, commitment and adaptation, followed by two illustrative case studies from pure business service industries. Finally we propose a few hypotheses.

WHAT IS SERVICE QUALITY?

Quality is derived from the Latin *qualitat* for "how constituted, of what kind." According to Webster's Dictionary (1977: 1474), quality is "any character or characteristics which may make an object good or bad, commendable or reprehensible," or "The degree of excellence which a thing possesses." Quality has a number of synonyms—for example, attribute, characteristics, distinction and nature.

One way of defining services is to compare them with goods. Sasser et al. (1978) have summarized them by the properties of intangibility, heterogeneity and inseparability. The intangibility of services implies that precise requirements, concerning uniform quality, for example, can rarely be set for services. This is especially the case for business services with a high labor content. Because pure services are heterogeneous their performance varies from one producer to another. Finally, the inseparability of the production and consumption of services implies that quality cannot be engineered and evaluated prior to delivery to a client. Also, in contrast to goods, services are experience goods; that is, services must be experienced before being assessed (Nelson, 1970). Experience properties are access, courtesy, reliability, responsiveness, understanding/knowledge of the customer and communication. A few services are high on credence attributes; for example, these are impossible to evaluate even after purchase (Darby and Karni, 1973).

Berry (1995: 32) stresses that "Quality is defined by the customer. Conformance to company specifications is not quality; conformance to the customers' specification is quality. Spending wisely to improve service comes from continuous learning about the expectations and perceptions of customers and noncustomers." Because of the high experience and credence attributes, service quality is determined by a set of imprecise individual factors such as the perceptions, expectations and experiences of clients. Service quality means different things to different buyers. Juran (1982) states from a client-oriented view that quality is fitness for use, and he stresses client utility and satisfaction. Grönroos (1984) focuses on client expectations and perceptions of quality using two generic dimensions of quality: technical quality and functional quality. The first determinant corresponds to traditional manufacturing quality control and is a prerequisite. The second is the process in which the client is a participant and co-producer. Functional quality indicates how a relationship evolves between the service provider and client. Therefore, the interaction between clients and service providers is important in the client's evaluation of service quality. Customers have an important role to perform in creating services (Mills and Morris, 1986). To sum up, service quality is a client-perceived concept.

In this chapter, we define service quality as a client-perceived concept based on what is good or bad, acceptable or unacceptable. To the clients this means the solving of problems faced by them and the delivering of solutions to them. It includes aspects such as punctuality, accuracy, service mindedness of the staff and speed of supplying services.

RELATIONSHIPS IN BUSINESS SERVICES

The services supplied by business service firms are based on their manpower resources. Business services are highly customized, which means that sellers start from the client's point of view and the problem solving is customized to the client's needs. Customization demands the use of judgment by the service supplier, and interaction between the service supplier and the service buyers (Lovelock, 1983). The second aspect implies active client participation in service production. Applying judgment is important to create scope for tailoring services to meet the needs of the individual client. High service quality means that the client is able to rely on the salesperson's integrity and have confidence in the salesperson's future performance because the level of past performance has consistently been satisfactory. Satisfaction is achieved when the service is delivered by someone who (1) applies correct judgment to detect and analyze the needs of the client (2) possesses skills, experience and other resources to develop the service offered to meet the needs of the client, and lastly (3) is in a position to deliver the services to the client. On all three counts, an intensive interaction between the service seller and the client is important.

Thus, we assert that the quality of services is created in the dyadic relationships between buyers and sellers. Our approach takes into account the perceptions and actions of both buyers and sellers in a relationship; the customer is not always right: sometimes customers need education from the seller to identify and understand their problems and the problem-solving process. The degree of client involvement in the service production and transfer process influences the criteria for service quality evaluation by the client (Goodman et al., 1995). The success of this process depends on how well the client's needs are identified, the qualification and skill of the employees who produce and deliver the services, and the efficiency and effectiveness of the media in transferring services to the client. Such exchange relationships are characterized by trust (Håkansson, 1982). Both partners interact continually and invest resources in building up and maintaining trust and in understanding each other's needs. The buyer's perception is shaped by these idiosyncratic exchanges and by his or her continuous participation in the service production and delivery process to create service quality. The buyers' perceptions of the quality of services supplied by a firm are subjective and will be based on their own experience with that particular service supplier. These perceptions are cumulative in nature. Previous service interactions affect the buyer's present perceptions toward the quality of service supplied by the seller, such that those clients who have repeatedly received services punctually, for example, will perceive a one-off delay in supplying services differently from those clients who have persistently received services late.

In business service markets, firms conduct business as a series of transactions to make commitments. Clients are willing to make a commitment only if the seller also makes a commitment in the relationship. Based on these considerations, it is appropriate to argue that one major approach to improving service quality is relationship enhancement and the reduction of uncertainty. The clients' perceptions of service quality will depend considerably on the quality of interaction and exchange with the service provider. The interaction between a buyer and a supplier is idiosyncratic, and different clients generate different types of interaction. They also use different amounts of them. Some services demand more interaction between buyers and sellers than others.

The development of relationships requires time and resources, but established relationships are durable. Service industries demonstrate a remarkable degree of stability in buyer–seller relationships (Sharma, 1991). Stable relationships reduce uncertainty. Central to the concept of a relationship is trust.

TRUST AND SERVICE QUALITY

Intangibility, heterogeneity and perishability are all important service characteristics influencing the level of trust between service providers and clients.
Trust plays an important role in assuring service quality when clients face uncertainty and can only imperfectly judge service quality, even after the point of
consumption. And the opposite is true: service quality is important in building
trust among clients and service providers (Rogerson, 1983). Uncertainty implies
that buyers lack knowledge about future events, which makes decision making
difficult. Trust reduces the need for information in the decision-making process
and makes reliance on power/dependence relationships unnecessary.

Several researchers have emphasized the importance, in a positive way, of
trust in service relationships (e.g., Crosby, Evans and Cole, 1990; Czepiel,
1990). In the absence of objective measures, past performance is generally regarded as the most important basis for trust. Trust allows confidential information to be exchanged between client and service provider. Relationships
deficient in the exchange of information develop conflicts and mistrust for the
buyers' perception of the relationship (Etgar, 1976). Distrust is negative for the
perception held by the buyers. We define trust "as a willingness to rely on an
exchange partner in whom one has confidence" (Moorman, Zaltman and Rohit,
1993: 82). Trust in a relationship has two dimensions: (1) the willingness to
maintain trust, or the commitment to the relationship, and (2) the capability of
maintaining trust, or the adaptations made in the relationship.

The client may interact with the service provider's employees or with physical
resources. The use of different media to interact with the counterpart has an
impact on the formation, development and maintenance of trust. Huber and Daft
(1987) posit a hierarchy of media richness: face-to-face communication, video-
phone, videoconference, telephone, E-mail, and so on, with face-to-face interactions giving a higher degree of trust than the other, impersonal forms of
media-based interaction. Face-to-face interaction is much richer in communi-
cating information, making an impression and giving a comprehensive picture
to the counterpart. Interaction and communication between buyers and sellers
can be formal or informal. The formal modes are made into routines and structured, while the informal ones are personalized, less routine and more spontaneous. Informal and face-to-face channels of interaction are more important in
international markets. Differences in cultures, languages and business traditions
make it more vital, but also more difficult, to establish trust in business transactions (Hofstede, 1984). It may take a longer time and may cost more to show
trust to foreign buyers.

Commitment has its roots in the past; it reflects the history of the exchange
relationship. Again, our definition parallels that of Moorman et al. (1992: 316).
"Commitment to the relationship is defined as an enduring desire to maintain
a valued relationship." Commitment escalates slowly over a period of time, as
both the parties make incremental investments in the relationship. These in-

vestments mark the buyers and sellers' adaptations to the relationship. Relationship-specific investment may take the form of a common history between the service firm and the client. We can distinguish between high-and low-contact services. By contact, we mean those situations in which the client interacts with any personnel from the provider's organization. Frequent interaction facilitates a two-way communication between buyer and sellers. This improves service quality. Cottrell (1994) reported that 87 percent of buyers indicated that they would purchase from a seller who kept in contact. Interaction allows buyers and sellers to influence each other. These influences may emanate from a direct request either by the buyer or the seller, although similar influences may arise from recommendations and particular guarantees or legal obligations (Mohr and Nevin, 1990). The influence of these tactics may produce different effects on clients' perceptions of service quality. For example, the use of means such as the inclusion of coercive legal obligations negatively influences buyers' perceptions of service quality. On the other hand, noncoercive means such as meeting a request by the buyer may be perceived as the selling firm's service-mindedness. This improves service quality.

Relationships consist of two basic components: interaction frequency (i.e., the number of times that the client interacts with the service provider in order to exchange values) and the interaction surface (i.e., the number of different people involved in the exchange at different organizational levels). Higher exchange frequency and a larger interaction surface improve the interaction and exchange of views and information between buyers and sellers. Frequent interaction and a high interaction surface are related to uncertainty concerning the exchange; the more unstructured the situation, the higher the uncertainty in the buyer-seller interaction. In more uncertain situations, the formal interaction media are easily overloaded, and informal interaction becomes imperative (Huber and Daft, 1987). More informal interactions are positively related to the desire of the buyers-sellers to forge long-term relationships instead of short-term exchange. Informal interaction positively transforms the attitude of buyers and sellers toward service quality. Commitment to a relationship manifests itself in (mutual) adaptation and relation-specific investments by buyers and sellers. In business service firms, these adaptations may require investments in interactive marketing and the appropriate recruitment and selection of employees. Frequent communication and a wide interaction surface may also improve service quality as the customer feels special (Czepiel, 1990).

Finally, high exchange frequency and a large interaction surface can bridge the gap between management perceptions of client expectations and the client's own expectation of service quality. Researchers note that what buyers perceive as high risk is associated with the limited availability of or inferior quality of information supplied by the buyer (Spencer, Engel and Blackwell, 1970). As interaction between parties increases, the parties share more accurate, timely and comprehensive information (Dwyer, Schurr and Sejo, 1987). Then, the service-supplying firm will have fewer difficulties identifying buyers' needs and trans-

Figure 16.1
A Typology of Buyer-Seller Interaction in Services

Service buyers

		Active	Passive
	Active	1	2
Service sellers	Passive	3	4

lating perceptions of clients' needs to suit their requirements. The gap between management and the client's quality perception will decrease. The more intangible the services, the greater the need to interact with the buyer before, during and after the sales transaction.

Business services are people intensive, so that adaptations concern individuals as well as organizational procedures and processes. Learning by doing is an essential part of adaptation. Adaptations may be made when companies initially start doing business with each other or, more continuously, as a result of day-to-day interaction. An adaptation process can be started independently, at the initiation of the other party or by mutual consent. Adaptation implies relationship-specific resource investment, and thus it would entail additional cost to switch to alternative relationships. This hinders opportunistic behavior and improves the interest of both buyers and sellers in continuing their relationship. Exchange partners value their long-term gains more than the short-term gains based on what Williamson (1975) calls self-seeking guile. Thereby, service industry firms have an incentive to improve service quality.

STRATEGIES FOR SERVICE QUALITY DEVELOPMENT

The preceding presentation does not imply that all service buyers and sellers are equally engaged in exchange. Indeed, buyers and sellers in a service exchange are not equally active in interaction and exchange of information with their counterparts. Some are more active; others are more passive. Active partners are characterized by (1) being good at supplying and disclosing information to their counterparts, and (2) being good at listening and interpreting the information supplied by the counterpart. Thus, four different situations evolve (Figure 16.1).

Optimum service quality is achieved in Cell 1, whereas the type of interaction characterized by Cell 4 is the least conducive to high-quality service production and delivery. Cell 1 also demands the highest adaptation and resource commitment by buyers and sellers. In Cell 1, both buyers and sellers are good at supplying information to the counterpart. This implies a willingness to ask questions and collect information, as well as a willingness to expose the firm to the counterpart, and by disclosing information on what the firm means by service quality and what are its components, what weights are awarded to the different components of quality in total service packaging, and so on. Meetings and discussions between buyers and sellers will be frequent, and the time spent together will be great and will involve a number of people. Discussions are all around, including areas of disagreement and conflict. The purpose is to air and manage conflicts and disagreements. Conflicts are solved in a constructive way, thereby better satisfying the clients' needs. This improves perceived service quality. To fit in Cell 1, both the buyer and seller will be investing relationship-specific resources. This is a demanding situation. Cell 4 is the opposite case. This is the one that demands least adaptation by the buyer and seller. Here, meetings and discussions are few, and the partners are secretive. Conflicts and dissatisfaction are not expressed to the counterpart. Thus, they may never be solved, and the service quality is low.

FINDINGS FROM AN INTERNATIONAL STOCKBROKER: CARNEGIE

The Carnegie Company was founded in 1932 and is Sweden's largest stockbroker. It has subsidiaries in 10 countries. There are about 380 employees, of whom about 60 to 70 percent work in the stock market and 60 percent are to be found outside Sweden. The turnover was 400 MSEK in 1994. The core business is in trade stocks, but one branch also works with the money market. Carnegie has both analysts and brokers, but it is the brokers who have contact with the client. There are institution brokers, private-client brokers, SAX brokers and traders (position takers, market makers). About 8000 transactions are made each working day.

The Product and the Company's Marketing Strategy

When an institution decides to do business, it contacts its broker at Carnegie. The company trades on the institution's behalf on the market, which may be the stock exchange, or outside the stock exchange or against its own stock. The client receives a statement the same day and settles within three days. Two days later, registration of the purchase or sale takes place. Often Carnegie, not the client, initiates the business, and the brokers begin the deal. Carnegie's own trade is secret. There are three ways of buying shares for a client: (1) The broker asks another client if he is willing to sell; (2) the broker makes use of the stock exchange and lets the SAX-broker carry out the purchase order and (3) Carnegie's own stock is used and the trader carries out the purchase. When the broker has done his part of the job, the merchandise must be supplied and paid. Only then is the business complete.

Most business is done by account, and therefore the clients must trust the broker. The stock analyses are done in Sweden and are not recorded in either London or New York. On the other hand, an attempt is made to adapt the analyses to the needs of British and American investors. Coordination between the brokers is based on common analyses of the companies and the macro factors of the particular country. The analyses are built on the assumption that the traders have a common view of the world—of, for example, movements of the U.S. dollar and of interest rates. This picture is built up and communicated in daily broker's meetings. The analyses are founded on data, including annual reports, financial reports and rating agencies. The stocks are arrayed according to purchase dignity. The differences are often small.

Client Relationships

Clients are primarily financial institutions, for example, insurance firms and banks. They have their own analysis department and employ graduates trained in economics and business. Carnegie also employs people with the same type of background (i.e., analysts and brokers). Contact with clients is separated into face-to-face contacts and impersonal contacts. Every broker knows the client's particular preference. All clients are unique, and a good broker knows what kind of information they want. The relationships are built on good reputation and trust, which one may build up over a long time but which can be destroyed in a day. The larger institutional clients often work with three or four stock brokers for reasons of security. Carnegie has to adapt to the clients' needs. One adaptation is that every client has his own broker. The clients want to deal with the same person if they have daily contact. Those who do not have daily contact need not use the same broker. The frequency of the clients' purchase decides how each relationship develops, which means that Carnegie must be aware of the clients' likely business volume.

The international clients urge an international outlook and require an understanding of how the international capital markets work. International commerce is more aggressive than Swedish commerce, and international clients demand detailed knowledge about the enterprises and require higher liquidity to enable them to buy and sell large positions because they are big themselves. The foreign clients' personal dependence is still greater than that of the Swedes. They are not so interested in the stockbroker in terms of the company itself; rather, they wish to have good contact with just one person so that they know where they stand. Stability is important in the client relationship and is attained by ensuring that the individuals responsible for particular clients remain with Carnegie. One builds long human relationships, so that the clients believe that Carnegie's quality is good. The relationship pattern is different in Stockholm and London; it builds on situations that the participants deal with unconsciously.

To sum up, trust is built on unique broker-client relationships that have a deliberate long-term outlook. Commitment consists of relationship-specific investments in information, through personal and impersonal communication.

FINDINGS FROM AN INTERNATIONAL SALES EDUCATION COMPANY: MERCURI INTERNATIONAL

Mercuri International (MI) was established in 1958 and is the world's largest sales education and development enterprise. Every year MI holds fifty thousand education days in its sales development courses, with a total of three hundred thousand participants attending from ten thousand customers. MI has 24 subsidiaries in 24 countries. The home offices are in Stockholm and Geneva. The headquarters' task is mostly one of coordination. The number of employees in the company worldwide is nine hundred, and the turnover is nine hundred MSEK. The consultants recruited often have experience from industry as sales managers or as MDs in the heads of marketing department. Many consultants are former MI clients.

The Product and Marketing of the Company

The product is to teach how to develop, to lead and to implement sales companies—that is, to teach how to create and manage sales companies. The business works on certain basic given, concepts and models concerning marketing and sales training, which are continuously adapted to client needs. Product development may be divided into three phases: (1) achieving certain structures; (2) determining MI's "beliefs" (i.e., what does MI believe insofar as leadership and sales are concerned); and (3) obtaining insight into how things really work. The difference between the competitors' and MI's products lies in how and in what way MI combines its resources. MI's concept is to standardize, formalize and coordinate the market plans of international clients. It has general and firm-specific courses. The general courses are made up of predeveloped products, which have been given by special product development groups. The firm-specific courses are tailored to meet specific needs. Twenty percent of the company's concept must be adapted to each country, with the greatest number of adaptations required for Japan and the Arab countries.

First, management is trained, followed by the sales managers and vendors. Eighty percent of MI's marketing is through personal sales, and 20 percent through advertisements, including direct mail, which can only create interest, not sell. MI works actively for large decision makers and to deepen client contact, to obtain the required information and to ensure that the right decisions are made. MI has a library of knowledge that the consultants use to tailor their off-the-shelf general courses. There are product development groups operating on an international level. The project groups are specifically put together for different purposes and are dissolved after the work has been accomplished.

The platform describes MI's concept, which is used internally and is also transferred to the clients. It presupposes that the client has a need and that he must be educated to ensure that he buys the right products or services. The platform is divided into three parts: the purchase platform, the working platform and the market platform. The platform may consist of the client's attitudes to the company, the company's products and the particular product adaptations. The platform is coupled to future sale conditions (e.g., repurchase frequency, purchase of system products and particular investment discussions that accumulate on the platform before the decision). Simple ways are required for describing and measuring a platform. This is done by mapping the most important connections, but exact measurement of the platform size should not be attempted. By dividing the market into different categories, each of which indicates the company's purchasing potential, a general measurement of the platform can be accomplished in terms of volume and number of companies.

The buying platform is made up of those clients on the market who have purchased during the measurement period. The platform is an indicator of the future sales of the same product, and forms a base of system sale of other products and services, as well as providing a measure of the stability of and risk taking involved in the sale. The working platform consists of that part of the market in which there is a current sales effort that has not yet been successful (e.g., clients that the company would like to have but has yet to secure).

Client Relationships

The clients are segmented according to sales. MI has a particular organization for the coordination and recruitment of multinational clients. The clients may be divided into four categories depending on what kind of contract is drawn up: (1) The client's mother company is completely responsible; (2) there are several separate contracts, each made with a different client unit; (3) contracts for a number of countries are drawn up at the same time; and (4) contracts are only made with one subsidiary. The clients are divided into categories according to their potential educational demand. MI has information meetings with about 10 prospective clients, who represent several companies, to reconcile the knowledge gap between them. Since it is easier to criticize people in a group than separately, education and conversion occur simultaneously.

For example, MI has built up an international sales organization for Mercedes-Benz (MB) in Europe. MB's main office has about 20 consultants from MI. The consultant's job is to give advice to and train the personnel. The other MB companies work with MI in a similar way. The MI consultants obtain their confidential knowledge about the company by visiting MB offices in Germany and other countries. MI also works as a consultant to Sheratons (SHs) to help them get IBM as a client. Before the first contact, one person from SHs was employed to collect information on IBM. When a critical amount of information had been collected, IBM was visited simultaneously by SHs and MI. Several people on different organizational levels and from different countries in which IBM is active were visited by representatives of SHs and MI in one day. The duration of contacts and the length and depth of experience are important. Being able to influence a client through another client is of great importance.

To sum up, trust is built on teamwork, based on a high interaction frequency and a wide interaction surface. Commitment is built on learning by doing.

DISCUSSION

The two cases show that service quality always develops in an interaction between buyers and sellers. A continuous flow of information takes place between buyer and seller, which reduces the buyer's uncertainty and increases trust between the parties. In the case of Carnegie, perceived service quality is made up of the specific, and unique, buyer and seller relationship. Every client has its own broker. Computer technology mediates and enhances the information exchange between buyers and sellers (i.e., buying/selling the right volume of stocks at the right time). In the case of MI, perceived service quality is built on a multifocal interaction between several buyers and sellers on different organizational levels, which is very time and resource intensive. In the service delivery process, MI visits the client on a daily basis, before the first contact is made with the prospective client. A lot of information is collected about the market in general and the client in particular. Both cases show that buyers and sellers are active in the relationship.

In the context of trust, interaction frequency and interaction surface are important; this is illustrated in the MI platform concept. Previously, someone from the seller and someone else representing the buyer monopolized the client relationship. Now several representatives of MI interact face to face with several representatives from the buyers at different levels and in many countries.

The interaction surface between seller and buyer has been broadened. This wide contact surface facilitates a variety of means of information exchange between MI and its international clients. It also improves contact and reliability; interaction becomes continuous and more personal. It helps MI to identify clients' requirements and the changes necessitated, and it thereby helps MI to come up with suggestions. This shapes the client's future needs, defining the problems in the client firm and making the client aware of them. The flow of information between MI and its clients concerns the type of education/training program to be instigated, its content and duration. Decisions are based on discussions between MI and the individual clients. On a daily basis, MI detects the client's needs, and both MI and the client are active in the discussion. The discussion concerns the important needs of the clients and the courses that are relevant and how these courses should be produced and delivered to the client. MI's marketing strategy is interactive. In the discussion, MI and the clients are exposing themselves to each other as they supply and receive information. Through discussions, prospective conflicts and disagreements are settled.

In the case of Carnegie, much information exchange is based on impersonal electronic media (e.g., phone and fax). Carnegie and its clients have a rather similar background with regard to education and experience. This makes information exchange less problematic, even when less personal media are used. Using impersonal communication media is preferred because many numbers and figures are communicated. These concern the price of a number of shares to buy or sell. In addition, the secrecy of the transaction is maintained. Frequent face-to-face meetings would be more likely to give rise to errors and may generate rumors and speculations in the market.

Carnegie also uses personal face-to-face contact when complex, but qualitative, information is supplied. These concern the analyses of firms, the economy, trends in the stock market and investment advice and are judgment-based information. Proper understanding involves grasping the assumptions made in the analyses: the methods of data collection, the analysis itself and any reservations about and limitations of the data, including peculiarities concerning the conditions. Involving a team of people to serve clients is positive for another reason as well: It conveys a message to the buyer that MI and Carnegie are "large" companies with a selection of resources to suit the needs of individual clients. MI and Carnegie can be trusted now and in the future.

Carnegie's contact surface with the clients is not as wide as MI's contact with their clients. But the contact frequency is high. Carnegie's brokers speak daily to the same client, and the contacts are continuous. Therefore,

H1: The higher the experience attributes in a service, the more important are the width of the contact surface between buyer and seller in forming the buyers' perception of the service quality.

H2:The higher the experience attributes in a service, the more important are existing good relationships with clients in forming the buyers' perception of the service quality.

Frequent interaction between the parties and a wide surface of contact does not necessarily eliminate all conflict from the exchange. There are frequent discussions and disagreements between MI and its clients as well as between Carnegie and its clients. In the case of MI, for example, these are related to differences of opinion on the educational needs in the client's firm. In the case of Carnegie, conflicts concern such issues as the perception of future trends in the stock market. However, the parties treat these conflicts as differences in opinion and as divergences in interpretation. These are "functional conflicts," a natural occurrence in any exchange relationships, not "conflicts of interest" between the parties. These functional conflicts have a positive outcome, for they stimulate discussion between the parties and introduce an element of newness and creativity in the relationship, preventing stagnation. The service quality generated in the relationships improves to suit the counterpart's needs. Therefore,

H3: The more constructive conflicts resolved between buyer and seller, the higher the perceived service quality.

Frequent interaction with the client prior to, during and after a service is supplied reduces the need for separate service guarantees to the customer. Since clients are engaged in idea generation as well as service production, an element of guarantee is built into the service production system. Buyers continuously influence the services MI and Carnegie supplies to them. Trust is enhanced. Developing and maintaining trust is also important because a direct measurement of service quality is not readily available in either of the two cases. MI supplies educational services, which influences the way salespeople think. But these effects can hardly be directly measured. Carnegie supplies brokerage services. What stocks to buy or sell, when and at what price is decided by the buyer or seller. That is, the loss or gain to take is determined by who makes the buy or sell decision. In both cases, buyers' perceptions of service quality are formed by the processes by which services are produced and delivered. Moreover, buyers' perceptions are cumulative. The success or failure of an individual transaction is put down to chance. To build trust, it is important to supply good quality services consistently. Perceptions of quality are based on aspects of the process such as the punctuality of the transactions, the ease of settling, and delivery of shares. Therefore,

H4: The higher the experience attributes in a service, the more important the service delivery aspects in forming the buyer's perception of the service quality.

The two cases revealed that commitment is a mutual phenomenon whereby each actor's commitment to the relationship is based on its perception of the other actor's commitment. For both parties, adaptations are made in incremental steps in day-to-day operations, and the outcomes of a long history of doing business materialize over time. These commitments are more readily made partly because the buyer and sellers have a long association and because the relationships are mutually rewarding. Finally, both MI and Carnegie are engaged in business with large national and international firms. Long-term association with these buyers is rewarding in another way—namely, for their reputation. It provides confirmation in the market that these firms supply good-quality services. This, in turn, helps MI and Carnegie to attract new clients and to recruit high-quality manpower. High-quality manpower is essential to the supply of high-quality services to clients.

MI made adaptations in administrative structure, routines and decision-making processes vis-à-vis the client. It is important for MI to acquire confidential company-specific information from the client to do the problem solving. In the case of Carnegie, adaptation concerns such issues as the price of shares, sales, when, where and the duration of the offer. In Carnegie, adaptation is also introduced through investment in computers, software and electronic media. These investments cost them 10 MSEK a year. Every employee has his own PC and is connected to internal networks (the back office) and to the Stockholm Stock Exchange and option traders (front office). The purchase and sale orders can be placed at any time and essentially from "anywhere." This is an important aspect in improving the quality of the service supplied to clients by Carnegie. Using electronic media improves the secrecy of dealing, and the speed and reduces the time taken to place and settle orders. These are all positive for the quality of services supplied to clients.

An important element that has a positive impact on service quality is Carnegie's international coverage. Carnegie's computer system is directly connected to markets in other Nordic countries and to other European equity markets. Today Swedish clients can buy or sell shares in other European markets through Carnegie. This is a significant addition to the services offered to clients. Carnegie is now perceived as an international stockbroker.

The resources used in adaptation are intangible (i.e., human resources, firms' goodwill and their reputation). In addition, individual consultants (in MI) and brokers (in Carnegie) commit their own name, reputation and prestige in the relationship. A breach in commitment is as unacceptable to the individual consultants and brokers as it is to their respective firms. Organizational adaptations were often made in the case of MI. Adaptations at an organizational level meant an increase in the number of people involved in face-to-face contact with the clients and the participation of different management levels in the interactions. The relationship between MI and its clients is independent of particular individuals. These are a source of continuity in the relationship.

MI and Carnegie sell services that are highly customized, which is to say that some adaptations always concern the service exchange: both the service process and its outcome. Adaptations concern individuals and their knowledge. In the case of MI, a certain team spends a long time and puts considerable effort into acquiring knowledge of the client's products, organizational structures and marketing strategies. This is achieved through being geographically near the client. MI comes to clients, which is more convenient for them. Frequently, MI's people sit in the same building as the client. In order to serve international clients, MI has established a number of subsidiaries throughout the world. Again, the quality of the service is improved by this arrangement.

H5: For internationally active service firms, a local establishment has a positive impact on service quality.

Significant adaptations of routines and organizations were made by both of the firms and their clients. Carnegie keeps its own stock of "in-house" shares. These in-house stocks help Carnegie to balance the supply and demand for a particular stock by clients. Imbalances arise for a number of reasons, namely, imbalance of demand supply of a particular stock in the market, a temporary delay in the delivery of the stocks for which the client has already paid, or stocks are "lost" in the course of delivery. Keeping in-house stocks is a mechanism for creating and maintaining credibility and trust with the clients. This shows the buyers that Carnegie possesses the internal strength as well as the willingness to keep promises made to the clients. It is expected that nothing will be leaked to their competitors. In the case of Carnegie, a lot of money is handled every day, and each transaction involves a large sum of money. In addition, the timing of the purchase or sale is crucial for profits and losses. The client also puts trust in MI and permits them to observe and discuss confidential business with key individuals.

Mutual adaptation is therefore an investment into the relationship and a precondition for the supply of high-quality services. These investments are relationship-specific assets. Commitment is viewed as a function of behavior, with firms and individuals becoming committed to each other through their actions and the choices they make over time. The process in which services are delivered is improved in this way. Consequently,

H6: The higher the commitment of the buyer and seller, the higher the service quality.

H7: The higher the adaptation between buyer and seller, the higher the service quality.

REFERENCES

Berry, Leonard L. 1995. *On Great Service—A Framework for Action*. New York: Free Press.

Berry, Leonard L. and Parasuraman, A. 1991. *Marketing Services*. New York: Free Press.

Bitner, Mary Jo. 1995. Building Service Relationships: It's All about Promises. *Journal of the Academy of Marketing Science* 23(4): 246–251.

Cottrell, Richard J. 1994, March. Proactive versus Reactive Customer Contact. *Mobius* 39: 25–28.

Crosby, Lawrence A., Evans, Kenneth R. and Cowles, Deborah. 1990. Relationship Quality in Service Selling: An Interpersonal Influence Perspective. *Journal of Marketing* 54(3): 68–81.

Czepiel, John A. 1990. Service Encounters and Service Relationships: Implications for Research. *Journal of Business Research* 20(1): 13–21.

Darby, Michael R. and Karni, Edi. 1973, April. Free Competition and the Optimal Amount of Fraud. *Journal of Law and Economics* 16(1): 67–88.

Dwyer, F. Robert, Schurr, Paul H. and Sejo, Oh. 1987. Developing Buyer-Seller Relationships. *Journal of Marketing* 51(2): 11–27.

Etgar, Michael. 1976. Effects of Administrative Control on Efficiency of Vertical Marketing Systems. *Journal of Marketing Research* 13: 61–78.

Goodman, Paul S., Fichman, Mark, Lerch, F. Javier and Snyder, Pamela R. 1995. Customer-Firm Relationships, Involvement, and Customer Satisfaction. *Academy of Management Journal* 38(5): 1310–1324.

Grönroos, Christian. 1984. A Service Quality Model and Its Marketing Implications. *European Journal of Marketing* 18(3): 9–18.

Grönroos, Christian. 1991. *Service Management and Marketing*. Lexington, MA: Lexington Books.

Gummesson, Evert. 1991. Marketing—Orientation Revisited: The Crucial Role of the Part-time Marketer. *European Journal of Marketing* 25(2): 60–75.

Hofstede, Geert. 1984. *Culture's Consequences: International Differences in Work Related Values*. Beverly Hills, CA: Sage Publications.

Huber, Georg P. and Daft, Richard L. 1987. The Information Environments of Organizations, In Fredric M. Jablin et al. (eds.), *Handbook of Organizational Communication: An Interdiciplinary Perspective*. Newbury Park, CA: Sage Publications.

Håkansson, Håkan, ed. 1982. *International Marketing and Purchasing of Industrial Goods. An Interaction Approach*. Chichester: John Wiley and Sons.

Juran, Joseph M. 1982. *Upper Management and Quality*. New York: Juran Institute.

Lovelock, Christopher H. 1983, Summer. Classifying Services to Gain Strategic Marketing Insights. *Journal of Marketing* 47: 9–20.

Mills, Peter, K. and Morris, James H. 1986. Clients as ''Partial'' Employees of Service Organizations: Role Development in Client Participation. *Academy of Management Review* 11(4): 726–735.

Mohr, Jakki and Nevin, John R. 1990, October. Communications Strategies in Marketing Channels: A Theoretical Perspective. *Journal of Marketing* 54: 36–51.

Moorman, Christine, Zaltman, Gerald and Rohit, Deshpandé. 1992, August. Relationships Between Providers and Users of Market Research: The Dynamics of Trust Within and Between Organizations. *Journal of Marketing Research* 29(3): 314–328.

Moorman, Christine, Zaltman, Gerald and Rohit, Deshpandé. 1993, January. Factors Affecting Trust in Market Research Relationships. *Journal of Marketing* 57: 81–101.

Nelson, Philip. 1970, July–August. Advertising as Information. *Journal of Political Economy*: 729–754.

Norman, Richard and Ramirez, Rafael. 1994. *Designing Interactive Strategy*. Chichester: John Wiley and Sons.

Parasuraman, A., Ziethaml, Valarie A. and Berry, Leonard L. 1985, Fall. A Conceptual Model of Service Quality and Its Implications for Future Research. *Journal of Marketing* 49: 41–50.

Rogerson, William P. 1983. Reputation and Product Quality. *Bell Journal of Economics* 14: 508–516.

Sasser, Earl W., Olsen, Paul R. and Wyckoff, Daryl D. 1978. *Management of Service Operations: Text and Cases*. Boston: Allyn and Bacon.

Sharma, Deo D. 1991. *International Operations of Professional Firms*. Lund: Studentlitteratur.

Spence, Homer E., Engel, James F. and Blackwell, Roger D. 1970, August. Perceived Risk in Mail-Order and Retail Store Buying. *Journal of Marketing Research* 7: 364–369.

Webster, Noah. 1977. *Webster's New Twentieth Century Dictionary of the English Language*. Cleveland: Collins.

Williamson, Oliver E. 1975. *Markets and Hierarchies: Analysis and Antitrust Implications*. New York: Free Press.

CHAPTER 17

Intellectual Property Protection and Foreign Direct Investment: A Global Pharmaceutical Industry Perspective

P. M. RAO

Intellectual property protection (IPR) is only one of many factors that influence foreign direct investment (FDI) decisions, even in the pharmaceutical industry where great importance is attached to it. The recently concluded Trade Related Intellectual Property Rights (TRIPs) Agreement under the Uruguay Round will have little effect on the flow of pharmaceutical FDI into the developing countries. Increasingly, global marketing strategies—driven by market forces and technological developments in the industrialized world—are likely to increase the degree of involvement by pharmaceutical multinationals with the developing world.

INTRODUCTION

Few facts are better established in modern economics literature than that industrial innovation in the form of new products and processes has been a major source of U.S. economic growth (Denison, 1985; Kendrick, 1980; Mansfield et al., 1977; Solow, 1957). The stock of knowledge that firms produce and maintain through investments in research and development, together with the training of workers and similar activities, constitute the asset base, albeit an intangible one, which is often referred to as intellectual property. Although the term *intellectual property* can be defined to include a wide range of intangible "assets" described in such terms as knowledge base and knowhow, for purposes of this chapter, it is grounded in investments in technology and property rights and refers to all technology-based intangible assets of a firm—an idea or a design for a new product or a process, a new molecular entity, a computer software package and the like—that may be protected as a property right under the legal framework that includes patents, copyrights, trademarks or trade secrets.

This chapter does not seek to belabor a well-established finding that firms operating in a competitive market structure are unable to internalize or appropriate the full economic benefits of their investments in the development of intellectual property (Arrow, 1962; Bator, 1958; Mansfield et al., 1977; Nordhaus, 1969). This is often referred to as the appropriability problem which arises because intellectual property is expensive to produce and cheap to copy. The high social rate of return on investments in intellectual property, combined with the appropriability problem, provide the argument for strong legal protection of intellectual property rights (IPR) through patents, copyrights and the like. Nor does this chapter purport to debate the fundamental importance of protecting IPR in preserving incentives for industrial innovation which benefits all nations, both the industrialized and the developing nations. Rather, this chapter, based on a review of research findings to date, presents three major themes. The first of these suggests that legal protection is only one of several means and not always the most effective means (even in the industrialized countries) by which profit-maximizing firms enhance the appropriability of their intellectual property development. Second, while foreign direct investment (FDI) is an important means by which technology is transferred from one country to another, IPR is only one of the many factors influencing the FDI decisions, and the empirical evidence on the relationship between the flow of FDI and a country's system of IPR protection is anything but strong. Indeed, the empirical evidence on this issue raises more questions than it answers. Third, and more important, continuing debate over IPR protection appears to overlook the point that firms devise a variety of global marketing strategies to overcome the appropriability problem. Such strategies do not necessarily insist that IPR protection in developing countries be on a par with that existing in the developed countries as a precondition for FDI. This chapter presents a global marketing strategy perspective of the IPR issues as they relate to the pharmaceutical firms in the developed world for which IPR protection is of immense importance. Specifically, this chapter contends that such strategies will be increasingly driven by technological developments and competitive pressures in their home markets, combined with the growing importance of the developing world's markets.

We will discuss these themes, drawing, in part, on the many pioneering empirical studies conducted by Edwin Mansfield (Mansfield, 1986, 1986, 1993 and 1994; Mansfield et al., 1977; Mansfield and Romeo, 1980). Notwithstanding the recently concluded Trade Related Intellectual Property Rights (TRIPs) Agreement under the Uruguay Round of the General Agreement on Tariffs and Trade (GATT), the IPR debate is ongoing and broader than the issues resolved in the TRIPs Agreement. Therefore, a full or even a partial evaluation of the many provisions of the TRIPs Agreement, although some of them will be referred to as appropriate, is beyond the scope of this chapter.

INTELLECTUAL PROPERTY PROTECTION AND FOREIGN DIRECT INVESTMENT DECISIONS: EMPIRICAL EVIDENCE

What do we know about how the flow of FDI and the related transfer of technology from the developed to the developing world is influenced by the developing world's system of IPR protection? This is a large and complex question to which Edwin Mansfield, among others, has attempted to provide some answers (Baldwin, 1979; Evenson, 1993; Mansfield, 1993; Mansfield and Romeo, 1980; Root and Ahmed, 1979). Although Mansfield's earlier research found no statistically significant evidence that IPR protection was related to U.S. manufacturing FDI in a given country, the preliminary results of a more recent and ongoing study (Lee, 1993) which he reported (Mansfield 1994) indicate a statistically significant relationship between the flow of U.S. foreign direct investment into a country and the relative weakness of its IPR protection at the aggregate manufacturing level. However, the results are inconsistent and less strong at the level of individual industries. Particularly surprising is the small effect of IPR protection on FDI in the chemical industry, which includes pharmaceuticals for which IPR protection is a major issue. Mansfield's findings indicate that a 10-point increase in the index of perceived weakness of IPR protection (measured in terms of percentage of firms believing that protection in a given country and in a given industry is too weak to invest in joint ventures, too weak to transfer the newest or most effective technology to a wholly-owned subsidiary and too weak to license the newest or most effective technology to unrelated firms) results in a decrease in U.S. manufacturing FDI of about $200 million. The data for this study were derived from a 1991 survey of a random sample of one hundred major U.S. firms in six manufacturing industries. Based on these survey data, Mansfield provides additional conclusions, including the following.

- Overall, India, Thailand, Brazil and Nigeria are perceived to have the weakest IPR protection and Spain, Japan, Hong Kong, and Singapore to have the strongest protection (Table 17.1).

- Most firms outside the chemical industry regard IPR protection as only one of many factors influencing their FDI decisions.

- Strong IPR protection is more important in decisions regarding advanced technology than in investment decisions.

- The composition of U.S. firms' FDI is affected by the countries' IPR protection. While investment in sales and distribution outlets is unaffected by weak protection, investment in facilities to manufacture components or complete products is affected.

- Technologies transferred to countries with weak IPR protection tend to be older than those transferred to countries with strong protection.

Table 17.1
Index of Perceived Weakness of Intellectual Property Protection, by Country, 1991

Country	Percent
India	44
Thailand	34
Brazil	33
Nigeria	33
Taiwan, China	31
Indonesia	27
Republic of Korea	26
Philippines	25
Venezuela	24
Mexico	23
Chile	20
Argentina	19
Hong Kong	18
Singapore	18
Japan	7
Spain	4

Note: Index for each country represents the average of the three separate means presented by Mansfield in tables 2, 3 and 4.
Source: Mansfield (1994).

- Industries, reflecting their particular circumstances, differ as to their evaluation of a particular country's IPR protection.

Evaluation of Empirical Evidence

While these findings significantly advance our knowledge in this area and are generally consistent with the results of other prior studies by Mansfield and others (Evenson, 1993; Mansfield, 1993; Mansfield and Romeo, 1980), several troubling questions remain, to which we now turn. For purposes of this chapter, at least four are worth noting.

The first of these concerns the nature of the IPR regime present in the newly industrialized countries (NICs) such as Korea, Thailand and Taiwan as they evolved from the developing to the industrialized stage. Of the three countries, Korea and Taiwan had, in the main, IPR regimes that were very similar to that of India in that neither had allowed chemical patents of any kind. While Thailand allows chemical patents with the exception of chemical vaccines (patents), its lack of patent protection for other categories is identical to India's (Evenson, 1993). Yet these countries, unlike India, were able to attract large flows of FDI and made extraordinary economic gains in the past two decades. Gunda Schumann, who has examined this issue at length, suggests that a country's move toward strong IPR protection may be as much a consequence of economic development as it is a cause of it. In particular, Schumann concludes that the greater a country's promotion of FDI and indigenous development in the high-technology field and the more it becomes export-oriented, the more likely, out of self-interest, it will move toward a strong IPR regime (Schumann, 1990). This appears to be the case with Korea and Taiwan and, to a lesser extent, with Thailand in the past few years. Thus, a strong IPR regime could easily follow rather than lead the inflow of FDI.

A second question concerns the fact that much of the research on IPR protection, as Evenson notes, is conducted from the standpoint of the industrialized countries (Evenson, 1993). More often than not, the studies presume that the direct and indirect benefits of FDI to the developing country far outweigh the direct cost in terms of losing the free-riding options to copy and reverse engineering and the indirect cost in terms of potential negative impact on local adaptive R&D (Evenson, 1993). This issue is particularly important for countries like India that possess considerable reverse engineering capability and are on the threshold of joining the NIC group.

A third question has to do with the fact that recent IPR research, with its almost exclusive focus on the developing countries, seems to ignore one obvious but important point. That is, the countries with the strongest IPR regimes, namely, the industrialized countries, are also the countries in which the greatest incentive and competence exist for imitation of innovations in general and reverse engineering in particular (Evenson, 1993). The incentive comes from the large potential payoff, given the size of the markets, associated with successful imitation. A high level of technical as well as legal competence, combined with the free and rapid flow of information through the communications networks within the scientific community and the movement of personnel from one firm to another, only helps to facilitate the imitation process with or without a patent. This raises the question as to the extent to which the source of the developing world's free-riding can be traced to the developed world. Research on this issue could help provide a different and useful perspective for the current debate on IPR protection.

The fourth and final question concerns the fact that the recent empirical literature that attempts to link the flow of FDI to IPR protection, including the Mansfield findings summarized earlier, does not appear to be consistent with some important theories of FDI as they relate to multinational enterprises (MNEs). Starting with Hymer (1976), a number of authors have argued that the problem of appropriability associated with proprietary technology is one of the major reasons why firms would rather engage in FDI than use other vehicles of cross-border economic involvement such as trade, licensing and joint ventures (Blaine, 1994; Buckley and Casson, 1976; Caves, 1984; Hymer, 1976). Buckley and Casson (1976) note that the strongest incentives for internalization (replacing licensing and other contractual exchanges with FDI, for example) occur in the markets for knowledge due to "market failure" problems uniquely associated with the production, transfer and sale of knowledge. According to these theories, FDI is a means by which firms attempt to overcome the problem of appropriability. Furthermore, they view the monopolistic power gained by exploiting firm-specific advantages such as proprietary technology—whether patented or not—as the MNE's *raison d'être* (Buckley and Casson, 1976). Thus, the appropriability argument becomes part of a theory of the FDI as well as a theory of the MNE. The point here is the that the relative strength of IPR protection plays no role in such theories of FDI. On the contrary, these theories, taken literally, seem to imply that, given the favorable incentives for FDI and given that a firm's competitive advantages lies in the proprietary technology it possess, the weaker the IPR regime it faces, the greater its incentive to engage in FDI.

Intellectual Property Protection in the United States

Six legal regimes constitute intellectual property law in the United States: patents, copyrights, trademarks, trade secrets, semiconductor protection and misappropriation (Benson and Raskind, 1991). Of these, patents and copyrights, because of their foundation in the U.S. Constitution and in various federal statutes, represent the highest form of protection. There are no federally created rights in trademarks, but there is a federal framework (the Lanham Act) which provides a system of registration and enforcement. Protection of trade secrets is grounded entirely in state law, and the scope of protection varies from state to state. Semiconductor protection is closer to the copyright regime designed to reflect the special needs of that industry. Misappropriation refers to a legal doctrine that protects against taking information of commercial value in cases that are outside the reach of laws governing intellectual property.

Empirical Evidence on the United States

The United States experience in IPR protection is relevant for two reasons. First, much of the ongoing debate concerning the definition of internationally acceptable "minimum standards of protection" has been led by the United States, and, as a result, other systems are often judged against the U.S. standards of law and enforcement (Mody, 1990). Second, and more important, the U.S. experience suggests that, overall, even the most uniform and perhaps strongest of legal regimes-patents and copyrights—may not provide adequate IPR protection.

Mansfield's pioneering empirical studies, among others, provide support for such a view (Mansfield et al., 1977). That firms find it difficult to appropriate the full benefits of their innovative efforts even with the strongest IPR regime is evidenced by Mansfield's finding that the social rate of return on investments in industrial innovation in the United States is, on the average, more than twice (56% vs. 25%) that of the private rate of return (Mansfield et al., 1977; Mansfield, 1986). A major reason for the much lower rate of private return is the inability of innovator firms, despite the strong patent protection, to prevent the benefits accrued to the imitators. In a study of a random sample of one hundred firms from 12 industries, Mansfield found that patent protection was essential for the development or introduction of 30 percent or more of inventions in only two industries—chemicals and pharmaceuticals.

Indeed, in six of the twelve industries—primary metals, instruments, office equipment, motor vehicles, rubber and textiles—patent protection had little or no effect on the development and introduction of innovations. Based on the results of this study, Mansfield concluded that while propensity to patent remains high even in industries where patents are relatively unimportant, the effect of the patent system on the development and introduction of innovations is quite small. Mansfield's findings were fully supported by a more comprehensive study conducted by Levin et al. (Levin et al., 1987; Winter, 1987). Based on interviews with research managers from 130 U.S. industries, Levin et al., found that, on a scale of one to seven, only 5 of the 130 industries rated product patents to prevent duplication as high as seven. The pharmaceutical drug industry was one of the five. If the effectiveness of patents as a means of protecting the returns from innovation is not ranked high in many industries, what are the alternative means by which firms overcome the appropriability problem? Levin and his colleagues addressed this question in their study. Respondents were asked to rate alternative means of appropriating the returns from their innovations. The authors found that, on the average, the highest ranked means of appropriating the returns on product and process innovations were "superior sales or services efforts" and "lead time." Across broad industry groups, the importance of "sales or service efforts" dominated product innovations, whereas "lead time" dominated process innovations. Other means of appropriating the returns that were ranked by the respondents were: "patents to prevent competitors from duplicating the product," "secrecy" and "moving quickly down the learning curve."

The findings by Mansfield and Levin et al. strongly suggest that, for most industries, legal protection of IPR is but one of many, and not even the most important, means by which firms maximize the appropriability of their innovations. The same general conclusion applies to legal protection of IPR in the form of software copyrights (Rao and Klein, 1994). The chemical industry in general, and pharmaceuticals in particular, are strong exceptions to this conclusion. The next section discusses how, even in the pharmaceutical industry where patent protection is strongest (i.e., among the industrialized countries), given the changing structure of the industry in the developed world, increasingly it is global marketing strategies rather than legal instruments that are likely to enhance the appropriability of drug innovations.

A GLOBAL PHARMACEUTICAL INDUSTRY PERSPECTIVE

The Developed World's View

Not unexpectedly, firms engaged in the production and marketing of patented and branded prescription drugs in the developed world are at the forefront of advocating strong IPR regimes in the form of patents everywhere. Such firms invest heavily in research and development, and their R&D intensity (i.e., R&D to sales ratio) in the United States is two to three times the average of manufacturing firms (Piccini and Rao, 1994). A widely cited figure by the industry in the United States is that it costs $259 million (in constant 1990 dollars) and $300 million or more in today's dollars to bring a new chemical entity (NCE) to the market (International Federation of Pharmaceutical Manufacturers Association; 1995; Pharmaceutical Manufacturers Association 1993). Because pharmaceutical R&D is a costly and risky activity, firms engaged in such activity seek strong patent protection to achieve maximum appropriability of their innovations. The paradox of drug patents in the United States and other industrialized countries is that, despite the fact that the chemical entity itself becomes public knowledge by the time the drug is approved for sale, patent enforceability is high, resulting in a high degree of appropriability. This is because imitation around a patent is difficult due to the exacting nature of a compound claim that covers the chemical entity, including any and all formulations or uses of the chemical entity (Winter, 1987).

Costs of imitation: Until the enactment of Trade Related Aspects of Intellectual Property (TRIPs), most developing countries and some industrialized countries such as Australia, Finland, New Zealand and Norway had not introduced patent protection for pharmaceutical products, although many had patents for processes (Nogues, 1990). As a result, pharmaceutical innovations produced in the United States and a few other industrialized countries became easy prey for imitation. Nogués cites a late 1980s estimate by the U.S. Pharmaceutical Manufacturers Association (PMA) of $1.4 billion sales of copied drugs per year, or 23 percent of the total patented pharmaceutical market, and 16 percent of the total pharmaceutical market in four countries—Argentina, Brazil, India and Mexico (Nogués, 1990). The incidence of imitation by this measure varies among countries, India being highest at 36 percent and Brazil lowest at 5 percent. Such estimates of the costs of imitation abound in the popular press and academic literature alike in the developed world and are often cited by the industry's representatives as the reason developing countries are less popular recipients of pharmaceutical FDI (Burstall and Dunning, 1985). An estimate for the mid-1980s placed the volume of total investment (FDI plus domestic investment) going to developing countries at about a third of that going to industrialized countries (Ballance, Pogany and Forstner, 1992). Moreover, with respect to research centers, the multinationals' involvement in developing countries compared with that in industrialized countries is even lower.

Table 17.2
Pharmaceutical Manufacturers Association, Member-Company Shares of Sales, Employment and R&D Abroad, by Geographic Area, 1991

Area	Sales (%)	Employment (%)	R&D (%)
Western Europe (EC, EFTA and Switzerland)	56.0	47.3	72.0
Japan	13.0	10.3	16.0
Canada	8.9	5.2	7.4
Latin America (including the Caribbean)	9.9	19.4	1.2
Asia/Pacific (from Pakistan to Southeast Asia, including China, Taiwan and the Koreas)	4.4	11.7	0.6
Australia and New Zealand	3.0	2.0	1.2
Middle East (including Turkey)	2.4	1.9	0.2
Africa	2.1	2.0	0.4
Central and Eastern Europe (including the former USSR)	0.8	0.2	0.2

Figures do not add up to 100 due to rounding.
Source: Pharmaceutical Manufacturers Association (1993).

Location of research facilities: While multinationals often locate research centers (these are generally associated with their respective foreign subsidiaries) outside their own borders in other industrialized countries, few such facilities are located in the developing countries (Ballance, Pogany and Forstner, 1992; Burstall and Dunning, 1985). The 1991 geographic distribution of PMA member-company R&D, sales and employment abroad illustrates this point further (Table 17.2). An extraordinarily high proportion of R&D expenditures abroad (95.4%) was in three areas of the developed world—Western Europe, Japan and Canada—which accounted for 78 percent of sales abroad. By contrast, a mere 2.4 percent of R&D went to Latin America, the Asia/Pacific (including the NICs), the Middle East and Africa compared to their share of sales of 19 percent and employment of 35 percent. However, we need to put these numbers in some perspective. First, multinationals, overall, perform only a small fraction of their total R&D abroad. Thus, only 15 percent of R&D expenditures of nonbank U.S. parents in 1993 was attributed to their majority-owned foreign affiliates. Second, R&D activity, because it suffers from some well-known ''market failure'' characteristics, is highly integrated into manufacturing.

As a result, the fraction of R&D performed by foreign affiliates in various

Table 17.3
Shares of U.S. Direct Investment Abroad and Research and Development
Expenditures of Nonbank Foreign Affiliates, by Geographic Area, 1993

Area	Direct Investment in Manufacturing (%)	R&D Expenditures (%)
Europe (including Turkey)	49.3	68.9
Canada	17.2	9.4
Latin America (including the Caribbean)	14.2	3.5
Asia/Pacific	7.0	8.2
Japan	6.7	7.9
Australia and New Zealand	3.9	1.7
Middle East	1.1	0.3
Africa	0.6	0.1

Note: R&D expenditures are for majority-owned foreign affiliates in all nonbanking industries.
   Europe excludes Eastern Europe, Central Europe and the former USSR.
Source: Bureau of Economic Analysis (1995).

countries is more in line with the proportion of FDI in these countries (Table 17.3). For example, 86 percent of the R&D expenditures of majority-owned U.S. nonbank foreign affiliates in 1993 went to Europe, Canada and Japan, which together accounted for 74 percent of U.S. foreign direct investment in manufacturing. By contrast, Latin America, the Asia/Pacific (including the NIC's), the Middle East and Africa accounted for 12 percent of U.S. foreign affiliates' R&D and 23 percent of FDI (Bureau of Economic Analysis, 1995).

Burstall and Dunning, in their analysis of international investment in pharmaceutical research, identify not one but several factors as influencing the choice of host country in which to locate research facilities. (IPR protection plays no part in their analysis because it is confined to multinational firms operating in the industrialized countries of Western Europe and Japan.) They include strength in the host country's science, large local drug market and need to adapt products to local requirements. The authors stress the first of these factors—quality of science in the host country—as the chief reason why Britain is a favorite country of foreign multinationals to set up substantial research facilities (Burstall and Dunning, 1985).

However, based on relatively low levels of FDI by multinational pharmaceutical firms in production and research in the developing countries, one must not minimize the importance of these firms in those countries. The data presented by Ballance et al. show that while foreign-owned firms are outnumbered by local firms in every country in their sample of 13 developing countries, their median market share is around 60 percent of the domestic market (Ballance, Pogany and Forstner, 1992).

The Developing World's View

Impact on drug prices: Several arguments have been advanced to suggest that the costs of IPR protection to developing countries, at least in the short run, could run very high without any offsetting benefits. The first of these concerns higher prices that will result from IPR protection. Judging from a comparison of pharmaceutical prices in the industrial countries with strong patent protection with those of developing countries, Nogués concluded that prices paid in the developed countries were more than twice those paid in the developing countries (Nogués, 1990). Pervasive and substantial price controls in many developing countries combined with limited controls in the developed countries (France and Italy are two major exceptions) is one obvious reason for this result (Ballance, Pogany and Forstner, 1992). Of particular concern to the developing world is the potential adverse impact of TRIPs on the price of essential drugs.

Mitigating Provisions in the TRIPs: Two provisions in the TRIPs agreement are intended to help mitigate the effect of sharp price increases in the developing world. First is the delay in the date of application of the TRIPs provisions to the developing world—five years after the entry into force of the TRIPs agreement for the developing countries and eleven years for the least developed countries. The second of these provisions is the continued availability of the compulsory license instrument, although its use, from the standpoint of the developing countries as well as some developed countries, is greatly limited. (International Federation of Pharmaceutical Manufacturers Association, 1995). For example, any compulsory license must not discriminate among different fields of technology. Thus, laws granting compulsory licenses only for pharmaceuticals such as the previous Canadian patent law violate TRIPs. Also, local market satisfaction through importation prevents the grant of a compulsory license to permit local working. Moreover, under the TRIPs provisions, the remuneration to the patentee who is subject to compulsory license is driven by the economic value of the grant rather than ''standard'' or industry average royalty rates. Other features of compulsory licensing under TRIPs include nonexclusivity, nonassignability and limitations on the scope and duration of a license to the authorized purpose.

Some authors have argued that the potential negative impact on the price of essential drugs would be minimal, in any event. Over 90 percent of the drugs on the essential drug list published by the World Health Organization (WHO) are not protected by patents, and they report, strengthening patent protection for new drugs would foster creation of substitute drugs that would drive down their prices (Rapp and Rozek, 1990). Others have argued that generally, TRIPs provisions, would on balance have the effect of increasing the cost of drugs sharply to the developing world without making any positive impact on global innovative activity (Rodrik, 1995).

Global Marketing Strategies

The previous discussion makes it clear that, in a market economy, an inherent tension exists between the need to grant temporary monopoly in the form of a patent to encourage development of new drugs and the goal of all countries—developing as well as developed countries—to make such drugs available at minimum prices. Public policy solutions invariably focus on the nature and degree of governmental intervention to balance the two conflicting objectives (Lall, 1985). They include, for example, not only the nature and degree of IPR protection (e.g., the scope of a patent, the life of a patent and the rigor of patent enforcement), but also the extent of price controls, more or fewer incentives to undertake research and development and foreign direct investment. It is also clear from the previous discussion that IPR protection is only one of many factors influencing the FDI decisions even in the pharmaceutical industry. Other factors include the size of the local drug market, growth opportunities, degree of price controls and, in the case of investment in R&D facilities, the strength of the host country's science. This chapter takes the view that, given certain unique characteristics of the industry—especially the segment that produces patented and branded drugs—and its changing structure in the developed world, perhaps global marketing strategies, driven by market forces, will increasingly supplant legal instruments and governmental interventions in mitigating the conflicting public policy objectives.

A global marketing strategy is concerned with, among other things, obtaining scale economies that reduce unit costs below those of national firms, developing and promoting global brands, access to low-cost labor (including R&D labor) or materials, ability to transfer ideas, experience and know-how from one country to another and access to strategically important markets (Aaker, 1995). It should be noted that the term *global marketing strategy*, as used in this chapter, is different from globalization of markets, although they are related. Global marketing strategy, as noted earlier has mainly to do with efficiency of operations and competitiveness, whereas globalization involves homogenity of demand across cultures and the extent to which marketing strategy will be standardized (Cateora, 1996). The following discussion concerns the pharmaceutical industry's characteristics, including recent trends and its changing structure. It also examines the opportunities and impediments for the evolution of global marketing strategies that—through a deeper level of integration in terms of FDI, including investment in research facilities and marketing infrastructure—are for the mutual benefit of developing and developed countries.

Industry Characteristics and Trends

Several industry characteristics and trends seem to favor moves toward a deeper level of integration with the developing world through global marketing strategies. Four of these characteristics are as follows.

High degree of specialization: Leading pharmaceutical firms are highly specialized in that they derive most of their revenues from pharmaceutical drugs (Scrip Reports, 1992). Moreover, most companies derive the bulk of their revenues from a few products. On the average, more than a fifth of the pharmaceutical revenues of the top 25 firms come from sales of a single product. A single drug such as SmithKline Beecham's Tagamet could account for more than half of that firm's pharmaceutical revenues in a given year (Ballance, Pogany and Forstner, 1992). Such a high degree of specialization, compounded by the post-launch risks, may induce firms to seek a more rapid penetration of the global market.

High proportion of sunk costs: The patented and branded segment of the pharmaceutical industry is not only R&D, but also promotion intensive. The average of the combined R&D and marketing costs of leading firms as a percentage of operating revenues in the United States, Switzerland and Germany in 1988 was estimated at 37 percent, about the same as their share of manufacturing costs (Ballance, Pogany and Forstner, 1992). These expenses, once made in the context of a dominant new drug in the firm's revenue stream and cost structure, cannot be recovered except through sales of that specific drug. Therefore, they become sunk costs. The presence of the high proportion of sunk costs in the cost structure, combined with a high degree of specialization, provides further incentive to maximize appropriability through rapid penetration of the global market.

Expiration of patents on popular drugs: In the United States, patents on roughly 80 of the 100 best-selling drugs had expired by 1990 and at least another 20 drugs were to have come off patent by the mid-1990s (Ballance, Pogany and Forstner, 1992). At the same time, the industry is not producing new drugs rapidly enough to replace those that lose market share to imitators when patents expire (Gambardella, 1995; Thomas, 1988). This will make new opportunities for producers of generics at home and abroad, thus placing even greater pressure on integrated firms to turn themselves into "dual producers" supplying both generics and patented drugs (Ballance, Pogany and Forstner 1992). The growing entry of producers of patented and branded drugs into the generic market would benefit consumers in both developed and developing countries.

Brand name: A strong brand name association in the home market—whether it refers to a particular drug, say, Zantac, and to the company which produces that drug and similar other branded drugs, namely, Glaxo—is another powerful reason to penetrate the global market as rapidly as possible. Given the potential for rapid spread of information to the medical communities across countries through standard reference books, professional journals and other means (at little or no cost to the producer) and given the dominant role played by doctors everywhere in drug prescription, the additional cost of promoting the same brand name in many other countries should be significantly smaller. Another reason is related to the point about sunk costs made earlier. A strong brand name in the home market is often a result of a high level of investment in promotion, much of it in the form of expenditures associated with salespeople aimed at physicians. To the extent such activities produce learning curve effects (in terms of reduction in real marketing cost per unit sold), they could then be used to quickly exploit opportunities even in the developing world where market potential tends to be smaller and price sensitivity greater. That is, the learning curve effects in the home country would enable a firm to sell profitably in the price-sensitive developing country markets.

Changes in Industry Structure

Two factors are particularly relevant to explain the changing structure of the industry, at least as it affects the large integrated U.S. pharmaceutical firms. They relate to changing technology and competitive pressures in the home market.

Technology: The emergence of biotechnology firms has caused what Alfonso Gambarella calls a change in the technological paradigm in terms of the drug discovery process. Drug research has shifted from a chemical to a biological basis. The chemical approach depends on scale, whereas the biological approach depends on rational understanding of the functioning of the human body (Gambardella, 1995). This change has the potential to strike at the structure of the pharmaceutical industry and provide new opportunities for international collaborative ventures between the developed and developing world. This can happen for several reasons. First, small biotechnology firms funded by venture capital are increasingly responsible for miracle drugs. This means that economies of scale in R&D are less important than in the past. Second, few or if any, of the key innovations in the biotechnology field are made by large pharmaceutical firms. Third, because of what Rothmann calls their rational design, remarkable efficiency and safety profile, the average development time of biotechnology-based drugs has been compressed to four to seven years, from the former ten years for a new pharmaceutical product, while at the same time reducing the risk of technical and commercial failure (Gambardella, 1995; Rathmann 1993). Finally, both collaboration and competition exist between biotechnology firms and large pharmaceutical firms. While many pharmaceutical firms have built in-house capability in biotechnology, their comparative advantage remains in large-scale bioprocessing or production know-how and worldwide marketing infrastructure and expertise. Similarly, the chief advantage of a biotechnology firm is its specialized R&D activity (Pisano, Wiejian and Teece 1988). Therefore, collaborative ventures between the two sets of firms are common and take many forms, including R&D contracts, licensing experiments, supply contracts, manufacturing agreements and marketing argreements (Pisano, Wiejian and Teece 1988). The significance of this change in the technological paradigm for the developing world can only be beneficial. This is because biotechnology has the potential to produce cheaper and safer drugs for the consumer, while at the same time reducing the risks of technical and commercial failures for the producers of such drugs. In addition, the change in the technological paradigm offers developing countries like India, which possess a strong scientific base, an opportunity to become a start-up player in the biotechnology field somewhat similar to its role in the emerging global software industry (Deolalikar and Evenson, 1990; Schumann, 1990).

Increased competition in the home market: Competitive pressure on firms producing patented and branded drugs in the home market is another reason why global marketing strategies that could produce beneficial outcomes for the developed as well developing world could emerge. There are many sources of competitive pressure in the United States. They include, as noted earlier, competition from producers of generic drugs, which in 1994 accounted for 37 percent of prescriptions, growth of managed care systems and prescription-benefits management firms (PBMs), all of which continue to exert pressure on the profitability of branded drugs (McGahan, 1994). Branded drug producers have been responding to these competitive pressures in several ways. They include acquisition of PBMs (e.g., Merck's acquisition of Medco), offering their own generic products (generic version of SmithKline Beecham's blood pressure drug, Dyazide) and developing milder versions (e.g., Merck's ulcer-treating drug, Pepcid) for the over-the-counter market (Freudenheim, 1992; Nichols, 1994). Moreover, there is competition among patented and branded drugs. For example, Humatrope (Lilly) and Protropin (Genentech) are close competitors for the long-term treatment of children with growth problems. Similarly, Tagamet (SmithKline Beecham) and Zantac (Glaxo) compete in the treatment of ulcer illness (Rapp and Rozek, 1990).

Yet another source of competitive pressure on the developed world's pharmaceutical industry should favor the developing countries. The pharmaceutical industry is a multinational industry in which firms originating in a few industrialized countries contest vigorously not only in each other's domestic and regional markets but also in the developing world's markets. While U.S. firms have a dominant share of the world market (43%), firms from only three countries of Western Europe—United Kingdom, Germany and Switzerland—hold 45 percent of the remaining market (Tancer, 1995). Moreover, there is some evidence which suggests that firms from the smaller industrialized countries— Ciba-Geigy and Sandoz (Switzerland) and Glaxo (United Kingdom)—maintain greater presence in terms of production as well as some research facilities across many developing countries compared to their U.S. counterparts (Ballance, Pogany and Forstner 1992). Given the competitive pressures on the U.S. firms in the home market their level of involvement with the developing world is also likely to increase.

This discussion provides reasons for a somewhat optimistic view—notwithstanding the inadequate IPR protection in many developing countries—of the prospect for greater level of involvement by the multinational pharmaceutical firms in the developing world. Global marketing strategies will increasingly shape the nature and level of the multinationals' involvement. Such a view is not without support from industry insiders. Dr. Otto A. Stamm, head of the

Patent Department of Ciba-Geigy and a significant industry figure in the IPR debate, put it best (Stamm, 1993: 224–255):

Patent protection tends to be rather of secondary interest for marketing strategy. . . . Especially important, above all in countries without effective patent protection are marketing steps that—varying from place to place—are independent of property rights. Such steps include customer orientation (e.g., the confidential relationship with doctors); satisfying real needs, which requires a true understanding of the consumer's interests; promotion by means of medical-scientific and other explanatory literature; a reliable distribution organization; readiness to take up suggestions from the realm of practice; good contacts with government authorities; commercial probity; market-oriented price strategy.

To be sure, this is not a case against patent protection. Rather, marketing strategy, especially promotional strategy, becomes a necessary complement to a high level of innovation activity in the pharmaceutical industry even when patent protection is strong (Piccini and Rao, 1994). Dr. Stamm's point above, which is consistent with the implications of this chapter, suggests that in countries where IPR protection is weak, marketing strategies designed to enhance the appropriability of innovations become substitutes for legal instruments.

Implications for Developing Countries

What specific implications does this analysis of the characteristics and changing structure of the developed world's pharmaceutical industry produce for the marketing strategies vis-à-vis the developing countries? The following is an outline of the direction in which some of these strategies might evolve and their impact on the developing world.

Globalization vs. adaptation: There is no reason to think that a single strategy will dominate among the large integrated firms producing patented and branded drugs. A high proportion of sunk costs (i.e., R&D and promotional expenditures) and a strong brand name in the home market, combined with a high degree of specialization, are strong incentives to pursue a globalized strategy with a high degree of standardization of marketing mix across cultures and countries. Growing harmonization of regulations through GATT and other mechanisms and growing universality of practice, therapy and other factors are additional incentives for globalization, especially in terms of product strategy (James, 1990). However, given the vast cultural, economic and infrastructure differences between much of the developing and developed world, a high degree of adaptation in terms of pricing, promotion and distribution strategies will be required. A recent survey of all major international brands marketed in Europe suggests that such adaptations are necessary even among the developed countries (Kapferer, 1992). It is important to note, however, that the need to adapt does not negate the incentives to leverage on large up-front fixed costs associated with R&D and promotional activities referred to earlier.

Pricing and branding: Potential adverse effects of TRIPs on drug prices in the developing world are and should be of concern to everyone, including the pharmaceutical multinationals, for several reasons, not the least of which is the fact that drugs are often substitutes for other, costlier forms of treatment (e.g., institutional care and surgery) which the developing world could afford even less. Here again, given that competitive pressure in the home market provides strong incentives for rapid penetration of global markets, multinationals could adopt discriminatory pricing and branding strategies, which could result in some drugs being sold at significantly lower prices in the developing countries compared with those in the developed countries. Simply put, such a strategy involves segmenting markets on the basis of their relative demand elasticities and devising a marketing mix appropriate for each segment. Such a strategy would result in lower prices for the more price-sensitive segments, the developing world in this case. This strategy is generally disguised in the form of private brands, generic brands or the same high-priced brand whose image is diluted by a less attractive and sometimes less convenient package and the like. Indeed, this is no more than a variation of the growing practice of firms producing patented and branded drugs in the United States to offer both the high-priced branded drug and a generic version of it, often at less than half the price of the branded drug after the expiration of the branded drug's patent (Freudenheim, 1992).

Investment in R&D facilities: As noted earlier, much of the investment in R&D facilities by the multinational pharmaceutical firms takes place in the home market. When it does go aboard, it goes almost entirely to other industrialized countries which are also their largest markets—Western Europe, Canada and Japan—and especially to countries with strong science bases. However, this pattern could change in the future. Countries like India with a strong science base and a large and growing market could become attractive sites for various types of R&D investment for several reasons. First, Gambardella suggests that biotechnology research is based not on scale but on scientific creativity and human capital organized around small, flexible and highly research-intensive firms that are often facing generally inhospitable capital markets (Gambardella, 1995; Rathmann, 1993). Given strong financial incentives combined with IPR protection, biotechnology firms appear to be good candidates for collaborative ventures in developing countries such as India. Second, the predominant part of drug development costs (over 70%) goes to clinical testing, especially testing for effectiveness, usually involving a large number of patients and hospitals. Given the high cost of testing in the industrialized countries and the ease of global communication, it may be cost effective to move some parts of the testing to developing countries with scientific capabilities. Third, competitive pressures in the home markets, combined with the declining levels of innovation, are likely to result in moving away from the traditional technology push strategy to a customer-driven strategy in which marketing plays a greater role in directing the focus of innovation (James, 1990). Such a change in orientation, since it would require a greater degree of interaction between marketing and research, could provide further incentives to move some investments in R&D to the developing world.

Investment in production facilities: In terms of the flow of FDI into the developing world, given the relatively small proportion of production costs—especially labor cost—and transportation cost in the cost structure, investment in marketing assets (infrastructure investments in distribution, promotion and information, for example) is likely to continue to dominate investment in production facilities. However, countries like India with substantial production capability and a large domestic market could serve as regional production centers for the large multinationals.

CONCLUSIONS

IPR protection is only one of many factors that influence FDI decisions, even in the pharmaceutical industry where great importance is attached to it. Perhaps IPR protection in relation to FDI is best viewed as an "environmental factor," albeit an important one. Judging from the U.S. experience, even the most uniform and perhaps strongest of all legal regimes—patents and copyrights—may not provide adequate IPR protection. Rather, firms across many industries seem to place greater emphasis on superior marketing as a means of protecting gains from product innovations. With respect to the pharmaceutical industry and the recent debate concerning the potential impact of the TRIPs agreement, IPR protection, in itself, would have little effect on the flow of FDI into the developing countries. Foreign direct investment in production facilities by pharmaceutical firms, much like FDI by firms in other manufacturing industries, seems to follow its largest markets, the developed world's. Moreover, the cost structure of pharmaceutical firms (the relatively small fraction of labor and transportation costs), combined with a highly standardized product, suggest that FDI in marketing assets will continue to dominate FDI in production facilities. Foreign direct investment in R&D facilities, when it takes place at all, seems to follow production facilities in other industrialized countries, particularly those with a strong science base. This again suggests that it takes more than IPR protection to attract R&D facilities into the developing countries.

Increasingly, global marketing strategies—driven by market forces and technological developments in the industrialized world—are likely to increase the involvement by pharmaceutical multinationals with the developing world. Among the important factors influencing such strategies are changes in the industry structure brought about by the emergence of biotechnology, increased competition from generics, declining levels of innovation, expiration of patents on branded drugs and the presence of a high degree of sunk costs in the cost structure of firms producing patented and branded drugs. These factors could force large pharmaceutical multinationals to adopt global marketing strategies in the form of a more rapid penetration of the global market through segment-specific pricing and branding strategies that could be favorable to the developing world and mitigate the potential adverse effects of the strong IPR protection required by the TRIPs. This could also create new opportunities for international collaborative ventures.

There is little doubt that a shift has taken place not only in the technological paradigm but also in the competitive paradigm within the pharmaceutical industry in the developed world. These shifts offer new opportunities for countries like India, with substantial production, innovation and export capabilities combined with a large and growing domestic market. However, successful exploitation of these opportunities will require that the focus of the current IPR debate be shifted from legal instruments to market-based strategies.

NOTE

This chapter is based on a revised version of a paper presented at the International Conference on Globalization and the Market Economy in December 1995 in New Delhi, India. The author thanks Rick Kriauciunas for helpful comments, Dr. Anthony M. Akel for his encouragement and the C.W. Post Research Committee for its support.

REFERENCES

Aaker, David A. 1995. *Strategic Market Management*. New York: John Wiley and Sons, 298–317.

Arrow, Kenneth J. 1962. Economic Welfare and Allocation of Resources for Invention. In R. Nelson (ed.), *The Rate and Direction of Incentive Activity*. Princeton, NJ: Princeton University Press.

Baldwin, R. 1979. Determinants of Trade and Foreign Investment. *Review of Economics and Statistics*.

Ballance, Robert, Pogany, Janos and Forstner, Helmut. 1992. *The World's Pharmaceutical Industries*. Prepared for the United Nations Industrial Development Organization. Brookfield, VT: Edward Elgar Publishing Co., 121–135, 139–250.

Bator, Francis N. 1958. Anatomy of Market Failure. *Quarterly Journal of Economics* (72): 351–379.

Benson, Stanley M. and Raskind, Leo J. 1991. An Introduction to Law and Economics of Intellectual Property. *Journal of Economic Perspectives* 5(1): 3–27.

Blaine, Michael James. 1994. *Cooperation in International Business*, VT: Brookfield, VT: Avebury, 36–58.

Buckley, Peter and Casson, Mark. 1976. *The Future of the Multinational Enterprise*. London: Macmillan.

Bureau of Economic Analysis. 1995, June. The International Investment Position of the United States in 1994. *Survey of Current Business*: 52–60.

Burstall, Michael and Dunning, John. 1985. International Investment in Innovation. In Nicholas Wells (ed.), *Pharmaceuticals Among Sunrise Industries*. New York: St. Martin's Press, 185–197.

Cateora, Philip R. 1996. *International Marketing*. Chicago: Richard D. Irwin, 317.

Caves, Richard E. 1984. *Multinational Enterprise and Economic Analysis*. Cambridge, MA: Cambridge University Press.

Denison, Edward F. 1985. *Trends in American Economic Growth, 1929–1982*. Washington, DC: Brookings Institution.

Deolalikar, A. and Evenson, R. 1990. Private Inventive Activity in Indian Manufacturing: Its Extent and Determinants. In R. Evenson and G. Ranis (eds.). *Science and Technology: Lessons for Development Policy*. Boulder, CO: Westview, 233–253.

Evenson, Robert E. 1993. Intellectual Property Rights, R & D, Inventions, Technology Purchase, and Piracy in Economic Development: An International Comparative Study. In M. Wallerstein et al. (eds.), *Global Dimensions of Intellectual Property Rights in Science and Technology*. Washington, DC: National Academy Press, 325–355.

Freudenheim, Milt. 1992, September 20. How the Big Drug Makers Are Imitating Their Imitators. *New York Times*: D5.

Gambardella, Alfonso. 1995. *Science and Innovation*. Cambridge: Cambrige University Press, 40, 161–167.

Hymer, Stephen. 1976. *The International Operations of National Firms*. Cambridge, MA: MIT Press.

International Federation of Pharmaceutical Manufacturers Association. 1995. *GATT TRIPs and the Pharmaceutical Industry: A Review*. Geneva, 1–16.

James, Barrie. 1990. *The Global Pharmaceutical Industry in the 1990s: The Challenge of Change*. The Economic Intelligence Unit, Special Report No. 2071. London: Business International.

Kapferer, Jean-Noël. 1992. *Strategic Brand Management*. New York: Free Press.

Kendrick, John W. 1980. *Productivity in the United States: Trends and Cycles*. Baltimore: Johns Hopkins University Press.

Lall, Sanjaya. 1985. Pharmaceuticals and the Third World Poor. In Nicholas Wells (ed.), *Pharmaceuticals Among Sunrise Industries*. New York: St. Martin's Press, 91–97.

Lee, Jeon-Yeon. 1993. Unpublished work toward a doctoral dissertation at the University of Pennsylvania cited in Mansfield (1994).

Levin, R., Klevorick, A. K., Nelson, R. R. and Winter, S. G. 1987. Appropriating the Returns from Industrial Research and Development. *Brookings Papers on Economic Activity*, 3.

Mansfield, Edwin 1968. *Industrial Research and Technological Innovation*. New York: W. W. Norton.

Mansfield, Edwin et al. 1977 May. Social and Private Rates of Return from Industrial Innovations. *Quarterly Journal of Economics* 91(2): 221–240.

Mansfield, Edwin and Romeo, Anthony. 1980, December. Technology Transfer to Overseas Subsidiaries by U.S. Based Firms. *Quarterly Journal of Economics* 95: 737–750.

Mansfield, Edwin. 1986, February. Patents and Innovation: An Empirical Study. *Management Science* 32(2): 173–181.

Mansfield, Edwin. 1993. Unauthorized Use of Intellectual Property: Effects on Investment, Technology Transfer, and Innovation. In M. Wallerstein et al. (eds.). *Global Dimensions of Intellectual Property Rights in Science and Technology*. Washington, DC: National Academy Press.

Mansfield, Edwin. 1994. *Intellectual Property Protection, Foreign Direct Investment and

Technology Transfer. International Finance Corporation, Discussion Paper Number 19. Washington, DC: World Bank, 1–43.

McGahan, Anita M. 1994, November–December. Industry Structure and Competitive Advantage. *Harvard Business Review*: 115–124.

Mody, Ashoka. 1990. New International Environment for Intellectual Property Rights. In F. Rushing and C. Brown (eds.), *Intellectual Property Rights in Science, Technology, and Economic Performance*. Boulder, CO: Westview Press, 203–240.

Nichols, Nancy A. 1994, November–December. Medicine, Management and Mergers: An Interview with Merk's P. Roy Vagelos. *Harvard Business Review*: 105–114.

Nogués, Julio. 1990. Patents and Pharmaceutical Drugs: Understanding the Pressures on Developing Countries. *Journal of World Trade* 25(6): 81–104.

Nordhaus, William D. 1969. *Invention, Growth and Welfare*. Cambridge, MA: MIT Press.

Pharmaceutical Manufacturers Association. 1993. *PMA Annual Survey Report: Trends in U.S. Pharmaceutical Sales and R & D*. Washington, DC.

Piccini, Raymond and Rao, P. M. 1994. Innovation and Product Promotion: A Different View. Proceedings of the *Association of Marketing Theory and Practice*, Jekyll Island, Georgia, 66–71.

Pisano, Gary P., Wiejian, Shan and Teece, David J. 1988. Joint Ventures and Collaboration in the Biotechnology Industry. In David C. Mowery (ed.), *International Collaborative Ventures in U.S. Manufacturing*. Cambridge, MA: Ballinger Publishing Co., 183–222.

Rao, P. M. 1995. Promotional Strategy over Patent Life: Recent Pharmaceutical Evidence and Its Implications. Proceedings of the *Association of Marketing Theory and Practice*, Savannah, Georgia, 32–39.

Rao, P. M. and Klein, Joseph A. 1994. Growing Importance of Marketing Strategies for the Software Industry. *Industrial Marketing Management* 23(1): 29–37.

Rapp, R. and Rozek, R. 1990, October. Benefits and Costs of Intellectual Property Protection in Developing Countries. *Journal of World Trade* 24(6): 75–102.

Rathmann, George B. 1993. Adopting IPR's to New Technologies: Biotechnology Case Study. In Michael B. Wallerstein et al. (eds.), *Global Dimensions of Intellectual Property Rights in Science and Technology*. Washington, DC: National Academy Press, 319–328.

Rodrik, Dani. 1995. Comments. In Anne Krueger (ed.), *Trade Policies and Developing Nations*. Washington, DC: Brookings Institution, 107–108.

Root, F. and Ahmed, A. 1979. Empirical Determinants of Manufacturing Direct Foreign Investment in Developing Countries. *Economic Development and Cultural Change*: 751–767.

Rozek, Richard. 1990. Protection of Intellectual Property Rights: Research and Development Decisions and Economic Growth. In F. Rushing and C. Brown (eds.), *Intellectual Property Rights in Science, Technology, and Economic Performance*. Boulder, CO: Westview Press, 31–46.

Schumann, Gunda. 1990. Economic Development and Intellectual Property Protection in Southeast Asia. In Francis W. Rushing and Carole Ganz Brown (eds.), *Intellectual Property Rights in Science, Technology, and Economic Performance*. Boulder, CO: Westview Press, 157–202.

Scrip Reports. 1992. *Pharmaceutical Company League Tables*. Richmond, United Kingdom: PJB Publications.

Solow, Robert M. 1957. Technical Change and the Aggregate Production Function. *Review of Economics and Statistics* 39: 312–320.

Stamm, Otto A. 1993. Intellectual Property Rights and Competitive Strategy: A Multinational Pharmaceutical Firm. In Michael B. Wallerstein et al. (eds.), *Global Dimensions of Intellectual Property Rights in Science and Technology.* Washington, DC: National Academy Press, 224, 225.

Tancer, Robert S. 1995, March–April. Trends in Worldwide Intellectual Property Protection. *The International Executive* 37(2): 147–166.

Thomas, Lacy Glenn. 1988. Multifirm Strategies in the U.S. Pharmaceutical Industry. In David C. Mowery (ed.), *International Collaborative Ventures in U.S. Manufacturing.* Cambridge, MA: Ballinger Publishing Co., 147–181.

Winter, Sidney G. 1987. Knowledge and Competence as Strategic Assets. In David J. Teece (ed.), *The Competitive Challenge.* New York: Harper and Row, 159–184.

CHAPTER 18

Environmental Changes and the Impact on International Marketing Strategies: The Case of the Textile Industry in Zimbabwe

ZORORO MURANDA AND
JAN-ERIK JAENSSON

The influence of the external environment on a firm's strategy in international marketing is a result of a combination of international market influences, domestic market influences and the internal structural weaknesses of individual firms. The poor performance of Zimbabwe's textile and clothing sector is the result of two and half decades of protection, economic structural changes in the domestic market, limited vision of opportunities in different international markets and inability to adapt strategy to quick changes in both the international and domestic market. Firms in this sector lack experience and knowledge of the wider external markets except for a few niches in Europe, the United States and the Southern Africa region. This has become a handicap in the firms' ability to internatinalize their operations.

THEORETICAL BACKGROUND

Perhaps the important question to be answered at this point is, What implications does environmental variable analysis have on company strategy? In the literature of marketing, the role of environmental analysis in influencing how organizations shape their future strategies has never been contested. However, there has been a debate on whether the environment should be regarded in marketing and strategy choice as simply a deterministic factor and therefore not influenced by the firm or, conversely, should also be considered as applicable.

The traditional marketing theory has tended to view the environment as a deterministic influence to which the organization adapts its strategies. McCarthy (1960) in his "4 Ps" model argued that the environment has uncontrollable factors that are external. In his view, the internal aspects of the organization can be managed, but the external environment is established and must be accepted as is.

The approach of environmental determinism has also been proposed within organizational theory where the natural selection model has claimed that environmental characteristics select organizations for survival and growth, according to how good a fit there is between their activities, structures, and environmental characteristics (Hannan and Freeman, 1977). Although the model does not explain why certain organizations and not others adapt to external requirements, it draws explicit attention to the environmental determinants that may facilitate or constrain change. This view was also reflected in empirical research by researchers such as Burns and Stalker (1969), Duncan (1972), Lawrence and Lorch (1967), and Neghandi and Reinman (1973). Hayes and Abernathy (1980) and Wind and Robertson (1983) argued that the firm must cater for its customers within the context of the firm's environment.

In general, marketing theory appears to assume that the organization confronts predetermined opportunities in the environment. Marketing strategies are therefore viewed as a set of adaptive responses. Under this situation, firm strategy and performance are dependent on the efficient and effective adaptation of company characteristics to environmental contingencies. This perspective has been challenged by recent theory and research in management. Some authors such as Pfeffer (1978), Pfeffer and Salancik (1978), Galbraith (1977), Aldrich (1979) and Porter (1979, 1980) have argued that firms can implement a variety of strategies designed to modify existing environmental conditions. Although these researchers do accept the impact of internal and external contingencies, their message is that strategy formulation can be used to create environments in which organizations operate. In Bradley's view (1985), it is not the marketing environment itself that is important but the firm's ability to cope with it, predict it, comprehend it, deal with diversity and respond quickly to it. The intention in such cases is to develop specific sets of strategies they believe can be used to manage the environment and the conditions under which such strategies are applicable.

Galbraith has categorized the strategies that can be used in managing the environment for the good of strategy formulation. His three categories are independent strategies, cooperative strategies and strategic maneuvering. According to Galbraith, independent strategies are the means by which the organization can reduce environmental uncertainty and dependency by drawing on its own resources and ingenuity. Cooperative strategies involve implicit or explicit cooperation with other elements in the environment, whereas strategic maneuvering includes strategies designed to change or alter the task environment of the organization. Galbraith implies that the firm's strategy formulation should be independent of the environmental deterministic view but proactive in its approach. In changing environments, variations in commitment to operating in such environments may be an important factor in explaining differences in environmental perception and therefore the strategies formulated by the firm. Managers are therefore supposed to be committed in their analysis because it contributes to how they formulate their strategies. According to Pettigrew and Whipp (1993), in order to appreciate how an organization reaches an understanding of its environment, we should consider the following:

- The process of understanding and assessment combines analysis, judgment and action.
- The process is shaped jointly by the dominant logic of an industry and the internal features of the firm.
- Environmental assessment occurs across the whole organization.
- Above all, analysis, judgment and action seldom reflect the well-ordered progressions of traditional planning manuals. The problems of recognition, acceptance and contest are legion.

These four aspects have a number of important implications for strategy choice and formulation. First, environmental assessment is a process, just as strategy formulation can also be regarded as a process. Second, the process of environmental assessment is not an isolated act in the firm. The influences of industry, firm characteristics and personal values do affect management's strategic options. Furthermore, the individual or collective beliefs of managers fundamentally affect the way they conceive the environment in the first place. Such beliefs are therefore very important to the way company strategy measures the effect of environmental variables. Third, each function of the organization engages in its own environmental analysis, but the critical difference between firms is the extent to which this is realized, built upon and exploited (Pettigrew and Whipp, 1993).

In international marketing, the international environment directly affects the firm's strategic options and as a consequence, determines the kind of structure (and strategy) most appropriate for international marketing operations (Bradley, Hession and Murray, 1985). An aspect of the international environment that receives little attention among analysts and managers alike is the need to develop strategies along multidimensional lines. In international marketing, it is myopic to consider exporting as the only or even the primary way of entering foreign markets, as has been the case with most firms in developing countries. Concentration on exporting as the transfer modality may have given rise to the unnecessary and fruitless debate regarding international market shares at both the firm and the country level. To be successful, a firm must identify and concentrate on its relative differential advantage in international markets (Bradley, 1985). According to Bradley (1985) and Domegan (1984), many of the countries' marketing ills apparently lie in the micro-software cell (the firm level) of the matrix. They argue that corporate management has failed to adapt to new global standards. To increase competitiveness at this level requires major improvements in the management of internal change in firms attempting to internationalize (Bradley, Hession and Murray, 1985). O'Mahoney (1985) contends that because of the weaknesses at the corporate management level, many firms in traditional industry (including the textile and clothing industries) failed to adapt to appropriate strategies and structures in the face of environmental discontinuity.

Success in international marketing, according to some authors, hinges on concentrating on the micro- or firm level and software aspects of corporate management for answers to the question of international competitiveness. At the same time, these firms cannot neglect the country or macrolevel and hardware aspects of economic policy. Perhaps one of the most important environmental variables that has affected firm strategy at the macrolevel more than anything else in developing economies (e.g., Zimbabwe) has been the widespread deregulation and change in the support systems installed by governments to support industries and firms, especially those engaged in international marketing.

Despite the pervasiveness of regulation and the critical role of strategic choice in determining firm performance, the intersection of strategic choice and regulation has been largely ignored. Mahoney and Murray (1980, 1981) have identified two types of regulation associated with firm strategy: social and economic regulation. Social regulation aims to regulate noneconomic activities across industries. Economic regulation, in Mahoney and Murray's framework, is typically directed at a specific industry. A primary purpose of regulation identified by industrial organization researchers is to limit excessive competition. Limiting competition also limits the strategy choices available to firms when they formulate their strategies. Mahon and Murray (1981) have pointed out that economic regulation may be the most important type of regulation from a strategic management standpoint because it directly affects the competitive dynamics of industries. They have also suggested that the speed of deregulation should be considered when examining firm-level regulatory effects on strategy.

Spulber (1989) has suggested the importance of the amount of time firms have to adjust to changes in regulatory policy. When regulatory change is implemented gradually, especially in step-by-step fashion over several years, firms have time to react to impending changes. This offers firms advantages that are not enjoyed when deregulation is abrupt or unanticipated. Schwert (1981) has argued that understanding the effects of regulation and deregulation can be complicated because regulators may intend one type of regulation, but the realized regulation may have different effects. This is especially likely when regulations are enacted under one set of environmental conditions and those conditions later change. Similarly, deregulation may have realized effects that are quite different from those intended (Spulber, 1989). The mismatch between national industrial strategies (as seen in deregulation) and corporate strategic needs may be attributed to the failure to recognize the interactions and hierarchical relationships that exist between macro and micro influences on competitive strategy. Murray, Bradley and Hession (1985), in their discussion of how public policy affects firms in international marketing, have observed that one of the clear defects in action by marketing support system (which includes support through deregulation) has been its predominant focus of the provision of support at project level—an essentially sub-strategic level at which support could be applied—without any necessary appreciation of the strategic merit or impact of the support intervention. Acknowledging the existence of a hierarchical system would allow the state support system and policy makers to understand the variety of strategic issues at each level in the hierarchy, the interrelationships, and the need to differentiate policy and support mechanisms to provide intervention in different ways at different levels where the greatest system-wide leverage might be obtained.

At the individual firm level, managers must therefore develop a deep understanding of how the state support system works so that it may be used in a variety of ways to reflect the complexities of the firms' strategic needs, especially in international marketing.

THE CHANGES IN ZIMBABWE

Economic development in Zimbabwe can be related to three eras: the colonial era (pre-1980), the "socialist" era (1980–90) and the new economic liberalization era (1990–). The most interesting part of the colonial era was the period during which Zimbabwe (then Rhodesia) was under sanctions. During this period, the government in power had tight control over the economy by virtue of the political environment then prevailing in the country. The individual firms had relatively few opportunities to formulate strategies without a lot of political environmental considerations. The economic policy thrust during this period was import substitution.

The "socialist" era was characterized by an economic management policy that was pro-socialist but had many distortions that reflected an interest in free market policies at the same time. Strategy formulation at the firm level continued to be highly influenced by tight economic controls as had happened during the past era, but now the firms were able to engage in international marketing without the international environment distracting them through sanctions.

The new economic liberalization era started with the introduction of the Structural Adjustment Program in 1990, which in many ways shows that the economy had not been performing as expected. For industrial firms, this should have been a blessing because most economic controls had to be removed, but it turned out to be the "killer" of a lot of enterprises. Between 1991 and 1995, the number of companies in this sector declined from 280 to 200.

THE TEXTILE INDUSTRY

Background

The textile and clothing industry in Zimbabwe employs about two thousand people working in about 220 clothing manufacturing companies. This figure represents approximately 10 percent of the total workforce in the manufacturing sector. The industry contributes approximately 6 percent of the gross export earnings, a share that has been consistent over the past 30 years. The industry is largely concentrated in the Harare and Bulawayo areas. This probably is a result of the developed infrastructure in the two areas. In a study involving 30 exporting companies in 1994, it was found that established companies that export some of their products export an average of 20 to 25 percent of their individual production. The average production quantity for most of the established companies is approximately twenty-five thousand pieces per month. Smaller companies, which are on the lower limit of export capacity, are within five thousand to ten thousand pieces per month. Research shows that most established companies in this industry are 15 to 20 years old, with most new companies having been established in the past 5 years following the opening up of the economy in 1990. Despite recent problems, the textile and clothing industry had been growing quite phenomenally. For example, between 1980 and 1991 the industry grew by about 500 percent.

Problems of the Textile and Clothing Industry

Exports of the textile and clothing industry started showing negative values in 1992–93 when export performance declined about 25 percent overall. Two fundamental events led to the change in the operational environment of the industry. First, the government introduced the Structural Adjustment Program in October 1990 which created a new economic environment. Second, South Africa which absorbed approximately 60 percent of Zimbabwe's textile and clothing products until 1991–92, was experiencing major political and economic changes that resulted in new trade policies mainly in the form of raised duties in order to protect their own textile and clothing industry. In May 1992 South Africa, which was the biggest export market in the region, raised its import duties to about 70 to 100 percent for any imports beyond the quota. For most Zimbabwean exporters, this meant that textile and clothing products entered South Africa at the new rates minus 17.5 percent in the form of rebate.

The liberalized economy opened the domestic market to competition by reducing tariffs on imported textile and clothing products. This situation meant that textile and clothing firms had to fight for their market share in the domestic market while trying to diversify into the international market. The domestic environment now faced other external problems that accompanied the new economic dispensation. These included:

- an average annual inflation rate between 1994 and 1995 of up to 25 percent
- an interest rate of up to 35 percent
- a declining economic growth rate: 1993 (4.6%), 1994 (4.2%), 1995 (−1%)
- large currency devaluations between 1990 and 1994

- a small domestic market with low purchasing power and therefore very little pull-effect
- removal of export incentives by the government
- high transport costs to overseas markets
- stiff competition from imported and smuggled in second-hand textile and clothing products. At the height of illegal trade, up to 40 percent of textile and clothing products that were being purchased by people were second-hand items.

The 1991–92 period also witnessed environmental problems in the form of drought. Because of the textile and clothing industry's vertical dependency on good agricultural performance, the drought situation exacerbated the problems of the industry. By implication, therefore, it can be seen that the domestic market was no longer as reliable as it might have been in the past. In the international market, those firms that were exporting and those that attempted to enter new export markets were faced with the recession, which had affected most big markets such as the European Union and North America. It was therefore quite difficult to open up new opportunities in the international market. Although some of the firms had been exporting to countries in the region such as Botswana and Namibia, these markets had not been given high priority in the past and therefore could not sustain a sudden increase in the supply.

EXPORT MARKET SCENARIO AND COMPETITIVE POSITION

Zimbabwe's major export market is the European Union (EU). The future for that market seems to be growing because since Zimbabwe is a signatory to the Lome IV Convention its textile products to this market are not subject to any quotas or tariffs. For example, in 1991 Zimbabwe's exports to the major EU markets were as follows: the United Kingdom (40%), Germany (26%), the Netherlands (18.8%), France (5.1%) and the rest went to other EU markets. In 1994, of the total textile and clothing exports the major EU markets were as follows: Germany (23%), the United Kingdom (21%), the Netherlands (15%), France (2%) and Ireland (3%). Besides these EU markets, the other significant markets that year were the United States (15%), South Africa (5%), Botswana (4%), Namibia (4%) and the remaining proportion to other small markets.

Trends in the EU market point to a promising market for developing exporters such as Zimbabwe. Consumption of textile and clothing products has been increasing at a rate of approximately 7 percent per year in this market, although overall production during the past two decades has been decreasing. However, the major threats to a small exporting economy such as Zimbabwe are the East European, Asian and South American countries which are also very competitive in that market. As shown in the following country profiles, compared with other strong textile and clothing manufacturing companies, Zimbabwe's market position in this industry has some weaknesses that make it uncompetitive.

Thailand

Thailand has done well in the export of textile and clothing products, primarily because textile and clothing products were included under exporting zones, providing strong protection for this industrial sector. Thai government now limits investment flows into this sector as a matter of policy. Thailand's exports to developed economies are subject to Multifibre Agreements.

Brazil

Brazil's industry is characterized by high tariff protection of up to 56 percent for clothing items. Of all the output, only 5 percent is exported, mainly because the domestic market absorbs a substantial proportion of production. Its exports are subject to Multifibre Agreement restrictions.

Indonesia

In Indonesia, tariffs are relatively low. The industry itself is made up of both old and new production systems. The new system, backed by low labor costs, have made Indonesia's products competitive on the international market. Much of the growth of Indonesia's industry has been attributable to strong government backing, including duty drawbacks.

South Africa

South Africa's industry is still highly protective. In July 1995, the industry was scheduled to reduce protection from external competition over a period of eight years. Presently, South African textile and clothing exporters benefit from two incentive schemes:

1. The General Export Incentive Scheme (GEIS), which offers a direct payment to exporters
2. The Duty Credit Certificate, which grants discounts against import duties based on the value of the company's exports

In both cases, the value is awarded on a graduated scale according to the degree of beneficiation. Clothing exporters are eligible for an 18 percent General Export Incentive and a 30 percent Duty Credit Certificate. The GEIS was phased out in March 1997.

These country profiles show that government involvement in the development of the textile and clothing industries can be quite substantial. Because of this background support, these countries have an edge over Zimbabwe in the international market. Zimbabwe's textile and clothing sector's weaknesses are as follows:

- Only limited fabric resources are available to the industry. This is associated with the fact that import duties of fabric material outside EU and ACP countries would attract duties of about 40 percent. This kind of scenario makes it difficult to import higher quality fabrics from sources such as Asia without incurring very high costs. The situation outlined earlier limits the product range the industry can produce.

- Middle management was found to be very much unrepresented. According to a SwedeCorp study, this probably reflects the fact that most of the larger companies are run as family businesses with a rather old-fashioned management style and limited vision. Young dynamic managers are almost exclusively found among small-scale entrepreneurs.

- There is no export experience, and there is lack of interest to export in the industry. Companies that do export, export only about 20 to 25 percent of total individual production.

- Workmanship and quality of garments are mainly appropriate for lower to medium-oriented markets in such markets as the EU and the United States.

- Design and trend awareness are not keeping pace with those in bigger markets such as the EU.

- Prices for local exporters are comparatively higher for large quantities than those of other major exporters of textile and clothing products.

- There is little new investment in the sector, which implies that the present problems will probably be future weaknesses.

- Product promotion, especially with regard to exports, is very weak.

   Despite this bleak picture, the sector does have some strengths in Zimbabwe which could be exploited in international marketing, namely:

- Compared to international standards, the industry has very low wages and a skilled labor force. Therefore, the industry incurs low costs of production which are quite comparable to those of other textile and clothing exporters such as the Asian countries.

- The industry has some flexible production capacities with short lead times, and most established companies have quite a long experience in textile manufacturing.

- The industry has duty-free and quota-free preferences for garments exported to the EU countries. This gives Zimbabwe a big price advantage over many Asian countries.

- The manufacturers have a good image as serious and reliable business partners, especially in the EU markets where they have established niches.

- The industry has access to locally produced high-quality cotton.

   Given these problems, weaknesses and strengths, we can derive strategic directions to enhance export marketing for the sector. Most companies in Zimbabwe's textile and clothing sector are, by international standards, small and should concentrate on niches. The European market has already proved the viability of this strategy. However, survival in the international market calls for flexibility, which the Zimbabwean textile and clothing sector presently lacks.

Companies in this sector tend to concentrate on one or two markets without considering the advantages of diversifying their customer base.

An analysis of their problems in the regional market shows that the problems derive from their concentration in the South African market in the past without considering other potential markets. Diversifying into other African markets is a strategic option that has not received attention by most African exporters, including Zimbabwe's textile and clothing sector. Compared to the effort exerted in trying to penetrate the European and North American markets, entering the African markets should be easier given the similarity of the consumer's demand structures. Given that Zimbabwe only contributes about 0.2 percent to world trade in textile and clothing products, the strategic alliance is one option the sector could choose. Such alliances would be viable if pursued with larger and reputable companies such as those in the EU, Asian and North American markets. This kind of arrangement should help reduce resistance to their products by addressing common problems associated with products, such as fashion consciousness, brand loyalty and mentality toward products from development economies.

In the same vein, subcontracting arrangements could achieve similar strategic benefits. Larger companies that have been seriously affected by opening up the economy have the option of looking at the top markets in which they are exporting. This is because they have the capacity, technology and skilled workforce that would make them competitive even in the demanding markets in developed countries.

CONCLUSIONS

Zimbabwean companies, especially the textile firms, have made a poor assessment of the international trade environmental situation. The changes in the regional trade arrangements were not unexpected, but the approach of most firms to these changes appeared quite static. The firms had become accustomed to a stable environment, and therefore they could not redesign their strategies without appealing to the government to negotiate a market for them. The new, more turbulent environment was something they could not handle on their own.

Although diversification strategies would have been desirable, most firms instead continued to pursue concentration strategies that were no longer relevant for the given environment. The industry federation has been looking for external markets with the same stable arrangements as before, but this situation is no longer relevant in light of the liberalized economic situation. An alternative solution could have been for the firms to formulate their own entry strategies into new markets and redefine those strategies so that they could remain in the markets they already occupied. One other aspect that called for a reassessment of the environment and therefore a reformulation of the strategies involved the changes within the domestic market. Since individual Zimbabweans and firms could now import second-hand clothing at very low tariff duties, this would take away some of the traditional markets that the firms had held in the country. It therefore required that firms look more vigorously to the outside market.

REFERENCES

Aldrich, H. 1979. *Organizations and Environments*. Englewood Cliffs, NJ: Prentice-Hall.

Bradley, F. 1985. Key Factors Influencing International Competitiveness. *Journal of Irish Business and Administrative Research* 7(2): 3–14.

Bradley, M. Frank, Hession, Edna and Murray, John A. 1985. Public Policy Intervention and the Growth and Development of the Firm in a Changing Technology—Product–Market Environment. A paper presented at the Second Open International IMP Research Seminar on International Marketing, University of Uppsala, Sweden, September.

Burns, T. and Stalker, G. M. 1969. *The Management of Innovation*. London: Tavistock.

Domegan, Christine. 1984. An Evaluation Study of Marketing Management. Unpublished Master of Business Administration dissertation, Department of Marketing, University College, Dublin, 1984.

Duncan, R. B. 1972, September. Characteristics of Organizational Environments and Perceived Environmental Uncertainty. *Administrative Science Quarterly*: 313–327.

Galbraith, J. 1977. *Organization Design*. Reading, MA: Addison-Wesley.

Hannan, M. T. and Freeman, J. 1977. The Population Ecology of Organisations. *American Journal of Sociology* 82(5): 929–964.

Hayes, Robert H. and Abernathy, William, J. G. 1980. Managing Our Way to Economic Decline. *Havard Business Review* 58: 67–77.

Lawrence, P. and Lorch, J. 1967. *Organization and Its Environment*. Cambridge, MA: Harvard University Press.

Mahon, J. F. and Murray, E. A. 1981. Strategic Planning for Regulated Companies. *Strategic Management Journal* 2: 251–262.

Mahon, J. F. and Murray, E. A. 1980. Deregulation and Strategic Transformation. *Journal of Contemporary Business* 9: 123–138.

McCarthy, E. J. 1960. *Basic Marketing*. Homewood IL: Irwin.

Neghandi, A. and Reinman, B. 1973, May. Task Environment, Decentralization, and Organizational Effectiveness. *Human Relations* 26: 203–214.

O'Mahoney, Finola. 1985, Autumn. Renewal of the Firm Through International Strategies. *Journal of Irish Business and Administrative Research* 7(2).

Pettigrew, A. and Whipp, R. 1973. *Managing Change for Competitive Success*. ESRC Blackwell Business, United Kingdom.

Pfeffer, J. 1978. *Organizational Design*. Arlington Heights, IL: AHM Publishing Corporation.

Pfeffer, J. and Salancik, G. R. 1978. *The External Control of Organizations*. New York: Harper and Row.

Porter, M. E. 1979, March–April. How Competitive Forces Shape Strategy. *Harvard Business Review* 57: 137–145.

Porter, M. E. 1980. *Competitive Strategy*. New York: Free Press.

Schwert, G. W. 1981. Using Financial Data to Measure Effects of Regulation. *Journal of Law and Economics* 24: 121–158.

Spulber, D. F. 1989. *Regulation and Markets*. Cambridge, MA: MIT Press.

Wind, Yoran and Robertson, Thomas S. 1983. Marketing Strategy: New Directions for Theory and Research. *Journal of Marketing Research* 47(2): 12–25.

Selected Bibliography

PART I: CONCEPTUAL ISSUES

Axford, B. 1995. *Global System*. Oxford: Polity Press.

Brenton, T. 1994. *The Greening of Machiavelli*. London: Earthscan.

Catton, William R. and Dunlap, Riley E. 1980. A New Ecological Paradigm for Post-Exuberant Society. *American Behavioral Scientist* 24(1): 15–48.

Commoner, Barry. 1974. *The Closing Circle*. New York: Bantam Books.

Curwen, P. 1986. *Public Sector: A Modern Approach*. Brighton: Weatsheaf Books.

Curwen, P., Richardson, B., Nwankwo, S. and Montanheiro, L. (eds.) 1994. *The Public Sector in Transition*. Sheffield: Pavic Publications.

Daly, Herman E. 1980. *Economy, Ecology, Ethics: Essays Towards a Steady State Economy*. San Francisco: Freeman.

Drucker, P. F. 1978. *The Age of Discontinuity*. New York: Harper and Row.

Drucker, P. F. 1992, September–October. The New Society of Organizations. *Harvard Business Review*: 95–104.

Dunsire, A., Hartley, K., Paker, D. and Dimitriou, B. 1988. Organizational Status and Performance: A Conceptual Framework for Testing Public Choice Theories. *Public Administration* 66: 363–388.

Escobar, Arturo. 1995. *Encountering Development: The Making and Un-Making of the Third World: 1945–1992*. Princeton, NJ: Princeton University Press.

Etzioni, A. 1973, July–August. The Third Sector and Domestic Mission. *Public Administration Review*: 314–323.

Featherstone, M. 1990. *Global Culture: Nationalism, Globalization and Modernity*. London: Sage.

Forster, C. 1992. *Privatization, Public Ownership and Regulation of Natural Monopoly*. Oxford: Blackwell Publishers.

Frydman, R. and Rapaczynski, A. 1993. Privatization in Eastern Europe. *Finance and Development* 27(3): 43–53.

Goldsmith, J. 1994. *The Trap*. London: Macmillan.

Hall, Stuart. 1991. The Local and the Global: Globalization and Ethnicity. In Anthony D. King (ed.), *Culture, Globalization and the World System: Contemporary Conditions for the Representation of Identity* New York: Macmillan, 19–39.

Harvey, R. 1995. *The Return of the Strong: The Drift to Global Disorder*. London: Macmillan.

Held, D. 1995. *Democracy and the Global Order: From the Modern State to the Cosmopolitan Governance*. Oxford: Polity Press.

Kahn, H. 1977. *The Next Two Thousand Years*. London: Sphere.

Kay, J. 1987. *The State and the Market: The UK Experience of Privatization*. London: Group of Thirty, Occasional Paper No. 23.

Majone, G. 1994. Paradoxes of Privatization and Deregulation. *Journal of European Public Policy* 1(1): 53–69.

Marsh, D. 1991. Privatization under Mrs. Thatcher: A Review of the Literature. *Public Administration* 69: 459–480.

Martinez-Alier, Juan. *Ecological Economics: Energy, Environment and Society*. New York: Basil Blackwell.

Meadows, Donella H., Meadows, Dennis L. and Randers, Jorgen. 1972. *The Limits to Growth*. New York: Universe Books.

Meadows, Donella H., Meadows, Dennis L. and Randers, Jorgen. 1992. *Beyond the Limits: Confronting Global Collapse, Envisioning a Sustainable Future*. Post Mills, VT: Chelsea Green Press.

Mitroff, A., Mason, R. and Pearson, C. 1994. Radical Surgery: What Will Tomorrow's Organization Look Like? *Academy of Management Executive* 8(2): 11–21.

Mlinar, Z. (ed.). 1992. *Globalization and Territorial Identities*. Aldershot: Avebury.

Parry, G. (ed.). 1994. *Politics in an Interdependent World*. Aldershot: Edward Elgar.

Perry, J. and Rainey, H. 1988. The Public-Private Distinction in Organization Theory: A Critique and Research Strategy. *Academy of Management Review* 13: 182–201.

Ramanadham, V. 1984. *The Nature of Public Enterprises*. London: Croom Helm.

Shiva, Vandana. 1989. *Staying Alive: Women, Ecology and Development*. London: Zed Books.

Sikorski, D. 1993. A General Critique of the Theory on Public Enterprise. *International Journal of Public Sector Management* 6: 17–40.

Soros, G. 1995. *Soros on Soros: Staying Ahead of the Curve*. London: John Wiley.

Sternberg, E. 1993, November–December. Preparing for the Hybrid Economy: The New World of Public-Private Partnerships. *Business Horizons*: 11–15.

Veljanovski, C. 1989. *Privatization and Competition*. London: Institute of Economic Affairs.

Waters, Malcolm. 1995. *Globalization*. London and New York: Routledge.

Wilson, K. and Van der Dussen, J. (eds.). 1995. *The History of the Idea of Europe*. London: Routledge.

World Commission on Environment and Development. 1987. *Our Common Future*. New York: Oxford University Press.

Yamamoto T. 1992. Privatisation and National Interest. *The Waseda Business and Economic Studies* (28): 99–120.

Yarrow G. 1987. *Does Ownership Matter?* London: Institute of Economic Development.

PART II: REGIONAL ISSUES

Allard, Christian. 1990, November. Mexico for Sale: Gringoes Welcome. *Canadian Business* 63: 72–76.

Auteri, E. and Tesio, V. 1990. The Internationalization of Management at Fiat. *Journal of Management Development* 9(6): 6–16.

Bollard, Allan and Mayes, David. 1992, June. Regionalism and the Pacific Rim. *Journal of Common Market Studies*: 195–209.

Brand, Joseph L. 1991, October 17. The New World Order: Regional Trading Blocks. *Vital Speeches of the Day*: 155–160.

Davenport, Michael. 1992, June. Africa and the Unimportance of Being Preferred. *Journal of Common Market Studies* 30(2): 233–251.

De Melo, Jaime and Panagariya, Arvind. 1992, December. The New Regionalism. *Finance and Development*: 37–40.

Kinnock, Neil. 1994, Summer. Beyond Free Trade to Fair Trade. *California Management Review*: 124–135.

Krugman, Paul. 1991, December. The Move Toward Free Trade Zones. *Economic Review*: 5–25.

Lal, Deepak. 1993, September. Trade Blocs and Multilaterial Free Trade. *Journal of Common Market Studies*: 349–357.

Langhammer, Rolf J. 1992, June. The Developing Countries and Regionalism. *Journal of Common Market Studies*: 211–229.

Lipsey, Richard G., Schwanen, Daniel and Wonnacott, Ronald J. 1994. *The NAFTA: What's In, What's Out, What's Next*. Toronto: C. D. Howe Institute.

Naon, Horacio and Grigera, A. 1996, Summer. Sovereignty and Regionalism. *Law and Policy in International Business*: 1073–1180.

Panagariya, Arvind. 1994, March. East Asia: A New Trading Bloc? *Finance and Development*: 16–19.

Petersen, Christian E. 1992, May. Trade Conflict and Resolution Methodologies. *Conflict and Peace Economics*: 62–66.

Taggard, Jim, Wheeler, Colin and Young, Stephan. 1994. The Training of International Managers: The Strathclyde Perspective. *Journal of Teaching in International Business* 6(2): 1–19.

PART III: GLOBAL INVESTMENT ISSUES

Agarwal, Sanjeev and Ramaswami, Sridhar N. 1991. Choice of Foreign Market Entry Mode: Impact of Ownership, Location and Internationalization Factors. *Journal of International Business Studies* 23(1): 1–27.

Aharoni, Y. 1986. *The Evolution of Management of State Owned Enterprises*. Cambridge, MA: Ballinger Publishing.

Ahluwalia, Montek S. 1994, Spring. India's Quiet Economic Revolution. *Columbia Journal of World Business* 29: 6–12.

Aswicahyono, H. H. and Hill, Hal. 1996. Determinants of Foreign Ownership in LDC Manufacturing: An Indonesian Case Study. *Journal of International Business Studies* 26(1): 139–158.

Austin, J. E., Wortzel, L. H. and Coburn, J. F. 1986, Fall. Privatizing State Owned Enterprises: Hopes and Realities. *Columbia Journal of World Business* 21: 51–60.

Baer, W. and Birch, M. 1992, Fall. Privatization and the Changing Role of the State in Latin America. *Journal of International Law and Politics* 25: 1–25.

Bartlet, Christopher A. and Ghoshal, Sumantra. 1989. *Managing across Borders: The Transanational Solution.* Boston: Harvard Business School Press.

Beamish, Paul W. 1984. Joint Venture Performance in Developing Countries. Unpublished doctoral dissertation, University of Western Ontario, London, Ontario, Canada.

Bhagavati, J. 1993. *India in Transition: Freeing the Economy.* Oxford: Clarendon Press.

Boardman, A. E. and Vining, A. 1989, April. Ownership and Performance in Competitive Environments: A Comparison of the Performance of Private, Mixed and State Owned Enterprises. *Journal of Law and Economics* 32: 1–33.

Caves, D. W. and Christensen, L. R. 1980. The Relative Efficiency of Public and Private Firms in a Competitive Environment: The Case of Canadian Railroads. *Journal of Political Economy* 88: 958–976.

Dunning, John H. 1993. *Multinational Enterprises and the Global Economy.''* Reading, MA: Addison-Wesley.

Harrigan, Kathryn R. 1985. *Strategies for Joint Ventures.* Lexington, MA: Lexington Books.

Heath, J. (ed.). 1990. *Public Enterprise at the Crossroads.* London: Routledge.

Hennart, J. F. 1991, April. The Transaction Cost Theory of Joint Ventures: An Empirical Study of Japanese Subsidiaries in the United States. *Management Science* 37: 483–497.

Jensen, M. C. and Ruback, Richard. 1983, April. The Market for Corporate Control: The Scientific Evidence. *Journal of Financial Economics* 11: 5–50.

Kang, Jun-Koo. 1993, December. The International Market for Corporate Control: Mergers and Acquisitions of U.S. Firms by Japanese Firms. *Journal of Financial Economics* 34: 345–371.

Killing, J. Peter. 1983. *Strategies for Joint Venture Success.* London: Croom Helm.

Kojima, Kiyoshi. 1978. *Direct Foreign Investment.* London: Croom Helm.

Kumar, N. 1990. *Multinational Enterprises in India.* London: Routledge.

Kumar, N. 1994. Determinants of Export Orientation of Foreign production of U.S. Multinationals: An Inter-Country Analysis. *Journal of International Business Studies* 25(1): 141–156.

Lall, S. and Mohammed, S. 1983. Multinationals in Indian Big Business: Industrial Characteristics of Foreign Investments in a Heavily Regulated Economy. *Journal of Development Economics* 13: 143–157.

Lipsey, Robert E. 1993. *Foreign Direct Investment in the United States: Changes over 3 Decades.* Working Paper No. 4124. National Bureau of Economic Research.

Lipsey, Robert E. 1994. *Outward Direct Investment and the U.S. Economy.* Working Paper No. 4691. National Bureau of Economic Research.

Markides, Constantinos and Ittner, Christopher. 1994. Shareholder Benefits from Corporate International Diversification: Evidence from U.S. International Acquisitions. *Journal of International Business Studies* 25: 343–394.

Mathur, Ike, Nanda, Rangan, Chhachhi, Indudeep and Sridhar, Dundaram. 1994, March–April. International Acquisitions in the United States: Evidence from Returns to Foreign Bidders. *Managerial and Decision Economics* 15: 107–118.

Morck, Randall and Young, Bernard. 1992, August. Internationalization: An Event Study Test. *Journal of International Economics* 33: 41–56.

Porter, M. E. and Fuller, M. B. 1986. Coalitions and Global Strategy. In M. E. Porter (ed.), *Competition in Global Industries*. Boston: Harvard Business School Press, 315–342.

Ramamurti, R. 1987, July. Performance Evaluation of State-Owned Enterprises in Theory and Practice. *Management Science* 33: 876–893.

Ramasway, K. and Renforth, W. 1995. A Comparative Study of Commerical Profitability, Managerial Efficiency and Public Interest in SOEs and Private Firms in India. In S. B. Prasad (ed.), *Advances in International Comparative Management*. Greenwich, CT: JAI Press.

Shirley, M. M. 1989. *Reform of State Owned Enterprises: Lessons from Bank Lending*. Washington, DC: World Bank.

Toyo Keizai. 1989. *Japanese Overseas Investments (by Country) 1989*. Tokyo: Toyo Keizai.

Toyo Keizai. 1994. *Japanese Overseas Investments (by Country) 1994*. Tokyo: Toyo Keizai.

UNCTAD. 1995. *World Investment Report, 1995: Transnational Corporations and Competitiveness*. New York and Geneva: United Nations.

Veljanovski, C. 1987. *Selling the State: Privatization in Britain*. London: Weidenfeld and Nicolson.

Vickers, J. and Yarrow, G. 1988. *Privatization: An Economic Analysis*. Cambridge, MA: MIT Press.

Wheeler, D. and Moody, A. 1992. International Investment Location Decisions; The Case of U.S. Firms. *Journal of International Economics* 33: 57–76.

Whitehead, C. 1988. *Reshaping the Nationalized Industries*. New Brunswick, NJ: Transaction Books.

Woodcock, C. Patrick, Beamish, Paul W. and Makino, Shige. 1994. Ownership-based Entry Mode Strategies and International Performance. *Journal of International Business Studies* 25(2): 253–273.

Yarrow, G. 1986, April. Privatization in Theory and Practice. *Economic Policy* 2: 323–364.

Xu, L. 1994. Inefficiency of State Enterprises, Ownership, Control and Soft Budget Constraint. Unpublished doctoral dissertation, University of Chicago, Chicago, IL.

PART IV: MANAGERIAL ISSUES

Dowling, P. J. and Schuler, R. S. 1990. *International Dimensions of Human Resource Management*. Boston: PWS-Kent Publishing Co.

Fernandez, J. P. 1991. *Managing a Diverse Workforce: Regaining the Competitive Advantage*. Toronto: Lexington Books.

Fernandez, J. P. 1993. *The Diversity Advantage: How American Business Can Outperform Japanese and European Companies in the Global Market Place*. New York: Lexington Books.

Geringer, J. M. and Herbert, L. 1989. Control and Performance of International Joint Ventures. *Journal of International Business Studies* 20(2): 235–254.

Hare, Paul G. 1991, Fall. Hungary: In Transition to a Market Economy. *Journal of Economic Perspectives* 5: 195–201.

Ibarra, H. 1993. Personal Networks of Women and Minorities in Management: A Conceptual Framework. *Academy of Management Review* 18: 56–87.

Jamieson, D. and O'Mara, J. 1991. *Managing Workforce 2000: Gaining in Diversity Advantage.* San Francisco: Jossey-Bass.

Johnson, Bryan and Sheehy, Thomas. 1995. *Index of Economic Freedom.* Washington, DC: Heritage Foundation.

Johnston, W. B. 1991, March–April. Global Workforce 2000: Work and Workers for the Twenty First Century. *Harvard Business Review*: 115–127.

Kogut, B. 1988, July–August. Joint Ventures: Theoretical and Empirical Perspectives. *Strategic Management Journal* 9(4): 319–332.

Konai, Janos. 1990. *The Road to a Free Economy.* New York: W. W. Norton.

Marer, Paul. 1991, May. Foreign Economic Liberalization in Hungary and Poland. *AEA Proceedings and Papers* 81: 329–333.

McKinnon, Ronald I. 1991, Fall. Financial Control in the Transition from Classical Socialism to a Market Economy. *Journal of Economic Perspectives* 5: 107–122.

Pucik, V., Tichy, N. M. and Barnett, C. K. (eds.). 1993. *Globalizing Management: Creating and Leading the Competitive Organization.* New York: John Wiley.

Srinivasan, T. N. 1987, September. Economic Liberalization in China and India: Issues and an Analytical Framework. *Journal of Comparative Economics* 11: 427–443.

Teece, D. J. 1985, May. Multinational Enterprise, Internal Governance, and Industrial Organisation. *American Economic Review* 75(2): 233–238.

Tung, R. L. 1988. *The New Expatriates: Managing Human Resources Abroad.* Cambridge, MA: Ballinger.

Tung, R. L. 1993. Managing Cross-national and Intra-national Diversity. *Human Resources Management Journal* 23(4): 461–477.

World Bank. 1995. *Workers in an Integrating World.* New York: Oxford University Press.

PART V: COUNTRY-SPECIFIC EXPERIENCES

Deo, Frederick. 1987. *The Political Economy of the New Asian Industrialism.* Ithaca, NY: Cornell University Press.

Devan, Janadas (ed.). 1994. *Southeast Asia: Challenges of the 21st Century.* Singapore: Institute of Southeast Asian Studies.

Gulati, Umesh C. 1989, April–June. Dynamics of Economic Restructuring in a Small NIC. *Indian Economic Journal* 37: 40–56.

Gulati, Umesh C. 1992, April. The Foundations of Rapid Economic Growth: The Case of the Four Tigers. *American Journal of Economics and Sociology* 51: 161–172.

Harris, Philip and Moran, Robert. 1991. *Managing Cultural Differences.* Houston, TX: Gulf Publishing Co.

Hossain, Ishtiaque. 1995, June. Bangladesh: A Nation Adrift. *Asian Journal of Political Science* 3(1): 32–48.

Tu Weiming, et al. (eds.). 1992. *The Confucian World Observed.* Honolulu, HI: East-West Center.

PART VI: SECTORAL AND INDUSTRY-SPECIFIC ISSUES

Benson, Stanley M. and Raskind, Leo J. 1991. An Introduction to Law and Economics of Intellectual Property. *Journal of Economic Perspectives* 5(1): 3–27.

Berry, Leonard L. 1995. *On Great Service—A Framework for Action*. New York: Free Press.

Bitner, Mary Jo. 1995. Building Service Relationships: It's All about Promises. *Journal of the Academy of Marketing Science* 23(4): 246–251.

Blaine, Michael James. 1994. *Cooperation in International Business*. Brookfield, VT: Avebury.

Crosby, Lawrence A., Evans, Kenneth R. and Cowles, Deborah. 1990. Relationship Quality in Service Selling: An Interpersonal Influence Perspective. *Journal of Marketing* 54(3): 68–81.

Czepiel, John A. 1990. Service Encounters and Service Relationships: Implication for Research. *Journal of Business Research* 20(1): 13–21.

Dwyer, F. Robert, Schurr, Paul H. and Sejo, Oh. 1987. Developing Buyer-Seller Relationships. *Journal of Marketing* 51(2): 11–27.

Goodman, Paul S., Fichman, Mark, Lerch, F. Javier and Snyder, Pamela R. 1995. Customer-Firm Relationships, Involvement, and Customer Satisfaction. *Academy of Management Journal* 38(5): 1310–1324.

Grönroos, Christian. 1991. *Service Management and Marketing*. Cambridge, MA: Lexington Books.

Hakansson, Hakan (ed.). 1982. *International Marketing and Purchasing of Industrial Goods: An Interaction Approach*. Chichester: John Wiley and Sons.

Hofstede, Geert. 1984. *Culture's Consequences: International Differences in Work Related Values*. Beverly Hills, CA: Sage Publications.

James, Barrie. 1990. *The Global Pharmaceutical Industry in the 1990s: The Challenge of Change*. The Economic Intelligence Unit, Special Report No. 2071. London: Business International.

Krueger, Anne. 1995. *Trade Policies and Developing Nations*. Washington, DC: Brookings Institution.

Mansfield, Edwin. 1994. *Intellectual Property Protection, Foreign Direct Investment and Technology Transfer*. International Finance Corporation, Discussion Paper No. 19. Washington, DC: World Bank, 5: 1–43.

Mansfield, Edwin and Romeo, Anthony. 1980, December. Technology Transfer to Overseas Subsidiaries by U.S. Based Firms. *Quarterly Journal of Economics* 95: 737–750.

McGahan, Anita M. 1994, November–December. Industry Structure and Competitive Advantage. *Harvard Business* Review: 115–124.

Nogués, Julio. 1990. Patents and Pharmaceutical Drugs: Understanding the Pressures on Developing Countries. *Journal of World Trade* 25(6): 81–104.

Rapp, R. and Rozek, R. 1990, October. Benefits and Costs of Intellectual Property Protection in Developing Countries. *Journal of World Trade* 24(6): 75–102.

Sharma, Deo D. 1991. *International Operations of Professional Firms*. Lund, Sweden: Studentlitteratur.

Spulber, D. F. 1989. *Regulation and Markets*. Cambridge, MA: MIT Press.

Trancer, Robert S. 1995, March–April. Trends in Worldwide Intellectual Property Protection. *The International Executive* 37(2): 147–166.

Wallerstein, M. et al. (eds.). 1993. *Global Dimensions of Intellectual Property Rights in Science and Technology*. Washington, DC: National Academy Press.

Wells, Nicholas (ed.). 1985. *Pharmaceuticals Among Sunrise Industries*. New York: St. Martin's Press.

Index

About the Contributors

JAIDEEP ANAND is a F.W.P. Jones Research Fellow and Assistant Professor at the Richard Ivey School of Business, University of Western Ontario, Canada. He earned his Ph.D. from the Wharton School, University of Pennsylvania.

SUBHABRATA BANERJEE is a Lecturer, Department of Management, University of Wollongong, Australia, He received his Ph.D. from the University of Massachusetts. His research interests include environmentalism, international business and indigenous ecology.

MIKE CUDD is Professor of Finance and Head of the Department of Marketing and Finance at Southeastern Louisiana University. He has published in the *Financial Review, Quarterly Journal of Business and Economics* and the *Journal of Economics and Finance*, among other journals. His primary research interest is in the area of mergers and acquisitions.

ANDREW DELIOS is a doctoral candidate at the Richard Ivey School of Business, University of Western Ontario. His research concerns the foreign investments of Japanese multinational enterprises (MNEs), and his dissertation examines the performance and survival of foreign subsidiaries of Japanese MNEs.

RAKESH DUGGAL is Associate Professor of Finance at Southeastern Louisiana University. His research has appeared in *Managerial and Decision Economics, Quarterly Review of Economics and Finance* and *Quarterly Journal of Business and Economics*.

UMESH C. GULATI has been a member of the faculty of East Carolina School of Business for more than thirty years. Earlier he worked at the ministries of Commerce and Industry and Finance, Government of India. He has contributed articles to professional journals in international business and economics and cross-cultural issues.

JAN-ERIK JAENSSON is Assistant Professor in the Department of Marketing and coordinator of the Africa Research Collaboration Program at the Umea Business School, Sweden. He obtained a Ph.D. in Marketing in 1997.

V. H. (MANEK) KIRPALANI is Professor Emeritus at Concordia University, Montreal, Canada. He has published several scholarly books and numerous research articles in the fields of marketing and international marketing. He has held leadership positions in leading professional organizations.

ANDERS MAJKGÅRD is a doctoral candidate in the Department of Business Studies, Uppsala University, Sweden. His research interests include service quality in the international market and internationalization of service industries. His research has been published in the *Journal of International Business Studies*.

ZORORO MURANDA is Chairman of the Business Studies Department at the University of Zimbabwe.

NIK RAHIMAH NIK-YACOB is Associate Professor in the Department of Marketing, Faculty of Business Management, University of Kebangsaan, Malaysia. She is an active researcher in the area of small- and medium-scale business marketing. She is a marketing consultant and has published extensively, including two books in the Malay language.

SONNY NWANKWO is Senior Lecturer in Strategic Management and Marketing at Sheffield Business School, Sheffield Hallam University, United Kingdom. Prior to entering academia he was a senior manager in the telecommunications industry. His most recent book is *Strategic Planning & Development: Developing Economies in Perspective* (1997).

NOËL O'SULLIVAN is Professor of Political Philosophy at the University of Hull, United Kingdom. His books on twentieth-century political thought have been translated into Spanish, Italian, Dutch and Czech. He is presently writing a book titled *European Political Thought Since 1945*.

A. BEN OUMLIL is Associate Professor of Marketing at the University of Dayton, Ohio. He has published widely in the areas of international marketing and inflation-related consumer behavior. He has published a book on inflation-induced consumer shopping behavior. He has also taught in overseas countries.

KANNAN RAMASWAMY is Associate Professor in the Department of Management and International Business at Florida International University. His current research interests include corporate governance structures, global strategy, privatization and mergers and acquisitions. His research has appeared in many academic journals, including *Academy of Management Journal, Journal of International Business Studies, Strategic Management Journal, International Management Review* and the *International Journal of Public Sector Management.*

C. P. RAO is a member of the faculty of the College of Administrative Sciences, Kuwait University. He was Eminent Scholar and William B. Spong Chair, Old Dominion University, and Wal-Mart Lecturer in Strategic Marketing and University Professor, University of Arkansas at Fayetteville. He has published extensively in the areas of marketing and international business.

P. M. RAO is on the faculty of the College of Management, Long Island University/C.W. Post Campus. Prior to entering academia he worked in the telecommunications industry. His research writings have been in the area of intellectual property protection.

MOHAMMED ABDUR RAZZAQUE is Senior Lecturer in the Department of Marketing, National University of Singapore. He has taught at the University of Western Sydney, Australia, the University of Khartoum, Sudan, and the University of Dhaka, Bangladesh. His research has been published in a number of international journals, including the *International Journal of Physical Distribution and Logistics Management* and the *International Journal of Consumer Marketing.*

WILLIAM RENFORTH is Professor of International Business and Head of the School of Marketing and International Business at Queensland University of Technology, Brisbane, Australia. He also serves as the current President of the Business Association of Latin American Studies. His research interests center on privatization, small firm exporting strategy, export distribution channel management and comparative marketing practices. His research has appeared in the *Journal of International Business Studies, Journal of Borderlands Studies, Management International Review, Columbia Journal of World Business* and *the Journal of the Academy of Marketing Science.* He has held prior teaching appointments in the United States, Trinidad and Nicaragua.

D. DEO SHARMA is Professor of Marketing at the Copenhagen Business School, Denmark. His research interests have focused on strategic alliances, government–TNC relationships and internationalization processes. His research has been published in the *Journal of International Business Studies, International Marketing Review, Journal of Global Marketing, International Business Review* and *Advances in International Marketing.*

A. V. SUBBARAO is Professor and Coordinator of the Marketing, Health and Human Resources section of the Faculty of Administration of the University of Ottawa, Canada. His doctoral degree is from the University of Minnesota. He has published over fifty research articles and has contributed chapters to six management books.

DAVID M. SZYMANSKI is the Al and Marion Withers Research Fellow and Associate Director of the Center for Retailing Studies at Texas A&M University. He received his Ph.D. in Business Administration from the University of Wisconsin–Madison, and has since been named the recipient of numerous teaching and research awards from Texas A&M University and national professional associations. His areas of research interest include international marketing strategy, personal selling and sales management and retailing strategy.

SUNIL VENAIK is a doctoral candidate at the Graduate School of Management, University of New South Wales, Sydney, Australia. His major area of research is management of multinational corporations, with special focus on technology transfer.

MANJIT S. YADAV is Associate Professor of Marketing and Faculty Fellow at the Center for Retailing Studies at Texas A&M University. He received his Ph.D. in Marketing from Virginia Polytechnic Institute and State University. His research focuses on consumer and managerial decision making and pricing strategy. He has published in a number of journals, including *Journal of Marketing Research, Journal of Consumer Research* and *Sloan Management Review*.

RAO, C.P.

ISBN 1-56720-075-3

90000>

EAN

9 781567 200751

HARDCOVER BAR CODE